THE SCIENCE OF GOD

Other Books by Ashish Dalela:

Time and Consciousness
Conceiving the Inconceivable
The Balanced Organization
The Yellow Pill
Cosmic Theogony
Emotion
Mystic Universe
Moral Materialism
Signs of Life
Uncommon Wisdom
Gödel's Mistake
Quantum Meaning
Sāṅkhya and Science
Is the Apple Really Red?
Six Causes

THE SCIENCE OF GOD

The Twelve Principles of Perfection

Ashish Dalela

The Science of God—The Twelve Principles of Perfection
by Ashish Dalela

Interior Design: Ciprian Begu

Published by Shabda Press
www.shabdapress.net
ISBN 978-93-85384-30-1

Dedicated to His Divine Grace A. C. Bhaktivedanta Swami Prabhupāda, who believed that the study of God was a science, and asked his followers to present the nature of God scientifically. He also believed that those who are studying nature through science can find God if they find the most fundamental reality. This is a small offering in the direction of that vision of presenting God's nature scientifically.

Contents

Preface

For a long time, I have thought of writing a book on the critique of Western philosophy from a Vedic perspective. Western philosophy is the source of many assumptions in modern science that prevail today, which have shaped the central dogmas of modern thinking, but they don't explain our experience, and if different theories are used to explain the world, then mutually contradictory descriptions about the world are produced.

Take for instance the Cartesian mind-body divide in which the body is defined as matter, and called *res extensa*, with the property of *extension*, due to which the external world is described as geometrical objects—points, dimensions, lines (which can be curved or straight), surfaces, and solid forms; algebra and calculus are just summarized expressions of geometrical forms. Due to this assumption, the perceptions of the five senses, such as taste, color, smell, and touch, must be reduced to geometry, which proves very hard both in terms of identifying what geometry corresponds to which sensation (e.g. there are no geometrical mappings of taste and smell today), as well as in why geometry is not perceived *as* geometry but as color, smell, taste, and touch. The latter is called the 'hard' problem of consciousness.

Our problems do not end here, because the concepts in the mind are relegated to a different substance, and *res cogitans*—as the mind is called—cannot have properties that the *res extensa* has. This means, for example, that theorems, paintings, music, or literature do not possess meaning in themselves. Rather, *we* give this meaning to a physical reality. In short, there is an active interaction between the mind and the body in every act of observation and interpretation, but how this interaction occurs cannot be explained.

Similarly, the mind has an emotive aspect, but because it is in the *res cogitans*, it cannot appear in the body. For example, your stress levels should not influence your heart rate, blood pressure, etc., which is patently false. Within the mind, the rational aspect must be used for science, while the emotive aspect—which is considered *inferior* to rationality—must be used for religion. Thus, after restricting religion to the mind, it is further restricted to emotions, which are, by definition inferior to reason. Thus, we cannot talk rationally about God, and we can only accept God on faith. God's rules and commandments are now guidelines for controlling the baser emotions in us, such as desire, anger, lust, greed, etc. These emotions must be subordinated to laws given by God, and if these laws are not followed, then God intervenes in nature (perhaps by altering the geometry) to punish us.

However, if these rules and commandments are replaced by legal edicts enacted by people-elected governments, some immoral laws are legalized, while many moral laws remain illegal. Thus, a clear conflict between religion and government is produced—after religion's role was restricted by the mind-body divide and instituting a distinction between reason and emotion. Now, the conflict between religion and government is solved by making religion a 'private matter'. God doesn't even intervene in nature, and has no role in punishing people who don't follow His rules. He doesn't even decide moral conduct. He is—if you wish—the gubernatorial head of the world, with no influence on our body or our public life. You can believe in God if you want, and worship Him in private. Or don't do anything at all.

The Cartesian mind-body solution wasn't meant to separate mind and body. It was meant to eliminate religion's role in our lives without seeming to do so. History has played along the trajectory that this divide defines.

But the mind-body divide itself suffers from many problems. For example, we cannot convert sensations to geometry. The emotive aspect is not inferior to the rational aspect; it actually rules over rationality. Emotions are not just in the mind; they are also visible in our body as tones of speech, as tremors in the body, as changing blood pressure and heart rate, etc. To control the body, the mind must intervene in the geometry, but this begs the question: Which aspect of geometry? Does the mind expand and contract the distances and durations—in which case the law of energy conservation would be false? Does the mind bend and twist space—in which case matter would be created and destroyed? Does the mind produce new dimensions in space—in which case all of scientific laws would be false? Regardless of which type of geometric modification is chosen, there is no way that the mind can impact the body, without violating principles of geometry. Thus, after removing God from the world, science must also attack the mind, and hopefully try to reduce it to matter, call it a mystery, or a hallucination.

Now, one of two things is possible— (1) the mind is real, and matter is not *res extensa* and the laws of science are false, or (2) the laws of science are real, but because we cannot explain sensations, thoughts, judgments, and feelings based on geometry, therefore, such mental entities must be illusions. This mind-body dichotomy forces materialism upon people, because the very existence of the mind violates science. Then we either try to reject and ignore the existence of the mind, or we fail to explain it away using geometry, and just call it a 'mystery' without agreeing to revise science.

In Vedic philosophy, the world is like speech, and comprised of three aspects— (1) the words which symbolize meanings, (2) the grammar which structures this meaning into sentences, and (3) the tones which modify the cognitive meaning with emotive undercurrents. This speech exists as a possibility and is selected by the soul to become its cognitive experience. As the soul moves from one experience to another, its focus shifts from one sentence to another, and this 'moving' of consciousness is called the 'change of body'—the past and the future sentences still exist as a possibility, and the present sentence is experienced. If we contrast this idea with the Cartesian mind-body divide, then (1) emotion is not just lust or devotion to God; it is objectively visible in the body and speech, (2) the fundamental property of the world and the observer is not geometry but *meaning*, (3) whatever we call 'geometry' is modified from the study of flat, open, and infinite space into a hierarchical, closed, and finite tree-like structure because meanings, grammar, and emotions are all organized from 'higher' to 'lower', (4) whatever we call the 'laws' of nature in science pertain not just to the motion of bodies, but also to the motion of the soul from one body to another, and (5) the latter are the laws of choice and responsibility, and thus morality is not just a natural law, but also the law that governs changing experiences.

In this process, all fundamental ideas underlying modern science—namely (1) the nature of space and time, (2) the idea of matter and force as geometry, (3) the idea of motion of physical objects, (4) the mathematical laws governing this motion, and (5) the separation of choice and responsibility from the physical world, are rejected in the Vedic description. This view of reality is then replaced by choice, possibility, and responsibility—the choice selects and rejects possibilities, and based on the selection and rejection it gets results and consequences: the results are seen immediately, but the consequences become possibilities to be reaped in the future. Our choices are ruled by our emotions; the cognition pertains to seeing the world as the possibility; and responsibility pertains to the relations with things that define our identity as *roles*. Choice, possibility, and responsibility, can thus, also be described as emotions, cognitions, and relations, respectively.

The 'mind' is defined as the 'knower' and more specifically as the many kinds of *senses*—that include the five senses of sense perception, the five senses of action, the four divisions of the 'internal sense' that perceives concepts, and judges them to be true, right, and good, and finally, a consciousness that controls them by accepting and rejecting the sensations (both internal and external). Conversely, the 'body' is redefined as 'known' and more specifically as 'sense objects' for the internal and external senses, as well as their properties. Due to hierarchy, the same thing can alternately be called an 'object' and a 'property', so we can just call them 'sense objects'.

Thus, the 'mind' and 'body' of Western philosophy are replaced by 'senses' and 'sense objects' in Vedic philosophy, and the body comprises emotions, relations, and cognitions as sense objects, just like the mind comprises emotions, relations, and cognitions as the sense contents. Now, 'science' is redefined as the changes to three things—(a) the nature of the senses, (b) the nature of the sense objects, and (c) the connection between the senses and the sense objects, or between the knower and the known.

This 'science' can also be described rationally, but it involves a different kind of logic and mathematics. The mathematics, in which we can include numbers (as individual entities) and structures (as their hierarchical organization), describe the sense contents, the sense objects, and the relation between sense objects and sense contents, which leads to experience. Numbers and structures pertain to the world of possibilities. The logic then pertains to the evolution of possibilities, and the attachment of consciousness from one possibility to another—that creates the change in experience.

In this logic, the senses can be described as *questions* and *problems* while the sense objects are described as *answers* and *solutions* to these problems. What we call 'experience' and 'change' is the combining and matching of questions to answers, or of problems to solutions. Some of these matches solve the problem, some of them exacerbate the problem, and some of them change the problem—i.e. lead to a new problem. Both problems and solutions have three aspects—a cognitive aspect, an emotive aspect, and a relational aspect. If the cognitive aspect of the problem is solved, then the matching of the problem and solution is 'true'. If the matching of the problem and solution exacerbates the cognitive problem, then it is 'false'. And if the matching of the problem and solution lead to a new cognitive problem, then match is 'neither false nor true' or 'both false and true'. Likewise, if the matching of the problem and solution solve the emotive problem, then the match is 'good'. If the matching exacerbates the emotive problem, then it is 'bad'. And if the matching leads to a new emotive problem, then it is 'neither good nor bad' or 'both good and bad'. Finally, if the matching of the problem and solution solves the relational problem, then it is 'right'. If the match exacerbates the relational problem, then it is 'wrong'. And if the match leads to a new relational problem, then it is 'neither right nor wrong' or 'both right and wrong'. All judgments are thus relations between problems and solutions, and logic emerges from the encounter between real elements.

Now, if all three problems—cognitive, emotive, and relational—are solved simultaneously, then experience comes to an end, until a new problem is produced. Under this situation, the knower or the internal and external senses are 'quietened', and the person becomes 'peaceful'. If one of these three problems are not solved, are exacerbated, or a new problem is produced, then the experience continues. But, if the problem is not solved, the previous experience becomes useless; if the problem is exacerbated, the previous experience becomes false, wrong, or bad; and if a new problem is produced, then the previous experience is neither good nor bad, neither true nor false, neither right nor wrong, or it could be both good and bad, both right and wrong, and both true and false. Our experience continues when the problem is not solved, when the problem is exacerbated, or when the problem is solved, but a new problem is produced by the solution.

What we call 'logic' is this complex dialectic between problems and solutions and creates the succession of the problems and solutions. This 'logic' changes the senses (e.g. when problems are exacerbated, or new problems are produced). This 'logic' changes the sense objects (e.g. when new answers are sought to the problems). And this 'logic' changes the connection between the senses and the sense objects (thus producing the experience of truth, right, and good, or knowledge, moral action, and happiness, or its very opposite, namely, false, wrong, and bad, or ignorance, immoral action, and suffering). The main conclusion from here is that ignorance, immoral action, and suffering cannot be separated. They are indeed three different types of things, but each can be the cause of the other, and each can be produced as an effect of the other. For instance, the quest for pleasure can produce immoral action, which is then justified by the ignorant ideas that our sole purpose of existence is the search for pleasure. Likewise, the ignorant idea that we exist only for our pleasure can lead to immoral action, which then leads to suffering. In brief, ignorance—which must be overcome through knowledge, through philosophy and science—is not merely the passive absence of the understanding of reality. It can also be actively pursued due to motivations for pleasure, or the absence of morality.

The critique of Western philosophy that I wanted to write would have countered the hopeless contradictions and inadequacies of the mind-body problem, the flawed and false ideas about matter, causality, space, time, and motion that exacerbate the contradictions and inadequacies as they are widely accepted, the problematic separation between truth, right, and good, and how focus on truth alone makes alternative thinking impossible.

But none of this can work, unless we address the root of all problems in modern Western philosophy and science, namely, that it arose out of its conflict with Christianity, and many of its unscientific and dogmatic ideas. These famously include the idea that the earth is flat, that human life, and indeed the earth is recently created, that the truth in religion must be established through power exerted by wars and conquest rather than by reason and understanding, and that a small group of nobility and priesthood preach austerity to the masses, while they lead a life of luxury and extravagance. The problems engendered by Christianity were unquestioned political power, societal disparities, and irrational and contrafactual ideas. In usurping the political power, reducing societal disparity, and returning to reason and fact, the baby was thrown out with the bathwater—the casualties of the European Enlightenment were God, the soul, morality, and all 'big questions' that had bothered and occupied philosophers for thousands of years. Change in ideas cannot emerge unless we throw the dirty bathwater and keep the baby. Keeping both or discarding both, leads to a problem.

The solution to the problem is understanding the true nature of God and the soul, morality and big questions, without the irrationality, unquestioned forced acceptance, and unfairness that previously accompanied these discussions. Over the centuries since European Enlightenment, many attempts have been made in this direction. Some of these accept the mind-body reciprocal influence, some argue that morality is natural rather than God-given, some even accept the soul, its transmigration, and liberation. All of them, however, have a problem with the idea of God, at least as a *person* who creates and controls the world. Therefore, all alternative religious ideologies—or "spiritual movements"—also tiptoe around Christianity, selectively choosing those ideas that they consider unproblematic, but always avoiding the elephant in the room—namely, the question of God. The outcomes of these alternatives are also predictable—they are not true rational alternatives to science, not good emotional substitutes for theistic religions, and not right replacements for an atheistic and immoral society. The more such attempts at truth, right, and good fail, the greater is the skepticism against any such alternative. The task therefore gets steeper with time.

But equally steep is our desire for utopia, especially as societal discrepancies mount, the investments in science begin to have diminishing returns, and the unhappiness and dissatisfaction in the individuals increases. All these are simultaneously coming to fruition at the present time. And this may then be the appropriate time to talk about the nature of utopia.

God is a sense of perfection and utopia in Vedic philosophy. He is the completion of knowledge, the fullness of happiness, and the embodiment of morality. In short, He is defined as *truth*, *right*, and *good*. I think most people approximately understand that God is goodness and righteousness (although despotic and tyrannical notions of God are not hard to find). The central question about God, even if we accept that God is beneficent and righteous, is whether the idea of God is true, and whether He exists! It is rather a simple question: Does utopia exist in reality or only in our minds? Can a perfect person exist, or are we merely dreaming of this perfection when all that we see in reality are selfish, ignorant, and immoral people?

In simple terms, the existence of God is a more important question than His goodness and righteousness. If God doesn't exist, then the idea of God is false, and notions of goodness and righteousness are also imaginary. This world—however painful and immoral it may be—is the only one. We have no choice but to exist and survive in this world and to make the best use of the available resources to create the most comfortable life possible. For sure, it will never be perfect, as it has never been perfect in the past. But through harder endeavors we can make it better. This is the most optimistic view of life without God. The cynical view, in which there is no such thing as morality or truth, just our individualistic pursuit of pleasure, is a more likely conclusion to be obtained, when God is believed to not exist.

Therefore, before talking about God, we must distinguish *utopia* from optimism and cynicism. If optimism declines, then we must choose between utter cynicism and perfect utopia. If optimism is high, then, both utopia and cynicism are rejected, and pragmatism about the present life is emphasized. This book caters to the presentation of the utopia of knowledge, happiness, and righteousness, but we will primarily focus upon knowledge.

If we can say that knowledge of perfection is true, then we can say that the pursuit of the knowledge of that perfection is also a valid pursuit. If perfection is itself impossible, then it cannot be a goal in life. Therefore, this book focuses on describing the nature of that perfection. If we can understand perfection in one case, then we can extend it to other things. Knowledge is such a thing. It covers the entire world, because everything is potentially knowable, although it may not be known perfectly. By understanding how knowledge can be perfected, we also understand utopia. If such perfection is possible, then it can be viable goal. If that goal can be attained, then such attainment becomes the perfect purpose of life.

This brings me to why I wrote a book on the critique of Western philosophy and called it *The Science of God.* The simple reason is that all modern philosophy begins in the desire to remove God from the study of nature, or limit God's role in this study, under the assumption that

God is either unknowable, or at least unknowable *rationally.* Science, as the pursuit of rationality is then defined as being fundamentally opposed to the idea of God. To separate the powers of the Academia from the Church, their concerns had to be separated, which underlies the mind-body separation framework of thinking, which leads to numerous scientific and philosophical problems. But their solution cannot be proposed rationally because all scientists and philosophers assume that the subject of God must also be irrational. We cannot critique science and philosophy without talking about the alternative, and if that alternative requires us to introduce God, then the discussion can never be carried out unless we address the central problem: the irrationality of the idea of God. The topic *The Science of God* is aimed to address this central problem and show why this idea is the definition of rationality.

This discussion of rationality can be undertaken in the context of modern philosophy. I will show in this book that there are 12 dominant ideas about rationality which define what we mean by knowledge, and they divide into six pairs which seem mutually contradictory in modern thinking. The conflict between these 6 pairs of ideas undercuts all rationality. Therefore, we don't have a good definition of what it is to be rational at present.

The six pairs of ideas that I will discuss in this book, and which I will describe as the fundamental principles of rationality, are as follows:

- Consistency and Completeness,
- Simplicity and Parsimony,
- Necessity and Sufficiency,
- Empirical and Rational,
- Operationality and Instrumentality,
- Stability and Originality.

Each of these principles often contradicts the other principles, and yet each of the principles is necessary because the other principles are inadequate and they do not adequately eliminate all that is not knowledge, nor do they effectively identify what knowledge is. For example, as knowledge gets more complete, it is also ridden with contradictions; if we remove contradictions, then we get incompleteness. As we make knowledge simple, we also make it very lengthy; as we make it short, we also make knowledge complicated. As we try to make knowledge sufficient, we produce unnecessary claims which can never be verified; but as we remove these unnecessary and unverifiable claims, our explanations become insufficient. As we collect more and more data, we make it impossible to analyze it rationally; as we get the ability to analyze rationally, we reduce the data. As we try to operationalize our knowledge, it becomes less and less instrumental in solving the day-to-day life problems; then as we try to make our knowledge instrumental in solving problems, we find that our theories can no longer be operationalized. As we talk about incremental progress in knowledge, we find that breakthroughs lie in originality; however, since originality produces instability, therefore, we seek the stability achieved via incremental progress.

What is knowledge? It is the coexistence of these opposites. It is completeness without inconsistency, parsimony without complexity, necessity without insufficiency, observation without irrationality, instrumentality without the inoperability, and originality without instability. Knowledge is perfect if all these contradictory qualities are present simultaneously.

But is this only the perfection of knowledge? Or is it perfection itself? For instance, can we apply the idea of perfection to making a perfect car or a house? The answer is that if we know the principles of perfection, then we can apply them to anything—including building a perfect house or a car. But it is not as easy to understand the nature of perfection while studying a house or a car. Perfection is that the house or the car must be consistent, complete, simple, parsimonious, necessary, sufficient, rational, empirical, operational, instrumental, stable, and innovative. All cars and houses are aimed to be perfect, but they trade off one attribute for another, which represents imperfection. Things in this world become imperfect if they are unable to reconcile these contradictory requirements simultaneously. The fact that we can apply the idea of perfection to anything in the world allows us to elevate the perfection of knowledge into perfection of anything.

That elevation allows us to say that *the knowledge of perfection is the perfection of knowledge*. Because by knowing the nature of perfection, we can make everything perfect. By this knowledge, we can also judge if something is imperfect, and why it is so. The study of what makes knowledge perfect allows us to apply the ideas of perfection to anything, and the reason is that 'knowing' is the most fundamental concept. Just as knowing that what makes something mammal, also allows us to apply the same epithet to cows and horses, similarly, knowing what makes knowledge perfect *defines perfection itself.*

This is then what I mean by the 'science' of God. It is the investigation, analysis, and study of what makes something perfect. And once we know what the idea of perfection is, then we can call that idea God. God is, therefore, not just a perfect being; He is that being Whose definition is perfection. There isn't a separate adjective of 'perfection' which stands apart from God and we use that adjective to judge whether God is perfect or not. If such an adjective exists apart from God, then we will ask ourselves: Why is God being judged by something other than God? Doesn't that constitute a contradiction in the definition of God, as the Supreme Absolute Truth?

Therefore, all the adjectives that can be applied to God, must constitute God Himself. As a result, in Vedic philosophy, God is defined as knowledge itself, beauty itself, power itself, wealth itself, heroism itself, and renunciation itself. We don't say that God is knowledgeable, beautiful, powerful, wealthy, heroic, and renounced, because that would mean that these qualities have a separate existence from God, and they are being used to judge God. By definition, God is the qualities by which He is described. In this book, I will summarize these six qualities as one idea—God is *perfection.* And these six qualities then define the meaning of the word 'perfection'. We all aim to attain perfection in our lives, and we define it as the attainment of greater knowledge, wealth, power, heroism, beauty, and renunciation. God doesn't need to become perfect, because He defines perfection itself.

The study of perfection involves the investigation of the conditions or criteria that define perfection. These qualities of perfection can be applied reflexively back to perfection itself to say that the definition of perfection itself satisfies all the attributes that are applied to call something perfect. For example, we can show how each criterion is consistent, but they are complete collectively. We can describe how each criterion is simple, and they are collectively parsimonious. We can delineate why each criterion is necessary, and they are collectively sufficient. We can demonstrate how each criterion is observable, but they are all collectively required to define what we mean by rationality. We can describe how each of the ideas is operational, and how they are instrumental. We can show how shifts from one attribute of perfection to another creates originality, but also how the shift brings greater stability in our knowledge. This is an objective definition of *perfection.*

To discuss perfection, we need a subject in the context of which we can discuss it. For example, we could discuss what makes houses and cars perfect, and then everyone will have to be aware of the mechanics of a car, or the architectural tenets underlying houses. This will prove to be harder, and not relevant to everyone. Therefore, I will not use houses and cars to study perfection. I will rather use 'knowledge' to do that. Knowledge is the most general concept, and it includes all concepts. Knowledge is also amenable philosophically and its nature has been debated endlessly for thousands of years. In contrast, very few people debate the perfection of cars and houses. Therefore, knowledge is an appropriate subject for discussing the nature of perfection. When we apply perfection to knowledge, we also define what it means to call something 'knowledge'. Everything that doesn't satisfy the criteria for perfection also cannot be called knowledge. And we cannot call that perfection a lie, a falsity, or non-existence, because then we would simply be left with imperfection, or the absence of knowledge.

When we study the properties of perfection, then we can understand why something is imperfect. And by knowing that imperfection, we can find that thing which is perfect. In the same way, if we embark on knowing the perfection, then we can find that which is the perfection of knowing. The methods of philosophy lay down many contradictory criteria for knowing. All these criteria are important, but they cannot always be applied to everything, because these things are not the perfect and ultimate truth. The ultimate truth is that which reconciles these contradictions, and by that reconciliation of such opposites, it can be called the perfection of knowing. Knowing that perfection is therefore also the perfection of knowing.

In this way, the study of God is a rational subject. The perfect thing to be known is God, but because people say that perfection doesn't exist, is elusive, or simply not well-defined, therefore, we can define God as perfection, and then study the different properties that constitute this perfectiveness. The discussion of perfectiveness involves philosophy. And the embodiment of this perfection is God. If we can define perfection, then we have defined God. And by knowing this definition, the possibility of

God's existence is established—it is the possibility of perfection. The next step is to explain how imperfection arises from the perfection, by removing aspects of this perfection. The imperfect world is a *part* of perfection, but not perfection itself. By studying the imperfect, we can also know the perfect.

This idea of God's existence hinges on the premise that the reader accepts the possibility of perfection and wants to understand how imperfection entails that something is missing from perfection. It is not necessary that you be so optimistic. You can also be cynical, and say: There is nothing called perfection, there is no such thing as perfect knowledge, it is not possible to know the nature of truth, and rationality is quite overrated. In that case, you are also welcomed to continue on your path of imperfection.

This book is meant for the cynic who may not believe in God although believes in perfection. The idea of God can be easily explained to such a cynic, rationally. This book is not meant for the cynic who either believes in God, but not in perfection (e.g. if the person believes that God is irrational, immoral, or jealous), or doesn't believe in either of these two. In short, your belief of God is not important; your belief in perfection is important. If you believe in perfection, then God can be presented rationally. But if you don't believe in perfection, then nothing at all can be discussed, because knowledge itself doesn't have to be perfect, and whoever claims to know something cannot be judged by any standards of knowledge. Then if someone says that "I know God" the statement cannot be judged true or false, just as the statement "God doesn't exist" cannot be called true or false.

In brief, if you are not a theist, that is not a problem that this book cannot address. But if you are not a perfectionist, or don't believe in the possibility of perfection, then it is a problem that this book cannot solve.

One final note to the reader, who may have read some of my previous work. This book comes after a number of other books which have dealt with other topics, that generally did not discuss God so directly. Many of my previous books don't mention God at all or mention Him to the extent necessary for the discussion of other topics, such as the nature of matter, the nature of the soul, the process of creation, and so forth. Having spent so much time describing these topics, why change the focus now?

The answer to this question is that reality in Vedic philosophy is said to comprise three categories—*Purusha*, *Prakriti*, and *Jīvā*, or God, Nature, and soul. My earliest books largely focused on Nature. Then I wrote a few books about the soul and used the idea of the soul to describe both soul and Nature. All that discussion is pertinent, and I will recapitulate it when necessary. I am now turning toward the third major category in Vedic philosophy—namely God. My method and style don't change—i.e. don't stop asking the hard questions, be relentless in questioning every idea, frame the problem and the solution in an accessible manner, and leave the reader in a better place than where they started. I apply this method to discuss the topic of God in way that I believe has not been done before—not just in my writing, but in any other that I'm aware of. I approach the God question in a way that open-minded people of other religions can also appreciate.

What is perfection? When can we call something perfect? What conditions must something satisfy in order to be considered as being perfect? If you are not a cynic who believes that perfection is impossible, then this book will be useful for you. It describes the meaning of 'perfection'. Once this definition is obtained, then it also describes how Vedic philosophy presents God as these very qualities of perfection. In short, God is the definition of perfection. He is not just perfect; He defines perfection itself.

The religious people can perfect their lives by worshipping perfection, meditating on perfection. And the philosophers, scientists, and academics can perfect their lives by discussing, debating, and analyzing perfection. Their paths and methods can differ, but if the goal is the understanding of perfection, then the goal is perfect, and it can make our lives perfect. This is then the meaning of the word "God": the thing that is most perfect, and the science of God is the study of what we mean by perfection itself.

1

The Problem of Knowledge

The Definition of God

The Vedic scriptures describe God as the Absolute Truth that expands into many relative truths, and many 'worlds' are thereby created. These relative truths, or 'worlds', are the *proofs* of the *truth*, because from the understanding of the 'world', the source of the world—i.e. the Absolute Truth—is known. The proofs, however, are different from the truth, since a proof indicates an aspect of the truth but is not the full truth. Similarly, the world represents parts of the Absolute Truth, but is not itself that Absolute Truth. Ultimately, there is nothing else to be known other than the Absolute Truth; whatever we know in this world is the proof of the Absolute Truth.

This idea can be illustrated by an example. Suppose the truth is a subject called 'number'. To illustrate this truth there are hundreds of theorems about numbers that explicate their nature. All these theorems collectively prove the nature of 'number'. Many of these theorems were at one time not proven, but people still believed their truth. Thus, these properties about 'number' existed even if their proofs did not. And yet, even if the proofs exist, they are not the fundamental truth; they are only describing the theorems, which in turn describe the properties of the numbers. Quite simply, number expands into theorems, which then expand into the proofs of the theorems, and the expansion describes the thing it has expanded from. Each theorem or proof describes some properties of the numbers, and all the theorems and proofs collectively explain what we mean by number.

Since there are many theorems, therefore, we must be able to distinguish and sequence these theorems—the first theorem, the second theorem, the third theorem, etc. Similarly, we must be able to distinguish and sequence the steps in the proofs—the first step, the second step, the third step, etc. If we cannot distinguish and count the theorems or the steps, then we cannot know number. But in distinguishing and sequencing the theorems, we use numbers, and so we must assume the truth of numbers.

Thus, we can identify the two ways in which we use numbers, by calling them *description* and *demonstration*. There is an abstract truth called 'number' which expands into some properties {P}, which expand into some theorems {T}, which expand into some steps {S}. Then, {P} is a description of number, {T} is a description of {P}, and {S} is a description of {T}. However, even as {P}, {T}, and {S} are expanding from 'number', we must be able to count—i.e. distinguish and sequence—the properties, theorems, and the steps. In such counting, we also assume numbers. Hence, we can say that {P}, {T}, and {S} also *demonstrate* the properties of number.

The 'number' can exist even if we don't know its properties. The properties can be known even if we don't frame theorems about them. And the theorems can be known even if there are no proofs validating them. However, when properties, theorems, and proofs exist, then they must use 'number'. Due to this peculiar property, we can say that 'number' *transcends* its properties, the properties *transcend* the theorems, and the theorems *transcend* their proofs. But, since numbers are used to distinguish and count the properties, theorems, and proofs, therefore, numbers are *immanent* in them. As a result, we get two contradictory notions about numbers: they are transcendent, and they are immanent. To know numbers, we must assume numbers and use them. In that sense, the description of numbers, which refers or points to a transcendent reality, must also demonstrate the numbers.

The same idea is explained in Vedic texts by stating that the Absolute Truth is *knowledge* and the relative truths are the *expansions* of knowledge. The relative truths are the 'world', which can be compared to the properties, theorems, and proofs of 'number'. Each of these expansions describes the previous expansion, and ultimately the Absolute Truth. But, in so describing, everything assumes the Absolute Truth. Therefore, the Absolute Truth is transcendent to its expansions. And yet, the Absolute Truth is immanent in all the expansions, because we cannot know the expansion unless we presuppose the Absolute Truth. Since the expansion presupposes the source, therefore, they *demonstrate* this truth, and they *describe* it. The description cannot exist without the demonstration and vice versa. So, these two are not mutually exclusive, and yet, they are distinct. By the principle of demonstration, since everything is expanded from knowledge, therefore, it is also knowledge. But it is *referential knowledge* in the sense that it describes a truth beyond itself. However, since it cannot describe this truth without using the truth, therefore, what is described is also demonstrated, and the truth being described becomes immanent in the description. This immanence allows us to call even the 'proof' as some 'truth', but it is not the original truth. In the same way, we can say that everything in this world constitutes knowledge, but it is not the original knowledge from which it has been expanded.

Quite simply, there is a transcendent idea called 'knowledge', like there is a transcendent idea called 'number'. This idea then expands into many instances of knowledge, just like 'number' expands into many theorems. The *one* becomes *many*, however, the one is also immanent in the many.

Thus, the Absolute Truth is explained by describing the three ways of understanding it, called Brahman, Paramātma, and Bhagavan. Bhagavan is the transcendent truth—like the idea 'number'. Brahman is the expansion of Bhagavan, like properties, theorems, and proofs are expansions of number. And Paramātma is the immanent truth inside these expansions, just like the properties, theorems, and proofs can be counted using numbers.

This idea can also be made more intuitive by how we use grammar. The books on grammar describe a subject—grammar—that stands apart from the book. And yet, to describe the grammar, the sentences in the book must use grammar. The subject called 'grammar' is transcendent. The book is the expansion of the grammar. And the grammar is embedded inside the book. By using grammar, the book describes grammar. If grammar did not exist, then the book cannot come into existence. But when the book exists, then it describes grammar, and although the book also uses grammar, it is not grammar itself. You read the book not to know the book, but to learn grammar. The grammar is transcendent, and the grammar is immanent.

In knowing the world—i.e. grammar, theorems, proofs, and steps—we must satisfy the conditions that make something 'knowledge'. These conditions are just like the properties of 'number' or the 'rules' of grammar. The properties of number are immanent in the theorems, proofs, and steps, and the rules of grammar are immanent in the sentences that describe the grammar. If these properties and rules are not satisfied, then we cannot call something 'knowledge'. For example, if the sentences in the book on grammar do not satisfy the rules of grammar, then we would say that the book on grammar is ungrammatical, and hence it cannot be 'knowledge'. Likewise, if steps in the proof were jumbled such that the first step was made the last step, and the last step was made the first step, then we would say that this sequence of steps is not a proof, and hence it cannot be 'knowledge'.

In short, whatever is 'grammar' and 'number' must exist in the description of grammar and number, otherwise, those things are not grammatical and not numbered, and hence they cannot be representations of grammar and number. If we replace 'grammar' and 'number' with 'knowledge', then whatever doesn't follow the properties and rules of knowledge cannot be called knowledge. This requires us to distinguish the *object* called 'number', 'grammar', 'knowledge' from the *properties* of these objects. The properties can exist in other objects too, and they must exist for them to describe their respective objects. If the property described by a book or a sentence doesn't exist in the book or sentence that describes it, then whatever the book or sentence describes, cannot be called a description of that property.

If this idea seems difficult, then we can employ a completely physical example. Let's suppose that we are measuring the weight of an object using a weighing scale. The measured object has some weight, but the weighing scale must also have some weight. If the weighing scale had no weight, then it could not measure weight. In this case, the weighing scale is the description of the weight of the object it measures, and it must also have the properties that it is describing in the object. Thus, from the perspective of the scale, the property of weight is both transcendent and immanent. The immanence means that the weighing scale can also be weighed using another weighing scale, so it satisfies the conditions of possessing a weight.

You might say that we are just twisting words. If we use physical examples, then there must be something wrong with the way we are using *language*. This is not true. A weighing scale indicates two properties: (1) its own mass, and (2) the mass of the object it measures; there is a difference between the weight it *possesses* and the weight it *describes*. The described weight is transcendent, and the possessed weight is immanent. Physics theories don't use this terminology because they convert the 'described weight' into *acceleration*—according to gravitational theory, an object pushes another weight and causes it to accelerate, and the amount of acceleration is due to the described weight. Thus, the second way of using the word 'weight' is converted into a different word— 'acceleration'. The problem is not solved, but it is obfuscated. I am only clarifying what is obfuscated within a physics theory.

Now, we can replace the concept 'weight' with the idea 'knowledge'. This concept can be applied to anything because everything is knowable, and by knowing it, we get knowledge. However, before we know anything, we must know the criteria for calling something knowledge—i.e. we must know the meaning of the concept 'knowledge'. The concept 'knowledge' can be applied to anything—e.g. you can say that knowing the weight is also knowledge. However, knowledge is not a weight. Therefore, in one sense, everything is an instance of knowledge, because they are different types of knowing. And yet, none of these instances are the criteria for something to be called knowledge. Thus, even if something is *not* a weight, it can still be *knowable*. However, if something is not knowable, then it also cannot be a weight. As a result, knowability is embedded inside the property of being a weight. And weight is a part of everything that is knowable. And yet, knowing the weight is knowledge, however, knowledge is not a weight.

If the concept of knowing still seems difficult, then it is because all concepts are difficult. They follow what we can call a *non-dualistic logic*, which must be contrasted to the conventional *dualistic logic*. Dualistic logic is based upon the separability of things: Each thing is different from the other thing, and each thing is only one thing; it is upon this basis that we develop the notions of identity and difference. However, when we use concepts, this separability begins to break down. For example, to counter the idea that each thing is different from the other thing, we can say that there are two apples; each apple is different from the other apple, but as the representations of the idea 'apple', they are also identical. Likewise, to counter the idea that each thing is only that thing, we can ask: What about the concept apple? It exists in many apples, which are different from each other, so the concept apple has millions of representations, and yet, as the concept that is represented, it is one thing. Again, that one thing is not only one thing.

Getting used to the non-dualistic logic is imperative if we want to understand knowledge, because there are many departments of knowledge—physics, chemistry, mathematics, logic, economics, sociology, psychology, etc. Each such division presents knowledge; therefore, we can say that economics is knowledge. But we cannot say that knowledge is economics. Everything knowable embeds the meaning 'knowledge', and by that embedding, we call that knowable some form of knowledge. However, the idea 'knowledge' is different from everything. As a result, knowing that something is an apple can be called knowledge. But knowledge cannot be called an apple. The principle of identity—i.e. if A is B, then B is A—is broken. And that breakdown of dualistic logic must be seen in knowledge too.

Illusion and Knowledge

The Vedic texts describe this world as an 'illusion'. This presents a straightforward contradiction when we call this world 'knowledge'. But these two positions can be easily reconciled if we understand how the illusion is created through an agency called *māyā*, which means "it is not".

What is māyā? It is what we call the *focus* of consciousness, due to which we can see only one thing at one time. When our consciousness is focused in this way, when we see one property, we also say that it is *not* the other properties. For example, while experiencing an apple, our consciousness alternately shifts from perceiving the smell, taste, color, shape, size, distance, direction, etc. Then it also withdraws from these sensations and tries to combine the data of the senses into a concept, but that concept is not sensations. Therefore, while cognizing something as an 'apple' through the mind, the consciousness is defocused from perceiving the sensations. Then the consciousness again withdraws into what is known as the 'intellect' and compares the idea of an 'apple' against previous known versions of the idea *one by one*. Thus, for instance, if the apple is green, then the intellect will recall from memory the instances in which some green thing has been called an apple. If no such thing exists in the memory, then the perceived object will not be called an apple. The key point is that we never see the apple *at once*. We see it piecemeal—sometimes we see color, shape, size, distance, and direction, one by one. Then we try to apply varied interpretations to this data set of the senses—one by one. Then we withdraw into the intellect and judge against the memory of past such idea applications—one by one.

This process of perception is therefore called the *modes of nature*. Each type of perception is a *mode*. The interpretation of the data is a *mode*. The judgment of the truth of the interpretation is a *mode*. Even seeing the different parts of the apple are *modes*. These modes are not seen simultaneously, because our consciousness toggles between the modes. This toggling can be called the dominant-subordinate modalities of our experience. Indeed, the different things we perceive in this world—flowers, fruits, birds, fishes, humans, etc.—are also varied dominant-subordinate structures of the modes. Thus, the variety of the world is the variation in the mode structures, and our perception of the world is also a variation in the mode structures.

When one mode is perceived, the other modes are hidden, or out of consciousness. And this shifting pattern of the modes constitutes the *focus* or the *attention* of consciousness—we see only one mode at a time.

This problem exists in epistemology too: sometimes we say that observation is necessary for perception, and sometimes we say that concepts or reasoning are important. These two schools of epistemology are called empiricism and rationalism. And we are unable to reconcile them because we need some reason to interpret the sense data, and when data is interpreted in a certain way, then we get a selection bias—other data is ignored. Therefore, false theories of nature are produced due to our selection bias.

For example, classical physics models planets and our bodies as *point particles*. All the details about shape, size, color, taste, and smell are neglected, and some properties like 'mass' and 'charge' are assigned. We assume that we can measure all these properties at once, but atomic theory shows that we cannot. In atomic theory, we can measure only one property at one time, which is just like our perception—we can either see form, or color, or distance, or direction, at one time. The process of shifting from one property to another is rapid, but it is not *simultaneous* perception of the world. This idea, however, creates serious problems in science: How can the world be called 'objective' if we cannot perceive everything simultaneously? And the answer to that problem is that this is how material perception is.

The nature of the material experience is such that we must toggle from one mode to another, and due to this toggling, we cannot see everything simultaneously. In each vision, we see one thing, and we consider that to be the only truth. Our vision is just like those of the five blind men trying to perceive an elephant. They cannot see the elephant, because our perception is itself influenced by the *modes*—we are more likely to see one thing than another. These modes hence *focus* our consciousness on one thing, to a point where most people cannot see things from another perspective.

Epistemology is also a victim of this problem. Each philosopher sees one method of knowing, and claims that it is the only method, or the complete method, although it is not. When contrary methods are recognized, then we find it hard to reconcile them, because they are indeed different. To correctly perceive the method of knowing—i.e. what we call 'knowledge'—we must be able to *simultaneously* see all these things, and we cannot unless our consciousness is also 'purified' of the modal style of perception.

Of course, the choice in consciousness ensures that we can focus on certain things as opposed to others. And choice also creates a limited perception, but that is not the reason that the material experience is called an illusion. The real reason is that these modes are automatically toggling their state of dominance and subordination due to *time*. Due to this toggling, the world *changes* automatically and whatever changes is called 'unreal' because 'reality' is described as that which doesn't change. But that doesn't mean that the world truly doesn't exist. It rather exists as the modes, which keep changing, and that change includes the changes in our attention. When consciousness is 'purified' of the modes, then the changes in our focus ends, and we can keep a *still* consciousness. But this stillness is not just the absence of a changing focus, but also the ability to see multiple modalities at the same time. This state, in which the world is objectively changing but our consciousness is fixed, is then called the true knowledge of this world.

In this state, we can obtain the perception of God because our perceptive capacities have been stilled, and we are not toggling between the modes rapidly. That perception of God is the ability to see many modes at the same time, and in some sense, we begin to perceive the whole truth, rather than merely the parts or aspects of this truth. This perception is also described as 'detachment' in the sense that as we get 'farther' from the world we perceived, we begin seeing the bigger picture, instead of the details. However, this description alone would be improper as it would entail the ignorance of the details. The correct description is that we are farther in the sense that we can see many parts simultancously, and due to this simultaneous vision of parts, which is otherwise attained if we are 'far', in one sense, we are far from the perceived world. But in another sense, we are close to everything since we are not seeing one thing at a time; we are seeing all of them.

Thus, if the problem of simultaneity of the modes is resolved, then there is no contradiction between 'attachment' and 'detachment', or between being in this world, and being outside this world, or between calling this world an illusion vs. calling it knowledge. All these contradictions exist due to modal perception, and they cease to exist without the modes.

The Theory of God's Knowledge

Based on this principle, a distinction is drawn between our consciousness and God's consciousness. Our consciousness in the material world is conditioned by the modes, due to which we see only one thing at a time. God's consciousness is completely free of the modes; therefore, He sees everything at the same time. Our focus of consciousness makes our knowledge an ignorance of all that we don't know. But God's omniscience prevents the existence of ignorance. This doesn't mean that God may not focus on something; as a person, He still can exercise His choices to focus. But that focus is self-driven; it is not forced by the influence of time.

To see God, then, the essential prescription is to be able to enhance our perceptive capacity, and the ability to see multiple aspects of reality. There are various gradations of this advancement. They begin at the lowest level of being able to obtain better knowledge of small parts of reality. And they culminate in the ability to perceive the whole truth—i.e. God. The principle of advancement is the same: instead of seeing one thing at a time, we are now seeing more things. However, this 'more' can keep increasing, and it culminates when we see the whole truth, i.e. God. Even when we are not seeing God, we can still talk about the aspects of God, which become dominant and subordinate, and exist in various things to different degrees. And we can call all these things 'knowledge' because all the principles of knowing are present in everything—to lesser or greater extents. Some principle of knowing may be applied more prominently in some cases, because that thing is prominent in that mode. However, that doesn't entail that one mode contradicts the other. That contradiction is the result of our experience being conditioned by the occurrence of one dominant mode.

The trouble thus far has been that we are neither well-versed with the nature of God, nor well-versed with all the conditions of knowing. For example, does a collection of theories that mutually contradict each other's claims—even though they are logically proven (based on contradictory assumptions)—be considered true? What about a theory that incompletely describes reality—i.e. it describes some parts of the reality correctly, but doesn't describe the other parts of reality? Can we consider an incomplete description of nature knowledge? What if a theory employs thousands of complicated assumptions? Can we say that if the theory describes the world correctly, then it must be knowledge even if it uses numerous highly complex assumptions? What about a theory that seems very rational and logical, but can never be tested? Or something that seems rational, but hasn't yet been observed to be true? Can we say that empirical criteria for knowing are not necessary if the rational and logical picture is itself compelling?

The point is that we don't have a clear answer to all these questions. As an example, we know that our physics theories are not always consistent; although they are logically sound and empirically proven in their respective domains, they are logically contradictory. If we said that logical consistency is necessary for something to be called knowledge, then all these physics theories would become ignorance. Likewise, we also have beautiful theories that seem quite rational, but they might not be proven empirically. If we said that empirical proof is necessary for something to be called knowledge, then all mathematical theorems that have no application in the world would become ignorance. As we go on broadening the criteria for knowledge, we find that it becomes harder and harder to call something knowledge. Indeed, much of what we call knowledge currently then becomes ignorance.

This is where the philosopher begins to scratch his head. He would like to say that a working theory of nature that has helped us build useful technology, that seems to save lives, or provides comforts, must be knowledge, although it is not logically consistent with other theories, and sometimes may not be fully proven empirically. These pragmatic concerns about wanting to claim progress in knowing through our endeavors has marred our quest for the definition for what it means to know. In this book, I want to get past this problem by saying: Here are the essential criteria for knowing that we must accept, because if we don't, then some form of ignorance (which we can clearly understand to be ignorance) would become truth. Once we establish these rules for calling something knowledge, then these rules must be *universally* applied—universally because knowability is universal. If some theory or doctrine doesn't fit that criteria for knowing, then it cannot be called knowledge. This is an exercise in pure epistemology.

But once we identify these conditions, we must also ask: Can we apply these principles simultaneously, and what would that application look like? The answer is that as we broaden our description of the world, more and more criteria for knowing must be applied. Thus, for instance, in knowing the apple, the problem of consistency between the different aspects of an apple doesn't arise because an apple is red, round, and sweet, not blue, cubical, and bitter. This problem would arise if we were trying to formulate a theory that accommodated both these opposing types of qualities. Then we would have to say that consistency among descriptions requires us to revise our description in a way that knowledge can include the knowing of opposing qualities. Likewise, if we were looking at a simple object, then the concerns about the description being simple doesn't arise. It arises when the reality under consideration becomes very complex. Thus, as we broaden our horizons in knowledge, all the criteria about knowledge must be borne to bear, and these criteria are therefore applicable to the Absolute Truth, or that truth of which every other relative truth is only a partial aspect.

To the extent that knowing this truth is very difficult for us at the present, because our consciousness only focuses on one thing at a time, better knowledge cannot be acquired unless we improve our consciousness. We will remain ignorant and illusioned unless we free ourselves of the 'focus on one thing at one time' type of awareness. When this restriction is lessened, then we can also begin to understand God, and eventually we see God *in everything*. The reason we cannot understand God right now, is because God is knowledge, and we don't understand what it truly means to know, by applying all the criteria of knowing. If we can see God in everything, then even if everything is removed, the vision of the conditions of knowing still remains. This type of consciousness, which is exclusively focused on the conditions of knowing, without applying these conditions to knowing anything can be called 'God consciousness' in the sense that it uses the complete criteria for knowing, which is also the vision of all perfection. This is the vision of God, which helps us see God in everything, but even if everything is removed, we can still see the conditions by which we see. Now, epistemology is also not different from the understanding of God.

Knowledge as Absolute Truth

Thus, I don't wish to confine myself to the traditions of epistemology as they have existed thus far. I want to combine these traditions, and show why they are *aspects* or parts of the complete method of knowing, and unless they are combined, we don't have a good definition of knowledge. Knowledge is widely accepted to be the Universal Truth, because it applies to everything—by definition a Universal Truth is that which applies to everything. In so far that we claim to be able to know anything, this Universal Truth must be seen inside each thing. If a skeptic counters that we can know anything, I can offer: Your arguments for why things are not truly known is a side-effect of the fact that there are many criteria for knowing, and if all the criteria are not satisfied, then we truly do not know. Therefore, your reasons for skepticism is the absence of one or more of those missing criteria. Thus, rather than accepting the skeptic's argument for claiming that nothing is truly known, we must state the reasons why they are not known, and if these reasons are presented, then they define how we can know.

Once we define the criteria for knowing anything, and these criteria can be applied to knowing anything, then 'knowledge' becomes the most fundamental concept or idea. It is based upon this idea that we can derive all other ideas. For example, in knowing something to be an apple, we are invoking the idea of knowledge. However, in knowing something to be an elephant, only the idea of knowledge would be invoked; the idea of an apple will not be invoked. Granted that both 'apple' and 'elephant' are universals, 'knowledge' is a more fundamental universal, simply because it applies to everything we can know, although 'apple' and 'elephant' do not. If something is applicable to everything, then it becomes the Universal Truth.

However, the criteria for knowing are different from the knowledge of individual things, by the condition that knowing an 'apple' is knowledge, but knowledge is not an apple. The very means by which we define One Universal Truth that applies to everything, also makes that Universal Truth the Absolute Truth in terms of which all other truths are *judged* to be true.

For instance, let's say that the set of all the conditions that define something to be true is {X}, and let's suppose for the moment that {X} is finite. Then by virtue of the claim that {X} is not an apple or an elephant, we can say that {X} is different from all other concepts, but only identical to *itself*. That is, to know the criteria for knowing what we mean by knowledge, we must invoke knowledge. The definition of knowledge must therefore satisfy that same definition. For example, suppose we say that knowledge must be consistent and complete, then this condition must apply to all the conditions of knowing—i.e. the conditions must themselves be consistent and complete. Similarly, if we say that knowledge must be simple and parsimonious, then that definition must also apply to {X}—i.e. all the criteria for knowing must be simple and parsimonious. This entails that we cannot come up with self-contradictory criteria for deciding what is knowledge, because that would entail that knowledge is itself an incoherent idea. Similarly, our criteria for knowing cannot be incomplete such that some things that can be called knowledge are excluded from the definition of knowing itself. In simple terms, the criteria for knowledge must apply to the criteria as well.

This reflexive nature of the criteria of knowing can be understood easily if we say that the conditions of knowing (which we can call the Absolute Truth) is also a *person* because the act of applying the criteria for knowing to those criteria entails a self-conscious nature of these criteria. Since these criteria can be applied to everything to determine if they are knowable, therefore, God as the Absolute Truth is the precondition for the world to exist—i.e. to be knowable. Since the conditions of knowing can exist without anything else being known, therefore, God can exist when nothing else exists. Then, since God can exist all by Himself, therefore, He must be considered the cause of everything else—i.e. the conditions of knowing must be applied repeatedly to create the many forms of knowabilities. Since all these things can be known, therefore, in knowing anything, God's existence is intrinsically proven. In one sense, God doesn't need a separate proof, because He is defined as the conditions by which we know anything. In another sense, we can separate the conditions of knowledge from the knowledge *of* apples and elephants, so God is not merely immanent in all the known things, but He is also transcendent to these known things.

Therefore, epistemology cannot be separated from a rational and scientific study of God because: (1) there is need for a universal definition of knowledge in order for anything to be known, (2) this universal definition of knowledge pertains to knowing everything, and so, knowability is immanent in everything that is ever known, and (3) knowability stands apart from everything, because the conditions of knowing something are logically prior to anything being known, (4) the reflexive application of the criteria for knowing to those criteria entails that the criteria for knowledge is self-aware, and (5) this self-awareness exists when nothing else exists, and (6) this self-awareness is the very definition of 'God'. Therefore, 'God' is yet another *name* for the conditions of knowability or the meaning of 'knowledge'.

Philosophers and scientists prefer to use the term 'knowledge' and religious people prefer to use the term 'God'. In Vedic philosophy, these terms are replaced by *paramam-satyam* or the Supreme Truth. Since the Supreme Truth gives rise to subsidiary truths, which are judged to be true by the criteria defined by the Supreme Truth, therefore, they are called *relative truths*. In contrast, the Supreme Truth is called the Absolute Truth.

Thus, there are many names by which we can call the same thing. Someone can say 'knowledge'; another person can say 'God', another person can say 'Supreme Truth', someone else can use the terms 'Universal Truth' or 'Absolute Truth'. They are all valid terms, although they refer to slightly different nuances of the same idea. Once we understand why that Absolute Truth is knowledge or knowability, then we see why they are the same. In this book, I will use all these terms interchangeably. The context of usage can make one term preferable over the others, but if we understand the larger context, then they all mean the same thing. This may seem surprising to most readers, as the discussion of knowledge is equated with the discussion of God, but this equation is inevitable as we have seen above.

Epistemology and Theology

If the Absolute Truth is defined as 'knowledge', then upon this basis we can talk about the 'science' of God: all the *criteria* that lead to knowledge. Remember that the criteria are satisfied in all genuine knowledge—e.g. if we know something as an apple, then the criteria for knowing is satisfied in the knowledge of something being an apple. However, the knowing of an apple is not the criteria for knowing itself, because it doesn't apply to knowing an elephant. Therefore, there is a distinction between the criteria that define something to be knowledge, and the criteria that define something to be the knowledge *of* apple, elephant, etc. As an example, a criterion for knowing is that the known must be observed; this criterion is called empiricism. Whether we know the apple or an elephant, this criterion must be satisfied. However, the specific sensations we obtain through empirical observation can differ. In the case of an apple, we would say that observation must reveal a certain shape, size, color, and these properties will be different for an elephant. Thus, the criteria that define something to be knowledge are more abstract principles—such as observation and reason—while the criteria that define something to be the knowledge *of* an apple or elephant are *refinements* of the more abstract principles that constitute knowing. As a result, we can say that knowing an apple is knowledge, but knowing is not an apple.

The trouble is: If observation is defined to be a criterion for knowing, then how do we *know* that it is a criterion? All the criteria for knowing must also be known before we use them, and to know these criteria, we must know them beforehand, which then leads to an infinite regress—how can we know the criteria for knowing, if we need to know them beforehand? Someone can now argue: This infinite regress in deciding the criteria for knowing entails that these criteria can never be known.

Hence, the concept of 'knowledge' is unclear, and whatever criteria we may use, we cannot be sure that these criteria necessarily lead to knowledge. It may be that because the criteria can never be known, therefore knowledge is impossible.

This question seems difficult because it pertains to the nature of consciousness, by which we know. Consciousness employs certain methods of knowing, which are its innate nature. The methods of knowing are not imported from outside ourselves; they are the very nature of consciousness. In trying to know all the methods by which we know, we are ultimately exploring the nature of consciousness. But why should we explore that nature if we already are that nature? Shouldn't the methods of knowing be obvious to us if we are those methods of knowing? The answer to this question, which constitutes the substance of this book, is that there are many methods employed by consciousness in deciding if something is knowledge. Each of us has the capacity to employ these methods too. The problem is that we don't *recognize* the use of these methods *formally* in epistemology, while defining the nature of knowledge. Indeed, because the multifarious nature of consciousness is not properly understood, there is a temptation in thinking that there is only one method by which we know, and therefore, certain knowledge can be obtained by employing only one method. Thus, all theories of epistemology—which propose and eulogize one method—remain incomplete. But if they try to induct more than one method, then a contrary problem is encountered—the resulting method seems contradictory.

The reason for this contradiction, is that *our* consciousness at present uses one method at a time. Each soul, in Vedic philosophy, is said to be 'conditioned' in a different way to prioritize one such method over the other methods, because they dominantly employ that method to know, and they think that everyone must either use that method, or they cannot know. Other people, however, use other methods dominantly, and they are therefore capable of knowing things in other ways that everyone is not.

For example, an empiricist would say that the mind is a blank slate and all concepts are simply generalizations of perceptions. A rationalist would say that the mind is hardwired with certain fundamental ideas using which we perceive the world, and then use that perception to develop new concepts. The fact is that there are numerous capacities for knowing available to consciousness, but some capacities are developed while others are not. To recognize these capacities, we must *develop* our consciousness. Then we can also apply the methods of knowing that previously did not seem viable. By implication, we can define a 'fully developed' consciousness that has all the capacities for perception, which can then be employed simultaneously, and they will then together constitute what we mean by 'knowing'—it is the insight about something obtained by using all the conscious abilities.

But this book isn't about how one goes about developing their consciousness. It is about identifying the methods using philosophical analysis. However, to the extent that this development is essential as part of epistemology, it must be referenced in our discussion about knowledge. In the analysis of knowledge, we can consider many approaches. First, we can look at the *reasons* different philosophers have propounded different methods; there are some good reasons why certain methods are necessary in some cases, although they may fall short in the other cases. Second, we can examine how different methods play complementary roles in addressing the problems of the other methods, and why such methods must be combined. Third, we can study the consequences of not using some methods—namely, that knowledge will remain uncertain or incomplete without all methods. Fourth, all capacities for knowing are present in everyone to varying degrees of prominence; while everyone doesn't use them always, we can understand, and extrapolate from this understanding of how others may use them.

In short, the conditions that prescribe knowledge are already prevalent, and present to varying degrees in different people. A mathematician is more adept at reasoning, and a surgeon more adept at observation. An engineer is generally a pragmatist, while a psychologist is often an idealist. An artist understands how beauty plays an important role in knowing the world, while an economist quantifies the world. It's not that a mathematician is incapable of observation, a surgeon incapable of reasoning, an engineer devoid of a mind, a psychologist devoid of pragmatic concerns, an artist unconcerned with quantities, or an economist incapable of understanding beauty. Each person has these capacities to varying extents, and they emphasize different aspects of the process of knowing as the dominant ways of knowing. My goal in this book is to unearth all such capacities for cognition, describe how they complement the other methods, and how collectively a certain set of criteria for knowing constitute the complete definition of 'knowing'.

Unless we spell out the rules that define the criteria for knowing clearly, we might sometimes prematurely claim knowledge, without satisfying all the criteria for knowing. Thus, a pragmatist might say that a theory is true just because it works, not recognizing that other theories could also work. A rationalist may claim that a rational description is true, without verifying the axioms upon which his reasoning is constructed. An artist may see the symmetries in a description and claim that the beauty of the description itself makes something true, even if there is no empirical confirmation or pragmatic application for their ideas. These, and many others, are the potential pitfalls of not defining what we mean by knowing, and to overcome these pitfalls, we must identify all the ways in which we can know, and something is knowledge only if confirmed by the use of all those methods.

Therefore, the study of the conditions of knowing is nothing more than philosophical analysis of the criteria that define knowledge. In this respect, the quest is identical to that in epistemology, which asks questions such as: How do we know? If we assume that there is only one method, then we would commit the traditional mistakes of epistemology, wherein all the conditions of knowing are not prescribed, and by satisfying only one condition, something could be called 'knowledge' in one case, but not in another.

These methods of knowing are the capacities for consciousness, and the original consciousness—i.e. God—thus defines the meaning of 'knowing': It is all the ways in which He can know. Therefore, in another sense, the endeavor for uncovering all the methods in which consciousness can know (although we may not presently use all such methods actively) can also be applied to asking: What do we mean by "God"? The erstwhile subject of epistemology now becomes the subject of theology. The definition of 'knowledge' now becomes a religious pursuit of understanding God.

The difference between epistemology and theology is simply that in the latter case we are talking about the meaning of 'knowing' from our perspective, and in the former case we are speaking about the meaning of 'knowing' from God's perspective. In the former case, 'knowledge' is immanent in all acts of knowing, and in the latter case, 'knowledge' is transcendent to all individual acts of knowing. The difference between theology and epistemology is also that all the conditions of knowing are not equally dominant for knowing the things in this world. However, for knowing God, we must use all the methods, i.e. all the criteria of knowing must be applied to know God. Thus, unlike other kinds of knowledge, where the criteria are not equally dominant, knowing God means knowing that which simultaneously requires the application of *all* the principles of knowing. In short, God can be defined as that object which necessitates all the methods, properties, conditions, or criteria or knowing simultaneously. Unless all these methods are applied simultaneously, we cannot know God. Hence, God is a special person Whose knowledge differs from the knowing of ordinary objects, and that specialty is that knowing God needs all the methods that are selectively and occasionally applied in knowing the other things of this world.

Thus, we have two definitions of God—the object of knowing and the methods of knowing. The object is one, but the methods are many. Epistemology is the study of all the methods of knowing, and theology is the study of one object. However, we cannot separate the object from the methods because God is a person and His awareness is the combination of all methods. When we do epistemology, we study all the methods of knowing. And when we study God, then we know the person who employs all these methods. He is the embodiment of all the methods in fullness, and we are the partial representations of these methods. Therefore, His knowledge encompasses everything, and our knowledge encompasses only a few things.

Theology and epistemology cannot be separated because God is self-aware—i.e. He uses all the methods of knowing to know Himself. Since His consciousness is all those methods, therefore, what He knows through that awareness is indeed the methods of knowing. Thus, when we know other things by our consciousness, we *use* the methods of knowing. But when we know ourselves, then we use the methods of knowing to know those methods of knowing. If our methods of knowing are partial, then we know ourselves as that incomplete knower. And since God's methods of knowing are complete—which define His *omniscience*—therefore, He knows Himself as the complete knower. Therefore, the stark difference between the object of knowing, and the method of knowing, is useful when we know things other than ourselves. But that distinction must be dissolved when we know ourselves. In that sense, we can say that epistemology is the study of all the methods, as they are applied to knowing other things. And theology is the study of all the methods as God uses them to know Himself. Accordingly, if we want to know God as He knows Himself, then we too must apply the same methods that God uses to know Himself. Of course, it is possible that we may not be able to know God completely, as He knows Himself, because we cannot use all the methods simultaneously to the extent that God can. However, if we don't use the same methods as God uses to know Himself, then we cannot know Him. As our consciousness begins to approximate God's consciousness, our understanding of God begins to approximate the understanding God has of Himself. In principle, we can never achieve the same level of God understanding as God has of Himself. But to the extent that our consciousness can approximate God's consciousness, we can get a partial vision of God. Thus, a theoretical understanding of these methods simply helps us understand how God sees Himself, but that theoretical understanding is not a substitute for real experience. It is just the preliminary step toward realizing what knowing God means in terms of knowing.

Thus, the problem of infinite regress—namely, that the knower uses the method of knowing to know those methods—can be resolved only when the method of knowing is consciousness, and the application of that method of knowing to itself is self-consciousness. Epistemology is the study of how our consciousness knows. When this consciousness turns toward itself, then we know ourselves using the same methods as we know other things. For instance, if observation and reason are two methods of knowing the world, then these methods can be applied to knowing the self. That self, however, is both the method of knowing, and the object that is known by the application of the method. Therefore, self-awareness is the use of methods of knowing to know those methods by which we know. If our methods are incomplete, then our knowledge of the self using those methods is also incomplete. In the case of God, those methods are complete, thus, when He knows Himself as self-awareness then His knowledge is complete.

Thus, if we successfully collect all the methods of knowing, which constitutes a complete epistemology, then we can talk about the person who uses all these methods simultaneously to know everything. That person now becomes omniscient by virtue of knowing these methods. The discovery of all the methods of knowing is epistemology, and the discovery of the person who possesses all these capacities of knowing simultaneously is theology. Thus, the concerns of epistemology and theology cannot be separated. Rather, they must be united in the quest for the definition of knowledge as the collection of methods by which we know, and the understanding of the person who uses these methods simultaneously to be omniscient. Through the fact that both subjects ultimately deal in the nature of knowledge, or how perfect knowledge is acquired, they are also not starkly different.

The Six Qualities of the Absolute Truth

In this book I will be guided by the Vedic philosophical description of God or *paramam-satyam*, where He is described as possessing six qualities called knowledge, beauty, renunciation, power, wealth, and heroism. Each of these constitute the object to be known, and they also constitute the methods of knowing. In God's self-awareness, the method of knowing becomes the object of knowing. Therefore, we can say that as an object, God is the embodiment of these six qualities. But we must also say that these qualities are also the methods of knowing—i.e. God's consciousness. The former approach constitutes theology, and the latter epistemology. It is much harder to understand these topics through theology. It is easier to understand them as methods of knowing, or epistemology. This is what I will do in this book: analyze the methods to define the nature of consciousness. If that nature is understood, then God's nature is also known.

The term knowledge is stated to be the fundamental nature of God, and two criteria are applied to define knowledge—*completeness* and *non-duality*. In epistemology, these are known as completeness and consistency. The term non-duality is employed because the different aspects of reality are described using contradictory concepts, and to call them both 'knowing', we must say that these concepts are different *aspects* of knowing. For instance, the idea 'sweet' is not defined without the idea 'bitter'; 'hot' is not defined without 'cold', and 'smooth' is not defined without 'rough'. Therefore, when we call something 'hot', 'bitter', and 'rough', we are defining it in opposition to 'cold', 'sweet', and 'smooth'.

This not contradictory knowing; it is knowing something by *contrast* to other things, and all knowing (except the knowing of knowledge itself) is not just knowing what something *is*, but also what it *is not*. These contrasts exist for partial truths and they reduce as we obtain more *complete* knowledge. Ultimately, if complete knowledge is obtained, then its opposite—i.e. *ignorance*—ceases to exist. Therefore, knowledge is non-dual because it doesn't need to be defined as the opposite of ignorance. This means that if we define the criteria for knowing, then we don't need to define the criteria for ignorance. Whatever doesn't meet these criteria automatically becomes ignorance, and knowledge isn't co-defined with ignorance. However, the definition of 'ignorance' depends on the definition of 'knowledge'—it is the very opposite of knowledge. Therefore, if ignorance exists, then knowledge must exist *a priori*. However, if knowledge exists, then ignorance may not exist. This contrasts with other ideas which are co-defined with their opposites. Quite simply, knowledge is fully defined by the *positive* criteria, and doesn't need the elimination of the *negative* criteria. In philosophical terms we can say that we don't prove the truth by the method of elimination, or *reductio ad absurdum*, or falsification. By such methods, we just prove what truth is not. To also show what truth is, we must provide a positive definition—i.e. verification, confirmation, and affirmation.

However, upon closer inspection, we find that these two criteria do not sufficiently identify the nature of knowledge. For example, a theory of reality can describe the world using thousands of complex assumptions, and completeness and consistency of these assumptions doesn't entail that they are knowledge. Rather, knowledge is further defined by two additional criteria, namely, *simplicity* and *parsimony*. In other words, the assumptions underlying a theory of reality must be simple and parsimonious. Simplicity is a qualitative criterion, while parsimony is a quantitative criterion. Therefore, the ideas themselves must be simple, and they must also be a few ideas. The combination of simplicity and parsimony defines the meaning of 'beauty'. Thus, we must say: Knowledge must also be beautiful, because complicated and superfluous descriptions of nature cannot be called 'knowledge'.

Now, a new problem arises: Our notions of consistency, completeness, simplicity, and parsimony, heavily depend upon what we are describing. For example, if we just choose to describe an apple, then we might come up with a description that satisfies the above four criteria: The definition of apple can accommodate both red and green apples; it must not depend on what an apple is not; we must use the fewest assumptions to define the apple, and these must also be the simplest. In one sense, a consistent, complete, simple, and parsimonious description of the apple is knowledge. But a theory that applies only to the apple, and not the elephant, cannot be true. This means that the above four criteria are subject to the *data* we test it against. As the data set is broadened, the theory will fail the above four conditions. Thus, many theories can qualify the above four criteria for a small data set. But that does not mean that they are true. A true theory must also be universal, and it must explain a large data set simply, parsimoniously, consistently, and completely. Truth is applicable to all kinds of variety.

Obviously, the definition of 'knowledge' is now dependent on all that we call 'knowable'. As the 'knowable' reduces, more and more descriptions of this limited knowable begin to qualify as knowledge, and we now find that there are numerous theories that are equally simple, parsimonious, consistent, and complete, because the data *underdetermines* the theory. To solve this problem of underdetermination, we need to add more data to eliminate all except one theory. How much data do we need? We need as much data as necessary and sufficient to eliminate the alternatives. Necessity means that anything lesser will not eliminate some theories. And sufficiency means that even more data will not help us eliminate additional theory. Therefore, to the above four criteria, we can add the criteria of *necessity* and *sufficiency*. It defines a bound on the knowable world—the world must solve the problem of underdetermination without overdetermination. To address these issues, the world must be just the right amount of data to validate *one* theory.

When necessity and sufficiency are applied reflexively to knowledge, then we must say that 'knowledge' is necessary and sufficient to produce all the data that validates the knowledge. To understand this idea, we must look at the relation between cause and effect. For a cause to produce an effect, the cause must be *sufficient*, and something is said to be sufficient as a cause if the effect is present within the cause. By this sufficiency we know that a cause can produce an effect. However, the same effect could also be produced by other causes. How do we know that it wasn't the other causes that produced this effect? This requires *necessity* and it means that the effect must indicate within itself that it was produced by a cause. In short, sufficiency requires that the effect is within the cause, and necessity requires that the cause is within the effect. The effect being present within the cause is generally understood to be a physical existence—for example, if energy is transferred from one entity to another, an effect is produced, and that effect was within the cause because the energy was within the cause. By this transfer, however, the cause loses its energy. God is not that kind of cause; His causation is semantic. For instance, we can say that a 'mammal' is the cause of the 'cow' because mammal 'contains' the 'cow'. However, if 'cow' is removed from the 'mammal', then the 'mammal' is not reduced in terms of its meaning. Therefore, sufficiency indicates two things: (1) the cause contains the effect, and yet, removing the effect from the cause does not reduce the cause. Similarly, the cause within the effect is a symbolic existence, in the sense that we must know that it wasn't any other cause that produced this effect. For instance, just by looking at the 'cow' we can say that it is also a 'mammal'. Thus, both the cause and the effect are semantic; the effect within the cause exists semantically, just as the cause in the cause exists symbolically. In Vedic philosophy, the semantic cause of everything is Bhagavan; the semantic parts of this Bhagavan are called Brahman; and the symbolic existence of the Bhagavan in the Brahman is called the Paramātma.

If we think of physical causation, then there can be sufficiency in the sense that there is some physical energy transferred from one entity to another. However, we can never get necessity—i.e. knowing which cause produced this effect. As a result, all physical theories of causation become indeterministic because they can explain the effect from the cause, but not the cause from the effect. Given any effect, we cannot certainly say that it was a specific cause that produced it. If God is also treated as a cause in the same way, then there is no way to know that God produced the world, because the world could also have been produced in other ways—e.g. a 'big bang'. An atheistic theory of nature is hence based on the physical theory of causation, and there is no necessity for a specific physical cause to indeed be the producer of an effect. This necessity exists in semantic causality.

Semantic causality depends on the relation between concepts, which are organized in a hierarchy. The cow is within the mammal, and the mammal is within the cow, but this containment is not physical. Once the cow is manifest from a mammal, then the cow can be called a mammal. However, despite assigning the more abstract concept (e.g. mammal) to the less abstract concept (e.g. cow), there is still an asymmetry in the relation due to which we can say that a cow is a mammal (the property of being a mammal exists in the cow) but the mammal is not a cow (there are other kinds of mammals besides the cow). This asymmetry is the non-equality between the cow and the mammal, which can be called their mutual difference.

The same thing holds true for knowledge. The world as a specific type of knowledge is within the idea knowledge, and therefore this idea is the sufficient cause of the specific type of knowledge. The knowledge is also the necessary cause because the cause is present in the instance of knowledge, due to which we can call that instance a type of knowledge.

Thus, necessity and sufficiency pertain both to the data that has expanded from the knowledge, and to knowledge from which it has expanded. The expansion is necessary and sufficient to eliminate alternative ideas—if we begin studying the expansion and want to know the source from which it has expanded. Conversely, if we begin from knowledge, then the cause is necessary and sufficient cause of the expansions as all forms of knowledge are within the idea of knowledge, and even after these expansions have manifest from the original idea, they carry the property of knowability.

This idea is called God's 'renunciation' in two ways. First, God as the original *truth* has renounced everything that constitutes His *proof*. Second, in spite of renouncing the proofs of the truth, the truth still stands apart from the proof, such that the proofs refer to the truth. If the proofs were not renounced, then God would simply exist as the truth, but would not be known by anyone other than Himself. Likewise, if the truth itself became the proof, then we would say that something exists, but it doesn't prove anything, because the truth has ceased to exist apart from the proof. Thus, God's renunciation pertains to His independence from the proof, the ability to create the proof, and for the proof to be the way that He is known.

This means that if 'knowing' is the cause of everything, and 'knowing' is an idea, then all known things must also be ideas. This leads to a novel notion of materialism in which matter is not some 'stuff', but varieties of ideas such as color, taste, smell, many object-concepts, beliefs, and so on. If we apply the wrong idea to something, then we are not applying a wrong idea to some material stuff. Rather, we are applying a wrong idea to an idea, and this incompatibility between these ideas makes the ideas wrong.

Now, a new problem arises: If the world has expanded from 'knowing', and is a form of knowing, then how do we confirm that the world is indeed knowable? This is not such a straightforward idea as it might seem initially. The problem is that what we get in our sense perception and thought can be called 'phenomena' which are said to be different from the 'reality'. How can we know what a thing is, as opposed to just how it appears to us? This problem arises due to the existence of hallucinations, perceptual mistakes, and illusions. How do we know that we are not knowing incorrectly?

This is the domain of traditional epistemology, and two methods—called *rationalism* and *empiricism*—based on the existence of the mind and the senses are recognized. The empirical method relies on sense perception, but it is always incomplete because (1) we never have all the data, and (2) whatever data we have, could be a perceptual mistake, illusion, or hallucination. Whatever repetitions we perform to eliminate these errors could also be prone to errors. Likewise, the rational method relies on the mind, which interprets the sense perception to apply a concept, but whatever concepts we apply to the world can be problematic since (1) they depend on what we already know, and we are not assured to have all the concepts, and (2) even if we have the correct concept, we can apply it wrongly in specific cases. Again, whatever repetitions are used to overcome this problem can themselves suffer from the same problem of ignorance and misapplication.

The Vedic system describes a solution to this problem, namely, that all errors in perception and cognition arise from the 'impurities' of consciousness. Our senses and the mind are not blank slates; in fact, a blank slate cannot perceive or conceive anything. We perceive and conceive based on the concepts we have acquired in the past, and these concepts may not be the correct and *ideal* notions of something. For instance, there is a 'pure' color yellow, but we might think that alternative shades constitute the ideal 'yellow'. Likewise, there is a 'pure' sweetness, but our notions of 'sweetness' may not be pure. When we use these impure concepts to cognize the world, then things that are not so pure are considered perfect, and those things that are perfectly sweet or yellow, are considered to be not so perfect. Thus, after saying that the consciousness is not a blank slate, we must also say that it contains impure concepts, which must be purified in order to obtain correct perceptions and reasoning—i.e. for reason and observation to be useful methods for acquiring knowledge. If consciousness is not purified in this way, then all our reasons and observations are potentially incorrect.

The process of purification is *associating* with perfection. As the senses, mind, intellect, etc. associate with perfection, the concepts in terms of which we reason and perceive are altered. This alteration now helps us see the distinction between imperfect and perfect: whatever seemed perfect earlier now become imperfect and vice versa. The associating with perfection is called a 'spiritual process', and there are many such processes. In one process, we study the nature of perfection theoretically—as we are doing here. In another process, we mold our lives along the perfect ideals. In yet another process, we just meditate upon the nature of the perfection. And in a yet another process, we become devoted to serving perfection—i.e. God. Depending on the extent of a person's convictions, a different process can be used. For instance, someone who is not convinced that there is perfection, or what it is, can study this perfection theoretically, and this process is called *jnana-yoga*. Someone who has a theoretical understanding of perfection, can meditate upon it, which is called *dhyana-yoga*. Those who have visualized this perfection, can mold their lives after the perfection (*karma-yoga*). And those who have been able to change their lives can become devoted to the service of the perfection as the exclusive purpose of their lives (*bhakti-yoga*).

All these processes utilize observation, action, and reasoning, but they are progressive steps for realizing the nature of perfection. Therefore, the methods of reason and observation are not incorrect, however, the methods are understood differently in the Vedic system than in Western philosophy. In the latter, the mind and the senses are either blank slates (in empiricism) or they already carry the perfect ideas (in idealism). The Vedic system rejects this conclusion. It says that we have the *capacity* to know the ideal and be ideal. But we are not presently ideal. To become ideal, and to know the ideal, we must associate with the ideal—using one of the many possible methods. By that association, our consciousness is 'purified' and then we begin to see the world perfectly, and reason about it using the perfect concepts. Then, reason and observation are perfect methods for getting knowledge.

This claim, however, leads to the question: How do we know what is perfect? Unless we know what perfect is, we might associate with the imperfection, and that association will then not purify the consciousness. Therefore, before we associate with perfection, we must know what perfection is. How do we distinguish the perfection from the imperfection?

This is when *pragmatic* concerns are added to knowledge: the perfection is that which is freer of suffering. Those who know the truth, are also able to apply this truth pragmatically in this world and use that application to solve the problems of day-to-day life. The basic problem of life is suffering, which comes in many forms. If we can reduce this suffering, then we have the entitlements for claiming that we have knowledge. In short, we cannot decide what truth is based on reason and experience, if our reasoning and observation are themselves imperfect. To apply empiricism and rationalism, we must associate with perfection. But that association requires us to know what perfection is. And perfection it that which makes us free of suffering. We may not have the perfect ideas to observe and reason, but all of us know the distinction between enjoyment and suffering. And those who know the perfection must be able to tell us how we can reduce our suffering. Then, we can associate with those individuals, and that association will then purify us. Conversely, if someone claims to know the truth, but is unable to solve the problems of our life, then how can we know that he knows? Such a person is no different from all those who claim to know, but don't.

Thus, all transcendental quests for the nature of truth, and even mundane quests for knowing the nature of worldly reality whittle down to a simple problem: Can someone alleviate the suffering based on their knowledge? Even the prestige of modern science is based upon its ability to build technology that improves the quality of life. This technology includes medicine, housing, transportation, communication, economics, social structures, etc. The acquisition of knowledge needs effort and incurs costs. If we invest this effort and cost, what would be the test for the worthiness of that investment? Why would we take the effort and incur the costs unless it is proven to work? These kinds of pragmatic demands of the truth are not merely heuristics; they are also the expectation that knowledge must be *useful.*

Pragmatism leads to the *least action* theories of nature. Least action says that there is a quantity called 'action'—which we can loosely equate to effort or energy—that must be minimized to attain a certain objective. The objective is always the solution to a problem, and these objectives are already given to us by nature because our lives are already problematic. So, a theory of reality is that which gives us the shortest path to solving the problems. A problem might have many solutions; however, some solutions are also cheaper and easier than others. How do we know if something is better or worse? The answer is that we must lower the cost and maximize the value. Whatever solves the problem cheaply and easily is the best solution.

When pragmatism is reflexively applied to the other criteria for knowing, then we can say that we can pragmatically employ any of the previous criteria—consistency, completeness, simplicity, parsimony, rationalism, or empiricism—depending on whatever is easier and cheaper, if they also deliver what we want and need, and maximize the return on investment.

Pragmatism, however, also has a dark side, because it can also be interpreted as the rejection of all the previous principles. Thus, for instance, we can say that all prior principles of consistency, completeness, simplicity, parsimony, empiricism, rationalism, necessity, and sufficiency can be rejected if we don't find them working. Under the bright side of pragmatism, we say: "truth works". Under the dark side of pragmatism, we say: "whatever works is true". Under this darker view, the knower takes on an active role in defining the nature of reality rather than passively accepting its nature. The term 'knowledge' is redefined: truth is not always the *discovery* of truth; it can also be *invention* of truth. The criterion for invention is that something works. It is one thing to say that we affirm our knowledge by checking if it works against the day-to-day problems of life. It is quite another to say that whatever solves a particular problem of life must be the perfect truth.

This is when pragmatism must be extended to a broader set of problems. If a solution addresses one problem, but creates many more problems, than then do not have good solutions, or the solutions to those problems are hard and expensive, then pragmatically, it is not a good solution. A perfect solution is that which creates no new problems, while solving the stated problems. Ultimately, a perfect solution solves all the problems of life.

At present, we can see the darker side of pragmatism when science delivers some useful technology that solves the day-to-day problems of life; however, that solution then brings new problems, whose solution either doesn't exist, or becomes harder. As we try to solve the problems created by the previous 'solutions', we end up with a cascade of unsolved problems, which are ultimately substituting one problem with another. This is when we can pragmatically evaluate—is this solution knowledge or ignorance?

A side effect of the dark side of pragmatism is that knowledge begins fragmenting. Each department of knowledge says: "This idea is good because it works for me". We can use unique ideas, which do not apply in other cases, or may be contradictory to other cases, which may even be irrational or empirically not confirmable, which are neither simple nor parsimonious, can still seem to work in the short-term or a narrow problem. By a narrow focus, we lose sight of the broader reality, that it must be known consistently, completely, simply, parsimoniously, empirically, rationally, that which is necessary and sufficient, and is obtained at the lowest cost, bringing the greatest value. Instead of considering these broader criteria, scientists and philosophers define themselves narrowly in terms of their expertise in a subject, but those subjects are artificially crafted based on what works.

But pragmatism in this form doesn't work, because over time we find that the costs of the diversifying departments keep increasing, and the value that they generate constantly declines. At that time, pragmatism must be applied to itself, to say that some knowledge is too expensive, and it is better to invest our time and effort in something else that seems more productive! In trying to reduce costs, and maximize values, we generally tend to merge and combine things before we slim them down. Generally, the loser is paired with a winner because the winner can take on the burden of the loser. This leads to competition between ideas, theories, fields of knowledge, or even institutions that propound some theory, as they try to corner all the wealth and investment going into a particular idea. This competition is healthy if it is also fair—i.e. the idea that is more consistent, complete, simple, parsimonious, necessary, and sufficient is graciously allowed to be the winner. But pragmatism is different. The previous winners monopolize the resources and starve the competition by cutting off their supply lines to compete.

This unhealthy competition creates cycles of change in which the winners and losers oscillate between their powers and constantly try to weaken each other. The result is that knowledge is never obtained, unless the truth corners the resources, cuts off the supply lines for falsity, and monopolizes the discourse. Therefore, for knowledge to be obtained, we must say that *truth wins* and replaces the constant oscillations of dominance with stability. Under this stability, one type of theory is not replaced by another theory. With stability, we get continuous growth in knowledge, because the truth not only defeats the falsity, but brings whatever was good in the failed theory as well. The truth is that hero which is not only consistent, complete, parsimonious, simple, necessary, sufficient, lowest cost, greatest value, but also one that defeats the falsity and establishes the truth's dominance. But this dominance is not like the dominance of other false ideas. It is that dominance which creates permanence and stability in knowledge. If the truth doesn't win, then all other principles are neglected in the name of pragmatism, and the truth remains incomplete, inconsistent, large, complex, unnecessary, insufficient, irrational, unempirical, high cost, and low value.

But how can the truth win when it doesn't have the power and resources to win? And the answer is that falsity collapses due to its internal contradictions, while truth stands victorious because it is free of these inner conflicts. Truth wins because it brings unity, coherence, and harmony, while falsity loses because it causes disunity, incoherence, and discord. We have earlier noted that knowledge is consistent and complete, but consistency violates the fact that the world exists as opposites which must be reconciled. How can they be reconciled? The answer is that something becomes more dominant, and that 'winner' is understood as the universal truth. But what happens to the diversity? It may be subordinated by the winner, but it is also important, and unless it gets its dominance, it will create a conflict. The result of these inner conflicts would be the weakening of the truth.

Therefore, the meaning of the truth being stronger is that it is able to reconcile the contradictions by giving each idea a different role in the overall system of knowledge. The theory that was universally false, can be contextually true. If it is given a unique place in solving the problems where it doesn't create new problems, then we have satisfied pragmatic usefulness, without compromising the nature of the universal truth. For example, 'hot' and 'cold' are opposites, but they are valuable in different conditions—e.g. use 'hot' in winter, and use 'cold' in summer. Contradictions between 'hot' and 'cold' therefore do not need to eliminate one side (which would create a contextual problem in the summer). Rather, we can create a contextual role of that solution, such that (a) the opposites can coexist, (b) each side has its individual place, and (c) the ultimate truth is neither of these opposites. The heroism of leadership of truth is that it is beyond the opposites, but each opposite is given its proper role and place in the scheme of things. The weakness of falsity is that either one side is permanently removed, or it is permanently subordinated to create conflicts, or we toggle between the extremes in trying to find that truth which can solve the contradiction.

The truth that reconciles the opposites is the 'novelty' in knowledge since the opposites are parts of this broader truth. Likewise, since the opposites are reconciled by giving them varied roles, therefore, a greater stability in the knowledge ecosystem is created. Thus, newness or novelty in knowledge is justified if it brings greater unity and stability in our understanding. If newness just brings instability, then it is not knowledge. Thus, we can add two more criteria to knowledge—all that is new information and that which brings stability in our knowledge system is the greater truth.

The stability and novelty are established because the truth has greater internal coherence. This means that stability and novelty depend on consistency and completeness, but the quest for stability and novelty is an independent criterion by which we can seek greater knowledge simply because it is novel, or because it will usher greater unity within the diversities.

When we close the loop from 'consistency and completeness' to 'truth wins' because it establishes the consistency and completeness, then we can reflexively apply consistency and completeness back to the principles, conditions, or rules that define knowledge: the principles discussed here are consistent and complete; they complement each other rather than contradict each other; they overcome the limitations of the other methods, so they must be employed collectively as the definition of 'knowledge'. The consistency and completeness are not merely in the proofs that validate the truth; they are also in the definition of truth itself. Consistency entails that these principles are not contradictory, although they are individually incomplete—each principle overlooks some aspect of knowledge, and therefore doesn't spell out the meaning of 'knowing' completely. However, all the principles collectively solve the problems of the other principles. Therefore, all these principles are collectively consistent and collectively complete.

These six principles of knowledge are called the six properties of the Absolute Truth in Vedic philosophy. The principle of consistency and completeness is called 'knowledge' as it is the most fundamental criterion for the truth. The principle of simplicity and parsimony applies additional restrictions on the truth and is called 'beauty'. The necessity and sufficiency of the truth in causing the world, such that the truth stands apart from the world, and yet the world is 'expanded' from the truth is called 'renunciation'. Once the truth has emanated the proofs, then it must know the nature of these proofs to understand the truth. This requires the ability to comprehend the nature of reality through reason and experience, but since these methods suffer from the problem of imperfect senses and the mind, therefore, the purification of consciousness is necessary. This purified consciousness represents the 'power' of knowing, acting, and choosing—we can choose what we want to know and use, and then we can choose to know and use these appropriately. The process of knowing and using the world is long, and in that process, the knower and user becomes dependent on the world. From God's perspective, this interaction with the world is a *play*. From our perspective, this interaction with the world is a *struggle*. In either case, the knowledge must be pragmatically applied to play or to struggle. And pragmatism simply means that the costs of play or struggle must be minimized, and the values gained from that play or struggle must be maximized. The pragmatism about minimum costs and maximum value makes the play or struggle with the world—in which we seek and create things—a 'wealth'. It is all the desirable objects, the conveniences used in the play or struggle. Since wealth can be misused to undermine truth, therefore, truth is that which is victorious due to its novelty or uniqueness in bringing stability. This ability to defeat the warring opposites, and give them a place in the scheme of things where they show their usefulness is called 'heroism'.

The ability to conquer the warring ideas constitutes the "hard power" of heroism, but the ability to reconcile their positions by novelty constitutes its "soft power". This kind of truth not only subdues the falsity, but also attracts the truth-seekers toward it, rather than merely compelling them by force. If we study the history of philosophy, science, or religion, the initial attraction toward new ideas is their soft power, which allows them to gain hard power. But without the soft power, hard power becomes useless, because there is nothing intrinsically worthy in it. Such hard power undermines the previous principles, which then makes the hard power internally weak, and prone to defeat at the hands of other hard powers with the soft power. Thus, knowledge must exercise some hard power—i.e. it should be superior to the individual falsities. But it must also show the soft power—i.e. that it encompasses the diversities, and give them a place to exist in a system.

This kind of power is the 'heroism' within truth; it brings hard power to fight the battle against the hard power of falsity, and hence history and myths are full of glorious narrations of the victory of light over dark, good over evil, truth over falsity. But the reason these stories endure over time is because the victorious is also the light, the good, and the truth. Otherwise, we would replace these heroic stories with cynical ones where greater power—even if it is dark, evil, and false—wins over another power, which is equally dark, evil, and false, and the narration would merely about the battles between two dark and evil forces, with no ultimate purpose. The purpose or moral in the story appears when the winner is right, good, and truth. We would not know if it is so unless it wins. But after it wins, it must indeed prove itself to be right, good, and truth, and that process is harder, more important, and necessary for longevity, than winning a battle.

The Scientific Description of God

Our modern stories about God involve the narrations about the battles between truth and falsity, and people like to hear such stories. But these stories become meaningless cynical battles between two equally false and dark forces if the previous ideas of consistency, completeness, simplicity, parsimony, necessity, sufficiency, rationalism, empiricism, lower cost, and higher value, are not satisfied. The history of Western religion is especially marred by narrations of grotesque uses of hard power, without the rational basis and inner strength that must underscore religion as being different from all other falsities. If that quest for truth, simplicity and parsimony, necessity and sufficiency, rational and empirical basis, and pragmatic usefulness are missing, then religion simply amounts to a dark and evil hard power. To surmount this predicament, we must relook at the meaning of 'God'. If God is defined as the Absolute Truth, then religion can overcome the problems that have made it abhorrent to the intelligent class of people.

God is transcendent in all religions, but that is of no good to most people. It is God's immanence that makes religion attractive. The truth is not obtained by leaving this world and entering another world, especially if the existence and attainment of such a world is itself suspect. To enter and attain that world, we must overcome the suspicions and doubts about whether it exists, what its nature is, how that nature can be known and confirmed here and know, and how it is truth, right, and good. To achieve this, we must move away from the stories of winners and losers—which, by the way, may not be false—and focus on why God is a worthy pursuit, why this reality must exist, what its nature is, and how we can confirm its existence through the world that we can perceive and conceive. And this is possible only if we say that God exists in this world as immanent truth. He is the conditions of knowing, which must be applied to everything. By defining and describing these conditions, and showing that they are consistent and complete, simple and parsimonious, necessary and sufficient, empirical and rational, lowest cost and highest value, always victorious and never defeated, we establish two things. First, we complete epistemology as a *standard* for knowledge. Second, we see how this principle of knowing is immanent in everything and therefore must be used to completely know the truth. We are then equipped to ask: What is knowledge itself, as the embodiment of these principles, from which all the other knowables have expanded?

2

Consistency and Completeness: The Principle of Knowledge

Universals in Greek Philosophy

Our story about Western philosophy begins in Greek times, where philosophers were trying to define the *meaning* of words. They were primarily interested in some ephemeral words like 'knowledge', 'goodness', 'beauty', 'morality', etc. Since the problem of defining these words proved hard, therefore, a route of simplification was chosen. Why don't we define what we mean by an 'apple', 'rose', 'chair', etc.? The problem was that there are many kinds of roses, apples, and chairs. Something that is not normally called a chair can sometimes be used as a chair in some contexts. And certain things like 'beauty' and 'goodness' could even be completely private notions. The unproblematic ideas were geometric forms such as 'circle' and 'square', because you could provide a perfect definition of these concepts and get over the problem of subjectivity. This is one of the main reasons why much later during European Enlightenment, the world was described as geometry, because the definitions of geometrical objects are unproblematic. This basically means that Greeks could not solve the problem of meanings.

Returning to Greeks, and their attempts at defining words, even though geometrical definitions are easy, what happens when something is not a perfect circle or square? What do we call these things? If behind every word is a perfect definition of what that word means, and the word is merely a shorthand for that definition, then what will we call those things that are not perfectly square or round? We would need a definition for these too! So, for instance, a square that had rounded edges would need another name, just as a square with one side slightly longer than the other would need a name. That act of defining the imperfect things then leads to infinite words in language, and we might be better off not using any words. We might, for instance, just point to an individual thing and call it "this" and "that".

But if we resorted to only two words—such as "this" and "that"—then we would not be able to categorize and classify things into groups, and without such classification of things into generalities we could not claim any *knowledge*. Unless we define such words, we cannot frame *rules* about the world. For example, we cannot say that there are separate rules for 'particles' and 'waves' because to avoid the problem of multifarious geometrical shapes, we have given up all the words. Moreover, without concepts, we also cannot *communicate* our experiences to others. I cannot say, for example, that I had a dream about red apples, because nobody knows the meaning of 'red' and 'apple', and nobody else was present while I was dreaming. Likewise, I could not say that the "sky is cloudy" because nobody will understand what I mean, since they don't know the meanings of 'sky' and 'cloudy'. It would be impossible to live in such a society. Kings could not rule over a land, because they could not issue commands, ask for status and information, or use it to arrive at rational decisions, because all these things require the use of words, but our language only permits "this" and "that".

Again, you can see why Descartes chose geometry as the nature of the world—we could use these words accurately, and by claiming that the world was geometry, we could describe any shape by an algebraic equation without having to give it a name. Thereby, all the names, such as 'apples' and 'red' could be reduced to mathematical equations, avoiding normal language. Of course, this would mean that everyone had to know mathematical language, and should communicate only in that language. Philosophers and scientists were not concerned about that problem; if people chose to use inaccurate language, it wasn't their problem to figure out how their minds were working. Hence, the separation of the mind from the body was instituted.

Returning to the Greeks, while they recognized the problem with the use of words, they weren't yet ready to give up the use of language. They wanted to solve the problem, and their solution was like what Descartes did later, namely, that the words 'apple' and 'rose' could only be applied to *ideal* apples and roses. What is an ideal? You can pick any definition that you consider the best definition, and the meaning of the word 'rose' or 'apple' would be just according to that definition. The problem is that in reality no two roses and apples are truly identical, unlike circles or squares which can be identical. This would mean that these could not be called 'roses' and 'apples' by our ideal definitions. So, then, we return to the same problem: What do you call the things that are not conforming to the definition?

Now, the Greeks came up with another solution: when these words could not be applied to non-ideal things, then we can still use them by prefacing the words 'apple' and 'rose' with the epithet 'non-ideal'. We could also say that we are using these words approximately, and we don't truly mean that the thing in question is a 'rose' or 'apple'. Even then, the choice of what is approximately 'apple' and what is truly 'apple' is not straightforward. Approximations will work only if we agree upon the nature of the ideals. If everyone has their personal ideal, then they will have their personal approximations, and nobody will understand what anybody else is saying. Communication required that the ideals must be *universalized*. In short, there had to be a perfect definition of every word, which we hold in our minds, and we can then compare the real world against this ideal picture of perfection.

Thus, the doctrine of a pure and perfect world of ideals was framed, which is now called the *Platonic world* of ideas. It was a world that was purely idea-like, and Greek called these ideas *forms*. This world could be accessed through the mind, but everyone may not access this world perfectly. As a result, sometimes we might have non-ideal forms, and those people or societies which used non-ideal definitions were also non-ideal people. Effectively, a political doctrine of perfection, simply by the use of definitions, was baked into Greek philosophy, which led them to regard other societies that used other words or had other notions about what is ideal, *inferior.* Using this doctrine, a perfect man was tall, white, and muscular, and all other men were non-ideal. Their gods had to have such kinds of bodies, otherwise, they could not be called gods. In terms of humanity, men were ideal, and women were non-ideal, because there could be only one ideal human. These kinds of claims then led to all sorts of distorted ideas about society. Slavery was justified since the ideal men were subjugating the non-ideal men.

Emancipation from this world of non-ideal forms was now defined as the practice and pursuit of the ideal world, and the pursuit required changing our ideas about things into the *perfect* and pure Platonic ideals. In effect, a religious and political ideology was instituted within language itself. Centuries of wars were fought simply based on the notion that if some culture, language, or people were ideal, then they must be superior to other cultures, languages, or people. Therefore, our gods had to defeat their gods, our men had to enslave other men, and our cities had to demolish their cities, just in order to prove that we were indeed using the correct ideals. The importance of this belief has diminished in modern time, but hasn't completely disappeared. The West still believes that it has a superior culture, language, philosophy, religion, etc. and that gives them the right to subjugate others, because what use is some 'ideal' if it cannot be proven to be superior?

Notably, there is nothing wrong with ideals, if we use the correct ideals. For example, instead of saying that the perfect man was tall, white, and muscular, we could say that the perfect man was *moral*. The problem was in defining morality. Since Greeks could not define morality, therefore, perfection was reduced to shape, color, and size. Those who think that "philosophy is dead" don't understand its real socio-political power. It shapes people, civilizations, and societies in a way like nothing else. And because of that, false ideas can be more dangerous than no philosophy at all. Science too carries the philosophical presuppositions of the Greeks, because their failure to define everyday concepts have reduced science to geometry.

The success of this science means that there is some geometry. But the true geometry would be one in which morality could also be geometrical. The problem can therefore be rephrased as the understanding of the nature of space, or the geometry of space, which is something that I will discuss later. I will argue that the real geometry is that space is like an inverted tree, rather than like a box. In this inverted tree-like geometry, the branches closer to the root constitute abstract concepts like justice, beauty, humanity, etc. and the world indeed springs from these ideals through a succession of distortions by which all these ideals are polluted into non-ideals. The purpose of life is to 'cleanse' our polluted non-ideals into the pure ideals. Thus, there is a world of pure ideals, but it is based on the understanding of what we mean by 'perfect'. Shape and size are really low-level definitions of perfections, and therefore, almost irrelevant. When these irrelevant definitions of perfections are adopted as the only ones, then chaos ensues.

The Formalization of Language

Greek philosophy worked partially because philosophers were using *ordinary language* which allows casual use of words if the situation demands. For example, an imperfect circle can be called 'circular' when the situation so demands. It was implicitly understood that things are not truly circular, but since this world is imperfect, therefore, we must understand it by modeling it in comparison to a perfect world. Grave problems about the nature of words and their depiction of meaning where hidden in the process.

These problems came to light in the early 20th century attempts to formalize language as mathematics. There were three such problems. The first problem pertained to the fact that the same word can be used as different *figures of speech*. For instance, the word 'appraisal' can be used as a noun or a verb. In the former case, it represents a thing to be done, and in the latter case, it denotes an action. Similar kinds of nuances exist for other figures of speech. The same word, for instance, can be used as adjectives, nouns and verbs. How can we know the true meaning of the words unless we can discern which word represents which figure of speech? Mathematics doesn't have figures of speech, and hence, it cannot distinguish their meanings.

The second problem pertained to the fact that the same word could describe a class of people, or an individual. For instance, the word 'president' can mean a general class of people who head an organization or nation. And the word 'president' can also denote an individual. Only context delineates the true meaning of the words, which meant that to know the meaning we had to add contextuality. For instance, the same word can mean different things in different languages, cultures, and even specific cliques of people. Contextuality entailed two problems. First, the meaning of sentences could not be *universal*—it obviously wasn't true across all contexts. Second, to know the meaning, we had to add contextuality in language, which then required more such notions such a society, language, culture, etc. If all these things had to be incorporated in deciding meaning, then they had to be properly defined before we could use them in deciding meaning. But these words— 'society', 'culture', 'language', etc.—themselves bring a whole slew of meanings. For example, a society is defined by the rules and regulations enforced by a government, which could be in power due to one of many political systems. Likewise, 'culture' is collectively defined as art, music, customs, religion, and so forth. If we had to include this in our definition of context, then we would have to bring in numerous more words. Thus, the problem was that in trying to define 'context', we need literally infinite number of words, and the determination of meaning seemed impossible.

The third problem was that every individual can use the words in their unique way. For example, when someone says, "this idea seems interesting", he might just mean that he disagrees with it, but is too polite to say it. Language can sometimes be used sarcastically, euphemistically, or ironically. Unless we know the tone of speaking, and then map the tone to what someone is feeling at the time of speaking, we may not know the meaning.

To get around these three problems, 20th century philosophers tried many tricks, such as "all meaning is universal", "all meaning is contextual, but it has to be decided by the effects it leads to", or more pessimistically, "all meaning is grounded in one's consciousness, and nobody can know what you are saying, because nobody has access to your consciousness".

The problem is that regardless of which approach you adopt you start designating a huge number of sentences whose meaning is given by the context or by the individual as "meaningless". Statements such as "I am in pain" are obviously personal. If you say that either there is something objective about pain, or pain is meaningless, then you deny all human suffering. Ideas such as love and happiness obviously become meaningless. Even intersubjective relationships such as that between parent and child, or husband and wife, also become meaningless, because the relationship may have so many unique aspects that in trying to broaden the definition, we will start including those things that are not these relationships, and narrowing the definition will entail that many things that are these relationships are ignored. 20th century philosophy had a lesson—none of these approaches truly work. The utter failure of philosophy in solving the problems that it said it was going to solve (i.e. it chose its own problems), led people to pronounce that "philosophy is dead". This did not mean that philosophy as a discipline ceased to exist, but that it had nothing of relevance to tell us about the world.

Gödel's Incompleteness Theorem

Many philosophers at this time felt that there was something wrong with ordinary language, and if only we would use rigorous logical languages, then we will not have this problem. At least for the purposes of science, we must only use such logical languages. Thus, logicians and mathematicians set about trying to solve the problem individuality and contextuality for formal languages, which had to be used for the purposes of all scientific inquiry. To their surprise, and eventual disenchantment, the same problems appear in mathematics too. You see, the fundamental issue lies with words and the interpretation. It doesn't matter which language these words are encoded in. For example we can substitute all words by numbers, and we will still have the same problem, because a number too can be interpreted in the same three ways as ordinary words: (1) a number such as 'two' can denote the general idea of twoness which is found in all collections of two things, (2) a number 'two' can point or refer to the 'second' object—in a contextually defined sequence of things, and (3) the number 'two' can refer to a specific, individual thing, if we use numbers to designate such objects—words in computers are indeed denoted as numbers, for example. Thus, the same three interpretations of words arise in the case of numbers as well.

Kurt Gödel showed that we can designate specific sentences by numbers—the third use of numbers. Then we can speak about the properties of the number that designated the above sentence, *as if* we were talking about the properties of the number, rather than the properties of the sentence. Obviously, the properties of the number don't apply to the sentence. So, claims about numbers—when they refer to their own properties, or when they refer to the properties of objects they denote—would obviously be contradictory. Such properties can be assigned to any object; for example, we can speak about two being a prime number and designate a sentence as the second sentence in a theorem's proof, but claims about primality do not apply to the second sentence in the theorem's proof. Obviously, this would lead to logical contradictions and Gödel created such contradictions to prove that mathematics cannot entertain all kinds of statements about numbers. All these statements, which mathematics could not entertain—because they lead to contradictions—came to be thereafter known as 'undecidable' because you cannot consistently say if they are true or false. The fact was that they had to be kept outside mathematics; however, since mathematics could not deal with such statements, therefore, it was also *incomplete*.

Gödel's proof is called the *Incompleteness Theorem* because it states that if we tried to overcome this incompleteness, then the result will be contradictions. This problem arises because words in ordinary language have the properties of *representation* and *reference*: by representation, we encode the properties of an object into another object, and by reference we have this second object refer to the first. To encode these two properties, a symbol of meaning must have three aspects— (1) its existence, (2) its meaning, and (3) its reference. When we speak about such a symbol, we sometimes speak about the symbol's existence, sometimes its meaning, and sometimes its reference. In a physical reality, it is impossible to encode these three meanings. A physical object doesn't have representational and referential properties; it is just a thing-in-itself. The representational and referential properties are believed to exist in the mind, but when meanings are encoded, then symbols also possess these properties. If numbers are treated as quantities, then they only have the property of existence, not reference or representation. However, ordinary statements, which include statements *about* numbers, can have both representation and reference. For example, we can say that "numbers have the property of commutation" in which case we are representing the idea that $a + b = b + a$, for an infinite number of a and b. Similarly, we can say that "irrational numbers cannot be factored into integers" in which case we are using the term "irrational numbers" to refer to a class of numbers. Gödel's proof amounts to saying that these statements are true, but we cannot prove or disprove them in number theory. All proofs, if at all they exist, must involve actually summing up two specific a and b or trying to factor an irrational number and show that there are no such integer factors.

In most cases, this doesn't present problems for mathematics because we use the *reductio ad absurdum* method. For instance, to prove that an irrational number doesn't have factors, we can pick one such irrational number—e.g. π—and then show that it doesn't have factors by trying to factorize it, and by that exception, we have proven that irrational numbers don't have factors. In this process too, we are using the term 'irrational number' in two ways: (1) as a class of numbers, and (2) an individual number such as π. However, the first use of numbers—i.e. a class—doesn't enter mathematics as we solved the problem by just using the second usage of 'irrational number'. But in general, if we need to use classes, then we cannot employ them, because using such classes will lead to logical contradictions.

A simple example of this contradiction arises in trying to label statements by numbers. The label is a *name*, and the statement has a *meaning*. The name always *refers* to something other than itself. But if we do such labeling—which we must do, if we are going to convert ordinary language sentences (e.g. mathematical theorems) into numbers—then we can create contradictions between the *naming* and the *meaning*. Gödel proved how we can create such contradictions. He took an arbitrary statement like "P is false" and labeled it by the number P. His trick was in showing that in every possible numbering scheme there will be some statements whose meaning will contradict their name. So, now you can ask: Is P true? And the answer is that if it is true, then by its meaning it is false; if it is false, then by its meaning it is true. Again, by the *reductio* method, we can show a contradiction in one case, and that entails that the statement P: P is false is undecidable. That entails that all of mathematics is either inconsistent or incomplete.

In short, we can do arithmetic with numbers, but we cannot make statements about numbers or their properties and expect to prove or disprove these statements. And the fundamental reason is that to achieve that we would have to have an explicit role for concepts, which would then mean that sometimes a word denotes a meaning, and sometimes a name, and sometimes an individual thing, and we cannot know which case is which. This property of ordinary languages therefore exists even in mathematics, if mathematics has to have the *referential* power of ordinary language. If we take away that power, then mathematics also becomes infinitely incomplete because if we cannot make statements about numbers consistently, then we also cannot make statements about statements about numbers, or statements about statements about statements about numbers, consistently.

Turing's Halting Problem

A similar kind of problem was demonstrated by Alan Turing in the Halting Problem, which refers to the ability to know what a program is going to do, before it does it. This is an important problem due to malicious programs which can affect a computer's functioning. Turing demonstrated that it was impossible to know what a program will do without executing the program. Effectively, the damage would be known only after the damage was done. Ordinarily, programs are labeled by names, indicating the purpose they exist for. For example, a program may be called "Word Processor", which would be a *noun*. This program will contain instructions internally, which can be called *verbs*. The sequence of these verbs connects the computer's current state to the goal—a type of trajectory, if you will. Ideally, after each computer instruction is executed, we must get a new state—called by a noun—and if we are to sequence these nouns then we can get the final state or the goal. If you think of a trajectory, then you can interpret it in two ways: (1) as a sequence of points, which are called 'states' and denoted by nouns, and (2) as a sequence of steps that connect two successive states, which are called 'instructions' and denoted by verbs. The first instruction leads us to the second state, the second instruction to the third state, etc. To understand what a program does, without the program doing it, we must be able to interpret the same number (computer instructions are encoded as numbers) alternately as states and actions, or nouns and verbs. While executing a program, the computer will interpret the numbers as verbs, and while checking if the program is malicious, the computer will interpret the same numbers as nouns. Turing's proof amounts to saying that this is impossible in any numerical machine because machines don't know how to interpret or give meanings to numbers. A machine knows only how to parse a sequence of digits and match them to actions. We can cannot preface one instruction by another instruction and expect the computer to interpret the later instruction based on the previous instructions; such a machine would be called a *Contextual Turing Machine*, and contextuality necessitates a *hierarchy* in which you can enter a context and leave a context. Human readable languages have contexts, but machines do not understand these contexts. A machine executes an instruction *atomically*, not based on the *context*.

A classic example of contextual interpretations is sometimes presented while discussing the abilities of computers to understand meanings. This example involves the meanings of the sentence "I saw a man on the hill with a telescope". This sentence can be interpreted in various ways as follows:

- I saw a man using a telescope. The man was on a hill.
- I saw a man. I was on the hill, looking through a telescope.
- I saw the man. The man was on a hill and had a telescope.
- I was on the hill. I saw a man. The man had a telescope.

Each of these sentences has a different grammatical structure, which must be understood hierarchically. However, a computer operates sequentially from left to right. A program compiler converts the hierarchy in a program into a sequence of instructions and in that process, we also lose the ability to describe the words as 'nouns' and 'verbs' since the figures of speech are another *dimension* of meaning, besides the word meanings.

Ordinary language sentences combine different *kinds* of words, such as nouns, verbs, adjectives, etc. A mathematical statement, on the other hand, must add quantities of the same type. For instance, if you add two quantities in a mathematical equation, they must have the same *dimensionality*. We cannot add apples and oranges in mathematics to get a total number of fruits, because that requires us to see that apples and oranges are also fruits, which would in turn require a conceptual hierarchy, similar to grammar. If at all we add two numbers that denote apples and oranges, the computer will not know that the result of that addition is conceptually different from the added quantities. In the same way, the computer also cannot know if some word is a noun and another word is a verb. Without knowing the conceptual hierarchy and the hierarchy among the figures of speech, there is no knowledge of meaning. And if meanings cannot be known, then we cannot know if a statement is true of false. This fundamental problem leads to the inability to decide if a program will crash upon execution, or it will run successfully. It leads to the inability to know in advance what the program will do upon execution, unless it is executed. These are issues of program semantics, and semantics is necessary for programs too, otherwise, there are questions about such programs—e.g. Will a program halt? Will a program do something malicious? —that cannot be answered. Such statements are also true or false. But a computer cannot decide if they are true or false.

The Source of Incompleteness

The problem of incompleteness arises because each symbol has three kinds of properties—its use, its representation, and its reference. Each word can be an individual representative *instance* of that idea, or a *reference* to that instance of the idea, or a specific use to which that idea is being put to. For example, the word 'appraisal' sometimes is the representation of the idea of an evaluation (e.g. there was an appraisal); it is sometimes the name by which a specific event is referred to (e.g. today I had my appraisal); and sometimes it denotes an action (e.g. I performed an appraisal). In each case, there is a word, which has a universal meaning, but the meaning is adapted into either a common noun, a proper noun, or a verb, based upon the context.

This idea is described in Vedic philosophy by speaking about three *modes* of nature, which are called by various names, but for ease of our understanding, we can just use one such nomenclature in which they denote universality, individuality, and contextuality. For instance, sometimes when we use the word 'table' we mean the idea table. Then sometimes the word 'table' refers to a specific instance of that table. Then again something that doesn't have the form of a table can also be used as a table within a context. The same thing may then be called by other names in other situations.

This complexity can be demystified if we understand that the universals are ideas, and the individuals combine with the universals to create symbols of these ideas. An ordinary object is a combination of many such elementary symbols, which gives the combination many properties. When we perceive such an object, we may filter some of these properties, and hence a block of wood may be called a 'table' or 'chair' in some context, because its property of being 'bed', 'firewood', or 'weapon' is ignored in such cases.

The three modes of nature are the basic ingredients to create a *symbol,* and they must be combined to produce a symbol. We can also say that the three modes of nature are the three aspects or *dimensions* of a symbol, and the world exists in this three-dimensional 'space' of the three modes. Since the symbol exists in such a space, therefore, it always has all the three dimensions, and therefore, it is always a combination of these modes.

This 'space' not just three-dimensional, but also hierarchical like an inverted tree, with a root that divides into trunks, branches, twigs, and leaves. Each of these is like a sub-space inside a super-space. As a result, we can talk about a whole-part relationship, and when the world is described in this way, then its source—the Absolute Truth—is the whole, and the manifestation from this whole is its parts. The parts are *within* the whole, so in that sense, the manifested world is within the whole or the Absolute Truth.

Finally, both the whole and the part must be treated as concepts, and that simply means that the whole doesn't *reduce* to the parts. Rather, it stands independent of the parts, such that the parts may not exist, but the whole will still exist. Also, the parts may exist, but the whole is neither increased nor decreased by this existence. To understand this idea, we can think of concepts like cow and mammal. The cow is a part of mammal, but a mammal is independent of cow. Thus, the meaning 'mammal' can exist even with the meaning 'cow' doesn't. We can also say that the 'mammal' is the conceptual *truth*, while the 'cow' is the *proof* or evidence of that truth. In essence, we may not understand 'mammal' unless we see individual types of mammals such as cows, horses, dogs, cats, etc. In the same way, it is very hard to understand the Absolute Truth as the idea 'knowledge', but by the observation of individual knowable things we begin to grasp the meaning of 'knowledge'. The proofs of knowledge help us understand the truth.

Of these three aspects, the universal and the individual aspects *seem* like mutual opposites, but because they are connected by the third aspect, they are not truly opposites. To understand this idea, we can think of the three aspects as the knower, the known, and the knowing that connects the knower to the known. The knower is the individuality, the known is the universality, and the knowing connection between them is the contextuality. The combination of the knower, known, and knowing constitutes *knowledge*. The known is the signified, the knower is the signifier, the knowing is the signifying, and the combination of these three things is the symbol. As a result, the original 'knowledge' is divided into three aspects, and every part of this 'knowledge' comprises of the same three aspects. That is, it exists as a three-dimensional entity comprised of knower, known, and knowing. We collectively call it 'knowledge', but it can also be deconstructed into three aspects. If these three aspects are not combined, then there is potential for knowledge, but there is no knowledge. In short, all knowledge, or what we call 'experience' is produced out of the combination of these three.

With this background, we can understand the source of the incompleteness, and the source is that the same symbol has three aspects, but only one of these aspects is *dominant* in one context. The word 'appraisal' can mean a common noun, a proper noun, or a verb, and the meaning is contextual. If we cannot use all these meanings, then the symbol is *incomplete.* And if in using these meanings we get contradictions, then the symbol is *inconsistent.* The *completeness* refers to the coexistence of these three aspects, and the *consistency* refers to these three aspects not being mutually contradictory.

When this symbolic reality is described in physical terms, then a caricature of knowledge is produced in which we cannot talk about the same thing having universality, individuality, and contextuality. Each of these three modes seem contradictory to the other modes, and therefore, only one mode is employed, which then makes the solution *incomplete.* In short, we trade off completeness with consistency, and we get incompleteness.

Dualism and Incompleteness

This problem arises because Western philosophy conceives mathematics as the description of the *physical* world which is devoid of contextuality, and therefore, of meaning. In Cartesian mind-body dualism, for example, the body is a physical substance that is called *res extensa* because it has only one property—the property of extension in space. What is space? It has three dimensions of length. By this extension, mathematicians apply geometry to the world, and all our sense perceptions—taste, touch, smell, sound, and sight—have to be reduced to geometry. Accordingly, if the mind is reduced to the brain, then the mind also becomes geometry. Now, every thought, belief, intention, judgment, or valuation must be reduced to geometry. The problem is that all geometry reduces to points and lengths. But length is just *one* among infinite other properties such as taste, smell, color, tone, pitch, etc. How can we reduce all these properties to one property? That inability to reduce infinite concepts to one concept—length—leads to incompleteness. The incompleteness in one case is that the length cannot encode taste; in another case, it cannot encode smell; in yet another case, it cannot represent beauty, justice, or knowledge. Thus, the incompleteness is infinite, because we cannot encode infinite such concepts using length.

Thus, a basic disconnect between sensation and reality is established at the outset (we will later see that these are called 'secondary' and 'primary' properties by empiricists). Cartesian dualism then puts all concepts into the 'mind', without explaining the nature of the mind, or how the body connects to the mind. Now, since the incompleteness arises due to concepts, and the concepts are in the mind, therefore, mathematics is forever incapable of dealing with concepts. And yet, we cannot avoid these concepts because mathematics is a language in which we can refer to things, represent ideas, and use mathematics as an object that is inputted into functions. Thus, we must be able to tell when we are using the same thing as an object, referring to that object, or talking about the meaning of that object. This physical conception of the world is false. The correct conception of reality is that there are 'senses' and their 'objects'. These senses exist at multiple tiers that lead to sensation by the five senses, idea intuition by the mind, the judgment of truth by the intellect, the perception of intention by the ego, and the assessment of morality by the moral sense. The knower is the senses, and the known is the objects. Each knower is a known, and each known is a knower. Therefore, the world must be described as *persons*. Each knower identifies some known as its self, creating self-knowledge. And each knower knows the others as different from the self, creating other-knowledge.

Thus, reality is conceived in Vedic philosophy as *persons*. Each person is the senses (knower), the objects (known), and their relation (knowing). And they know other persons by the same process as they know themselves. The process of self-knowledge is identical to that of other-knowledge, and unless we identify a common method by which the self and the other are known, we will keep having contradictory categories like 'mind' and 'body' in which the mind knows its own body in one way, and someone else's body in another way; the mind knows itself in one way, and someone else's mind in another way. And all these ways of knowing will present themselves as contradictory distinctions within knowledge. Knowledge will remain incomplete if one of these methods is rejected. And it will seem inconsistent if all these methods are included. That is not because the methods are contradictory, but it is because our conception of what the world is, is false.

Mind-body dualism underlies the fundamental problem of consistency and completeness in mathematics, and by implication in the rest of science, because it is a problem about the *language* that we use to describe the world. If our language itself is problematic, everything we say in that language is also problematic. Therefore, the incompleteness of mathematics must extend into every other field of science, making all those fields incomplete.

Mind-body dualism is really about a claim that there are certain things in this world that don't have a mind. This problem is parented as much by philosophy as by religion, because in Christianity, animals don't have a soul. Certainly, nature is not living. Even in humans, which are said to have a soul, an artificial distinction between races has sometimes been made to engender the idea that some souls are superior to the other souls. Many religions thus try to maintain 'racial purity' even today, because they truly believe that they are special, privileged people on earth, chosen by God. These unscientific and dogmatic beliefs are the foundation of mind-body dualism, because the key idea underlying science was a separation with the Church, the Church dealt with the mind, and only humans have a mind. The rest of nature, which includes our bodies, animals, nature, this planet, and by implication all the other planets in the sky, are all amenable to science, because the Church is concerned with the soul, only found in (some) humans.

If life can exist without the mind—e.g. in the case of animals—then the mind is not a necessary condition for living. Indeed, the idea that animals don't have a soul underlies the rampant killing of animals for human consumption. But philosophically, it also undermines humanity because if living bodies can exist without the mind and the soul, then the soul is just incidental to life. Factually, the living body can exist even without a soul, and it does in case of animals. So, this body can be studied, completely disregarding the soul. And science—even if studies the body—has no dependence on the mind. Therefore, the mind-body separation in philosophy is much less problematic because only humans have a soul, and by neglecting the mind, we are not really neglecting all that much. This problem would not exist in philosophy if it did not previously exist in Christianity. Modern philosophy carries forward the presuppositions of Christianity, although it amplifies them to such an extent that knowledge becomes impossible.

If we have to overcome this problem, then we must recognize that this duality doesn't exist. There is indeed a soul, distinct from matter, but that distinction is not so stark, because the soul has to know the world, and in so knowing, its capacities of knowing must conform to the nature of the world, and vice versa. In short, we must describe the world in terms of our capacities of knowing. When we do that, the distinction between the soul and matter would be like that between a knower and the known, connected by the process of knowing, which produces knowledge. Within the soul, there is the knower, the known, and the process of knowing, and all three are combined when the soul knows itself as self-awareness. Likewise, when the soul is embodied, then, there is a known (e.g. a human body), a knower (the senses), and their connection (of knowing). Then we can say that our experience, which combines the world and the soul, through a relationship, is also knowledge, similar to the knowledge called Absolute Truth.

With such amends, consistency and completeness would no longer be a tradeoff. Completeness would simply say: We need to describe the knower, the known, and knowing, in order to describe knowledge, and if knowledge is defined as the combination of the knower, the known, and knowing, then it is complete. Similarly, consistency would say: The knower, the known, and knowing are three complementary aspects of knowledge, and their co-existence is non-contradictory. But this doesn't mean that the knower, the known, and knowing are always coexisting. Knowledge is an optional byproduct of the combination of knower, known, and knowing, and this combination necessitates the existence of choices—which knower, combines with which known, through which process of knowing.

In short, consistency and completeness are possible if we see the world not as physical things but as conscious persons. Everything is a person, but the consciousness in some things is developed or undeveloped. This idea is explained in Vedic texts by stating that Brahman or consciousness is 'covered' by matter to produce the world of material experience. That consciousness or the soul has three aspects of knower, known, and knowing. Likewise, the matter which covers the soul also has the same three aspects of universality, individuality, and contextuality. The basic problem arises when we cannot distinguish between these three aspects—which exist in the soul as well as in matter. The three aspects in matter are the reflections of the three aspects in the soul. Thus, for instance, the knower is the individual, the known is the universal, and the knowing is the contextuality.

Indeed, in Vedic philosophy, even atoms must be described in terms of three aspects. They encode some meaning, so there is a universality. They are individual things, so there is an individuality. And their meaning is understood in relation to other atoms, so there is a contextuality. Atomism cannot thus be divorced from the study of what makes us *persons*. When atoms are understood as persons, then (1) they are known through concepts, (2) they are knowers and remain aware of the presence of other things, and (3) they interact selectively with some things at some times, just like persons. Atoms must therefore be described as symbols of meaning which combine the universality, individuality, and contextuality. And this understanding about atoms can come in science if we understand how we are persons.

Thus, if consciousness is seen as the *model* of everything, then if the atoms are used in mathematics, we can say that they also exist in three modes, and that would solve the paradox of consistency and completeness. Without the personhood, we will only have physical things, and without the three modes, the problem would remain intractable because we will keep thinking about the world without using modes, as they are not *symbols*.

Knowledge is Knowing

Lots of people claim to know, but if we ask them to explain what they know, they cannot. They can explain a few things, but not all things. Their explanations may also be contradictory, as different inconsistent ideas are used to explain different things. Consistency and completeness are therefore the conditions of *knowing*—i.e. when we can say that someone truly *knows*. We can assume that the world can be known, that it is not paradoxical and inconsistent, and that everything that exists can potentially be known. This is the immanent property of the world, that we must assume. However, that immanent property doesn't mean that everyone is knowledgeable about reality. Knowledge must be demonstrated by the ability to explain its nature. In Vedic philosophy, this knowledge—i.e. the ability to consistently and completely explain the nature of reality—is the very nature of God. He is the original source of knowledge (and the primal author of the "Veda"—which means "to know") because He can explain the nature of reality consistently and completely. His explanations are thus superior to all other.

Of course, from His perspective, He is merely explaining His nature, and how He has expanded into the world. But this ability to know oneself is not a given. Most of us, for example, are struggling to just understand our true nature, why we are constituted in a certain way, why we sometimes act irrationally, why we are unable to give up things that we don't like about ourselves, etc. Self-discovery is a journey, and some might say that it is the only worthy goal to ever be pursued. Even after we discover our mundane nature, we must still perfect it. For instance, there might be undesirable aspects about our nature, that we might want to give up. There might be attitudes and skills that we might wish to acquire. Without giving up those attitudes and acquiring new ones, we might feel incomplete. Due to the desires to change our nature, we might have inconsistencies in our nature, where we succumb to our tendencies some times and then try to overcome them at other times. God doesn't need a journey to know or perfect Himself. He is already perfect, which means that He is also consistent and complete. He is also fully aware of His consistent and complete nature, which is a sign of perfection (just being consistent and complete, and not knowing about it, would be imperfection). Thus, He can explain His nature consistently and completely, and that explanation would be the full truth.

Conversely, if we cannot explain reality consistently and completely, then whatever we claim to know is not 'partial knowledge' of reality. It is factually ignorance, because the criterion for knowledge is consistency and completeness. Thus, all the theories about reality that are currently inconsistent and incomplete, do not constitute 'knowledge'. Rather, they are different forms of ignorance in which something is claimed to be real, but it is not. The nature of contradictions and incompleteness in our explanation indicates that what we consider to be the truth is not actually the truth. God is free of such ignorance because He can explain everything consistently and completely, and therefore, He is the original source of knowledge.

If knowledge cannot be traced back to God legitimately, then we can test it for consistency and completeness. But even if someone claims to have received knowledge from God (e.g. as a revelation from God), we must still test it for consistency and completeness. The claims of revelation don't automatically qualify someone as truly knowledgeable. If they have received knowledge, they must also be able to explain it to others consistently and completely. Of course, this requires some patience in the learner too, especially if the learner is ignorant—the greater the ignorance, the longer is the journey to learning the nature of truth. Nevertheless, given such patience and eagerness to check if the claimant truly knows, the requirement of knowing falls back on the person who claims to know—i.e. can they explain everything consistently and completely? Revelation can be a source of truth, but authority is not itself a guarantee, because it can be faked. God is accepted as Absolute Truth not just because He claims to be the truth, but also because He demonstrates an understanding of the truth better than others. His authority is therefore proven by His understanding also.

3

Simplicity and Parsimony: The Principle of Beauty

Symmetry and Asymmetry

The question of beauty has been incessantly debated since Greek times in Western philosophy, but there are no good resolutions to this problem. Certain basic ideas like *proportion* and *symmetry* are generally accepted as marks of beauty, but these don't seem to be the only ones. A certain amount of disproportion and asymmetry also seems to lead to beauty. For example, in a person's face, we expect the two eyes to be of equal size, which we can call their symmetry. We expect the nose and the lips to be proportionate to the eyes, and the face to be proportionate to the body. Considering these demands, we can say that beauty is proportion and symmetry. However, when people pose for photographs, they also stand diagonally, tilt to one side, or bend their heads in one direction, because these things also seem to create beauty. If beauty is attributed to proportion and symmetry, why are disproportion and asymmetry also used in producing beautiful images? How can opposing qualities constitute beauty, and if they do, can we really describe the causes of beauty when the most obvious concepts of beauty coexist with their very opposites in constituting the nature of beauty?

This question is so fundamental that it is essential to get it out of the way before we discuss anything else. So, let us try to understand the nature of symmetry and proportion and their opposites—namely, asymmetry and disproportion—in creating beauty. To understand these ideas, we have to think of the world as knowledge, or concepts. In short, the world is idea-like. After we recognize something as a rose, then we also say that the rose is beautiful. If we don't recognize the rose, then we also cannot call it beautiful. Thus, the cognition precedes the aesthetic judgment, and beauty is therefore a property of knowledge. This simply means that we can study the nature of beauty as the properties of information present in an object.

All objects encode some information, and some objects are also symmetric. Symmetry and information are, however, inversely related. The greater the information in an object, the lesser is the symmetry in that object, and vice versa. Thus, imagine a universe that was identical in all directions. We would call that a perfectly symmetrical universe, as we can rotate that universe along any possible axis and the result of that rotation would be indistinguishable from the unrotated universe. This rotational symmetry would also entail that the universe is devoid of all directional information. For example, symmetry in all directions means that matter is distributed uniformly in all directions, and there is no clear sense of directionality.

Likewise, we can imagine a sequence of numbers comprised entirely of repeating 1's. The length of this sequence doesn't contain interesting information, because there is a symmetry—the same digit is repeated thousands of times. Conversely, if we have a sequence of 1's and 0's such that the order of digits never repeats, then the sequence is interesting, it is perfectly asymmetrical, and it carries as much information as there are digits in the sequence. Thus, the amount of asymmetry equals the amount of complexity and information. A perfectly symmetric system has minimal information while a completely asymmetric system has maximal information. Symmetry and asymmetry are therefore inversely related aspects of any system because some asymmetry must exist in a system for it to carry information.

The above description of symmetry and information is physical. A similar type of symmetry and information can be seen semantically. For example, to encode information, an information-carrying system must use symbols. These symbols represent opposites or dualities. In a computer system, this duality is represented by the digits 1 and 0, which are logically opposed (the digit 1 represent true, and the digit 0 represents false; physically, they are represented by +z and -z quantum spins). In everyday language, there are many such opposites, such as hot and cold, black and white, rough and smooth, etc. which constitute opposing qualities, and all information is encoded using the symbols of these properties.

These symbols are organized or structured in space using relations, which can also be described using opposing qualities such as left and right, top and bottom, front and back. Thus, we can replace the pair of opposite digits by many such pairs of opposites that represent hot and cold, black and white, rough and smooth, etc. Similarly, we can generalize the idea of a position of a digit in a sequence with a more general idea of position defined in terms of left and right, top and bottom, front and back. To achieve these things, we still need a third property, which we must constitute the *origin* and *perspective*. This becomes very important in a semantic system, not a physical system. For example, in a physical system, we can count the points from left to right or right to left. Likewise, we can begin our counting not at the beginning of the sequence, but at any arbitrary point in the sequence, and loop back to where we started. From a physical perspective, a change of 'reference frame'—i.e. the origin from where we count, and the direction in which we count—should not matter. But it matters when we start interpreting these points as denoting some alphabets, words, sentences, etc. because if we change the origin, then all bit sequences would be interpreted as different character or word sequences. A change in direction would entail that the front and back are switched, and 'face in the back' would not mean the same as 'face in the front'. In short, when we treat a system semantically, then we must choose an origin and reference frame (i.e. a sense of directionality). The origin will say where we begin counting from. And the reference frame will say which direction we count before the other directions. This is necessary even when we count digits, as we begin from the first digit and count from left to right, but since this is just the common convention, it remains unobvious.

Thus, a semantic system is comprised of three things— (1) symbols, (2) positions, and (3) an origin with a reference direction. A physical theory collapses (2) and (3) into a single 'reference frame' or 'space' because all directions in space are assumed to be equivalent. We cannot do that in a semantic system because it will be tantamount to saying that we can read a sequence of digits from the middle rather than the beginning and we will obtain the same meaning. It will be tantamount to saying that we can read a sequence of digits backwards instead of forwards and the result will not be different. The objectivity of information means that there is a preexisting convention by which information is encoded—e.g. from left to right. Nevertheless, someone else—i.e. not the author of information—can choose to read it differently. They may not get the same conclusion if they don't read it as per the conventions, but they can get something out of it. In short, there would still be some information, but it could be understood differently. A reader who doesn't follow the conventions has defined his origin and reference frame, as they start reading from some point and then decide to read in some order (e.g. forward to backward or vice versa). In simple terms, we decouple the information into three aspects of encoding.

Now, we can describe many kinds of symmetries. First, we can talk about a symmetry in which the opposite meaning words—e.g. hot and cold, black and white, rough and smooth, etc.—recur with the same frequency. If they do, then we can say that the text is symmetrical in the words; if they don't then we can say that some words are asymmetrically higher than the others. Second, we can talk about a symmetry in which the varied positions—e.g. left and right, top and bottom, front and back, etc.—have the same number of symbols. If they do, then we can say that the text utilizes all parts of the space available for encoding symmetrically; if it doesn't then we can say that only space in certain directions is available for encoding. These two types of symmetries can give us the ability to make some statistical predictions, because we can extrapolate the frequencies of words, and the place they are found and predict with some accuracy if a specific word would occur at specific place. However, this prediction won't give us what the system encodes as meaning, because the prediction isn't precise.

A third more precise kind of symmetry can be found by combining the above two symmetries. For example, we can say that the word 'hotel' is always found on the odd pages of a book, which would be better than saying that there is a 50% chance of finding the word 'hotel' on a page. Finally, a more profound kind of symmetry can be described by saying that the words 'hot', 'black', and 'rough' always occur on the odd pages, while the words 'cold', 'white', and 'smooth' always occur only on the even pages. And we can go on like this specifying the word occurrence based on paragraph on the page, the number of sentences from the top after which the word recurs, or the count of words before a word appears, etc. As we get more refinement, the symmetry is described to a more accurate level. Also, if many such symmetries can be identified, then we can say that the system is more symmetric. But you will notice that as these symmetries start growing, then the next page becomes more predictable based on the previous pages—you can easily predict what a page will state, if you have the read the earlier pages. Thus, as the symmetries increase, the amount of information reduces.

Now, we can look upon the world as a text, and say that if the world was totally asymmetric, then it will have maximal information, but we will not have a predictive ability about this information because nothing would ever repeat. Conversely, if the world was totally symmetric, then we will have minimal information, and we will have infinite ability to predict this information, because if we know one thing, then we know everything. This helps us see the importance of symmetry and asymmetry in understanding a system. The asymmetry in a system denotes information, and the symmetry is the order, repeatability, and predictability in this information.

Symmetry and Natural Laws

In short, the symmetry in information is identical to the ability to make predictions about the world. This predictability is the existence of natural laws, that help us predict the events in the world, based on what we know. If the information is maximal, then there is no order in nature, and that means that we cannot predict. The absence of order entails the absence of laws, and through such absence, we lose the ability to predict the events. Conversely, if the information is zero, then there is perfect order and predictability but absolutely no information. Using this criterion, we can define 'knowledge' in two ways: (a) the uniqueness in the world, and (b) the repetitiveness in the world. If the uniqueness is maximized, then the repetitiveness is minimized, and vice versa. In either situation, one kind of knowledge exists at the expense of the other type. If both kinds of knowledge must exist, then there must be a balance between the uniqueness and the repetitiveness. However, these types of knowledge are mutually contradictory, as increasing uniqueness decreases the repetitiveness, and vice versa.

The properties of knowledge that we discussed in the previous chapter—namely, consistency and completeness—pertain to the information or *content.* But if this was the only type of knowledge to be had about the world, then the world would have zero order, predictability, and we would never be studying laws of nature that summarize this information into a shorter form. Knowing the world would rather be simply cramming up the infinite bits of information in the world, and organizing it exactly as it is present in the world. Since this is not the case, therefore, we can say that there is *symmetry* in the world, due to which by knowing a fewer number of things, we can predict other things, and therefore, knowledge is eventually *finite.*

This finiteness of knowledge entails that nature is compressible, comprises some fundamental ideas, which we can call 'axioms' of our theory, that it follows some principles of rationality using which we can predict. This finiteness is not contrary to the infiniteness entailed by the myriad combinations of information that can exist even with the predictability of the laws. Let's explain this using the example of language. Each language is defined by a finite vocabulary and rules of grammar. This is the 'order' in language, namely, that it follows some rules and constitutes the *symmetry.* The 'uniqueness' in language is that we can use the vocabulary and grammar to construct literally infinite sentences, and this is the *asymmetry* in language. If our vocabulary and grammar were so stringent that we could only frame a few sentences, then the universe of sentences created by such rules would also be small, as only a few sentences would be considered meaningful. Conversely, if our vocabulary and grammar were so relaxed that many more things could be said meaningfully, then the universe of sentences would also be significantly larger. In other words, an increase in the rules of grammar and vocabulary reduces the size of the possible universe, and a decrease in the rules of grammar and vocabulary, increases the universe's size.

The existence of symmetry, laws, vocabulary, and grammar, simply indicate that reality is knowable by a *finite* individual, because what constitutes 'complete knowledge' is not *infinite.* That there are some fundamental principles of reality, some laws, and some axioms by understanding which we can know the whole truth, because everything in the manifest world is simply a mutation or combination of these principles, laws, and axioms. In short, we don't have to memorize all the possible books in the universe. We just have to know the vocabulary and grammar, because that much knowledge is adequate to knowing everything—even if we don't know everything. Thus, if you haven't read all the possible books, then in some sense, you don't know everything. But you know how to know those things. That meta-knowledge, which gives us the ability to know—constitutes *beauty*.

Beauty is different from 'knowledge' that must be consistent and complete, just as grammar and vocabulary are different from all the books written using the grammar and vocabulary. An infinite mind can know all the books, and the grammar and vocabulary. But a finite mind may just know the grammar and vocabulary, and he can still be said to know everything, because he has the tools by which he can read all the possible books. Indeed, if the grammar and vocabular are *generative*—i.e. you know the principles by which some basic sounds can be combined to create complex words, and how a basic set of grammatical rules can be used to construct any number of grammatical structures—then the universe can spring simply from this generative principle: those rules that are capable of creating the universe. If we know the same rules, then, in one sense, we know the complete truth. That complete truth is not having to read all the possible books. But it is knowing the basis by which a book could be written or understood.

Now we can say that the problem of beauty pertains to the fact that symmetry and asymmetry are always mixed. The former constitutes the regularity and predictability, and the latter constitutes the irregularity and unpredictability, and both must exist if (1) we want the world to have information, and (2) we want to be able to understand that information. If our rules of meaning are so restrictive, that numerous sentences become meaningless if they do not comply to the rules that create meanings, and correspondingly the information itself doesn't exist for us, then such rules will disqualify a lot of things that we consider at present to be 'knowledge'. Conversely, if there is so much information—since the rules of meaningfulness are relaxed—then the rules will qualify many more things that we would never now at present as 'knowledge', or things that should be known.

In short, if the rules are too lax, then our knowledge will be *incomplete* (because we would not know everything). And if the rules are too tight, then our knowledge will be *inconsistent* (because what we know would be false). That would now contradict the principles of consistency and completeness that we outlined in the previous chapter. To avoid these outcomes, we must say that there is not just information but that information is also rule governed. Those rules allow us to generate new information, and process existing information. If we know all these rules, then we can know everything, if we encounter it, and in that sense, we possess all the knowledge needed to know. Thus, we exert opposite criteria to make knowledge sufficiently complex that there is enough to know, and then sufficiently simple that we can know. Since these two things are mixed, therefore, we struggle to define beauty, because asymmetries are interesting as they yield new information, but if combined with symmetries, they also make the world knowable.

Two Criteria for Beauty

Having made this clarification, we can now turn to the primary question: What constitutes symmetry? Remember that this symmetry is not just physical repetitiveness of patterns. It is rather the ability to grasp and predict the complexity in this world. In this form, symmetry exists as the axioms and principles of our theory, which then lead to the formulation of the laws of nature. In simple terms, symmetry is nothing other than the natural laws by which we predict. Therefore, when we discuss the nature of beauty, we must be discussing: What are the most fundamental criteria for considering something an 'axiom', a 'principle' or a 'law'? Here I will argue that something can be called an axiom, principle, or law, only if it is *simple* and *parsimonious*. Ideas that don't meet such criteria of beauty—*simplicity* and *parsimony*—also cannot be considered natural principles, axioms, or laws.

Suppose you describe a part of the world with X axioms, and another part of the world using Y axioms, and the combination of these two worlds with Z axioms, such that $Z > \{X \mid Y\}$, then our axioms are growing as we add more and more aspects or parts of reality to our knowledge. The principle of parsimony says that we must reduce our assumptions, axioms, or fundamental concepts to a bare minimum. So, a theory that can describe the world with fewer axioms is necessarily better than a theory that needs more axioms—even though both theories may be consistent and complete.

One way to achieve this reduction in axioms is to combine these axioms. For example, we could combine the first two Newton's laws of motion, and claim that there are only two laws of motion instead of three, so we have reduced the number of laws, and hence our theory is now parsimonious. But this won't work, because, under such situations, we must apply another principle of simplicity. We must say: not only do we need parsimony, but each of the ideas used in an explanation must also be simple. We can get parsimony by combining things into a fewer number of things, but that cannot be permitted, or at least, we will not call that 'knowledge'. The need for parsimony doesn't mean that the fewer things can each be individually more complex; the fewer things must also be simpler things.

We can illustrate this problem with an example. All of us who have had to file income taxes at the end of financial year end up dealing with tax forms, which have numerous questions that seem irrelevant to us. But they are there because they are relevant to some people. Now, if you demand the simplification of tax forms, the government can create many forms uniquely customized for each category of individuals, and then, each form would be simpler, but there would be too many forms—i.e. the forms will no longer be parsimonious—and you will be wondering: Which form should I use? Given a certain amount of informational complexity, there is a limit to simplicity and parsimony. If we try to make things any simpler, then we end up with many simpler things, and then we have the problem of extravagance.

In general, when we have fewer ideas, they tend to get more complex. And when we have simpler ideas, then they tend to be numerous. Therefore, simplicity and parsimony are often contradictory. This contradiction is like that between completeness and consistency: we can easily get consistent theories of nature, but they will be incomplete. As we unify these descriptions, we get more contradictions. Similarly, as we get many ideas, they tend to be simple. But as we unify them, they get more complex. Knowledge thus requires that we employ a minimum number of simplest ideas. Now, we can define beauty in a very rigorous scientific sense in the following way.

If a theory P uses axioms inconsistent with a theory Q, and both P and Q are incomplete, then we conclude that both theories are false. To be true, there must be one theory that explains all that P and Q explain, and this theory must be consistent in the axioms, and more complete than P and Q. Moreover, a theory that is consistent and complete is true, but it is not necessarily beautiful. This theory might use thousands of assumptions, a very complicated predictive structure, which may be hard to grasp. But we cannot say that the theory is false because it is consistent in the axioms and complete in its predictions. Therefore, the quest for a better theory stops once we reach consistency and completeness. To create an even better theory, we must say that it must not just be consistent and complete, but also parsimonious and simple. In short, it must explain everything without contradictions, but also utilize the fewest possible assumptions, and each of these assumptions must be simple and intuitive. Thus, a theory that uses only 5 assumptions is beautiful, and a theory that uses 10 assumptions (for explaining the same thing) is ugly. Let's not forget that an ugly theory is also knowledge, since the criterion for knowledge is that a theory explains a topic. Thus, to knowledge, we must add beauty. And this addition is necessary in science; beauty is not a need only for art, literature, or music.

In literature, this necessity will say: If you can state the same thing in fewer words, then your literature is beautiful, otherwise it is ugly. But remember that the fewer words must not be so complex that nobody can understand them. So, not only must we use fewer words, but also simpler words. If we can say something complicated in fewer and simpler words, then the statement is beautiful. The criterion of consistency and completeness drives us toward greater complexity and numerosity—after all, everything in the world has to be described using a single theory, and that can mean that knowledge may not necessarily be a simple or parsimonious theory. The criterion of beauty, when applied to knowledge, works contrary to this trend. It says: things that can be simplified must not be complicated. In short, we understand things cannot be oversimplified, because oversimplification becomes ignorance and incompleteness. However, the criterion of beauty says that this complexity must be minimized without sacrificing completeness. When unnecessary complexification exists, then it is ugly.

There is some truth in complexity—if this truth is consistent and complete. By the process of unification, we can obtain truer theories, whose complexity keeps growing. For example, present atomic theory unifies the theories of matter and light, electricity and magnetism, strong and weak forces, etc. But this unification comes with an extraordinary amount of complexity—e.g. there are over 25 free constants. Therefore, in some sense this is knowledge; but this knowledge is not the ultimate truth because it is ugly. We have an intuitive sense that nature cannot have so many free constants, that are being set so precisely. This intuitive sense is 'beauty'.

Symmetry in Physical Sciences

We can enunciate the idea that symmetries are natural laws by taking a few examples. The law of conservation of energy is nothing other than the symmetry called the 'homogeneity' of time. In short, we can move along the time axis, and time neither expands nor contracts, it doesn't bend or twist. This property of time then leads to the principle of conservation of energy. Likewise, the law of conservation of momentum is nothing other than the symmetry called the 'homogeneity' of space. In short, as a particle moves along onc of the space axes, the space neither contacts nor expands, it doesn't bend or twist. The property of space then leads to the principle of conservation of momentum. Finally, the law of conservation of angular momentum is nothing other than the symmetry called the 'isotropicity' of space. This is a rotational symmetry in which as an object goes round and round, the angles do not expand or contract, they do not bend or twist, and the uniformity of the angles results in angular momentum conservation.

The term 'symmetry' can then be defined simply as *something that remains unchanged* upon change, and these things that remain unchanged define 'matter'. All conservation laws in physics, therefore, correspond to a *symmetry group*, which is the collection of all the operations or transformations that keep nature unchanged. For instance, during a collision of particles, the total energy remains unchanged, so this law can be stated as symmetry of nature. Similarly, if the total charge in charged particles is conserved, then that can be called another symmetry of nature. Our actions upon the world are now described as reflections, rotations, or translations of symmetric objects. The general idea of symmetric patterns now becomes the laws of nature.

The standard model of particle physics describes what is called CPT symmetry, where C stands for charge, P stands for spin, and T stands for time. If all the particles in this universe were replaced by their antiparticles (i.e. those with the opposite charges), if all their spins were inverted (e.g.

from +z to -z direction), and if time direction were inverted (i.e. instead of going from past to future, time would now flow from future to past), then we would never be able to distinguish this new world from the previous world. The combination of CPT inversion produces an invariance in the standard model, so it is a symmetry, and it constitutes a law of nature.

In this way, we can pick any conservation law, and describe it as a symmetry. Likewise, we can take any symmetry and call it a law of nature. The 'law' simply means something that remains invariant, after some variation has been performed. This affirms our previous discussion that symmetry is our ability to predict what will happen. This prediction may not completely single out the precise outcome, but it can restrict the possible outcomes (I will shortly revise this criterion to include the ability to make predictions). For instance, knowing the vocabulary and grammar doesn't fix the sentences, but it does eliminate numerous meaningless sentences (again, I will revise this criterion shortly, to say that grammar must be generative—i.e. it will produce only the meaningful sentences and not meaningless ones).

Now, the requirement for knowledge is that the symmetries must be simple and parsimonious. Reflection for instance is a simple symmetry, as are rotation, and translation. On the other hand, an operation that first reflects, then rotates, and then translates, is a complex operation. The nature of space and time, the types of properties we attribute to matter, and the laws by which these properties transform, constitute the symmetries, and the requirement for knowledge is that there must be a bare minimum set of symmetries that are each simple (rather than complex). If these symmetries are known, then we can describe anything in the world as a sequence of symmetry operations upon some original reality. By that knowledge we can say that everything is a transformation of an original truth, and therefore, there is truth inside everything, although through transformations, its nature has been hidden. If we untransform it, then we can see its real nature.

Symmetries in Nature's Evolution

In Vedic philosophy, nature is transformed by time in a cyclical manner. Nature, or matter, is eternally a possibility, and all these possibilities thus remain 'conserved'. Time converts these possibilities into a reality over the course of a universe's existence (which is also cyclical). This conversion involves two important things. First, nature comprises three kinds of meanings, and change is produced as a result of the variations in the combinations. Second, each such type of meaning is hierarchical, so by changing the meaning combinations, there can be variations in the dominant-subordinate patterns. This cyclical pattern of change presents a rotational symmetry in which an identical time returns on the completion of a single revolution, but because this system is hierarchical, there are smaller revolutions within a larger revolution that recur more frequently. As a result, hierarchical and cyclical time also constitutes new kinds of symmetries that are not recognized in modern science where the time is believed to be linear (and isotropic, although in practice we know that time cannot be reversible).

The symmetries of nature in modern science pertain to conservation laws, because these describe what remains unchanged even after change. However, since time is believed to be linear, nothing ever repeats temporally, therefore, the dynamical laws of motion don't present symmetries. But if time is cyclical, then all changes are simply the hiding and revelation of an eternal possibility and when a type of meaning is hidden, another type of meaning is revealed. Which hiding leads to which revelation constitutes a symmetry in time. As a result of this symmetry, even the dynamical laws of nature can possess symmetries, which will describe how temporal change is not truly a change, but only a temporary hiding and revealing of qualities. This type of symmetry is not possible in modern science (until time is itself treated cyclically) but it will be a law of nature in a hierarchical and cyclical universe. As a result, the dynamical laws, which are currently outside the purview of symmetries would also come with their purview, and we can say that all laws—both conservation and dynamical laws—are symmetries.

Therefore, when I speak about the simplicity and parsimony of axioms, principles, and laws, the narrow construal based on the laws of modern science would simply be that the material energy is conserved. But we can also speak about a broader notion of laws, axioms, and principles under which simplicity and parsimony apply to every single law of nature, including those laws that describe the succession of individual and collective states.

In the previous section, we discussed how symmetries in science do not determine the future states, but only remove many alternative states. We can now revise that idea. The filtered states are those that violate *how* nature will change. But the next state is within the possibilities afforded by 'how' but determined by *what* it will change to. This idea can also be stated in terms of the rules of grammar. At present, we only treat rules of grammar as the conditions that filter out some sentences as being ungrammatical and hence meaningless. This doesn't tell us which sentence must come next. If instead we treat grammar *generatively*, then the next sentence can also be predicted. Notably, the collection of all sentences exists as a possibility, and grammar, in the conventional sense of the word, filters out what cannot exist. Time is now the agency that selects these possibilities cyclically, and due to this selection, the sentences can recur, and that recurring pattern is a symmetry. It is like you are rotating a cube, and upon every 3600 rotation, you get precisely the same state again. But even if you rotate by 900, you still get a face that that has a different number, and if you knew how the cube was being rotated, then you can predict the next face that would be encountered. This means that the symmetries constitute the complete definition of everything—they define the *impossibilities,* and the succession of *realities*—and these two together constitute a complete prediction of the outcomes.

What is Simplicity?

Parsimony and simplicity seem nearly identical ideas, but they are not. Parsimony is a *quantitative* idea, and simplicity is *qualitative.* The former indicates 'fewer' and the latter means 'simpler'. For instance, if you had 100 axioms, then 10 axioms are parsimonious. This is quite straightforward. But simplicity is not. What is simpler than the other thing? The answer depends on whether we talking about *physical* or *semantic* simplicity. A physically simpler thing is also a smaller thing. If you have an apple, and you go on cutting it into smaller pieces, then the smaller pieces are simpler. But what happens when you reach the limit of this simplicity? A physicist would say that we get subatomic particles such as electrons and protons (which then comprise even simpler particles such as quarks). The question is: Is a quark really that simple? After all, it is governed by the same quantum theory that applies to the entire universe. Conceptually, therefore, it is as much a quantum object as any other particle. The only thing simpler about a subatomic particle is that it has a smaller mass, a smaller charge, that it exerts a smaller force. But a subatomic particle is not conceptually simpler. Just ask a kid to solve the equations of Quantum Field Theory and you will know what I'm talking about. Simplicity is the ease of grasping something, or things so fundamental that we understand everything else in terms of these concepts. The understanding of quarks requires many such simpler ideas, besides many more complex ideas. Those complex ideas make the theory inaccessible to children. Therefore, we can try to rethink our notions of simplicity.

In Vedic philosophy, the universe is created from simple to complex, and it is semantic. This universe can be visualized like an inverted tree in which the root is the simplest idea of *knowledge*, the leaf is the most complex idea that can be known, but to know that idea correctly, we must know all that goes between the root and the leaf—i.e. the concepts of intermediate complexity. Thus, for instance, 'animal' is a simpler idea compared to a 'mammal', which is simpler compared to a 'dog'. Why is it simpler? Because in describing a 'dog' we must invoke the idea that it is also a 'mammal' and an 'animal', but in describing a 'mammal' or an 'animal' we don't have to invoke the idea of a 'dog'. Quantitatively, we need more *words* to describe a 'dog', fewer words to describe a 'mammal', even fewer words to describe an 'animal', the word 'life' must say that it is a type of 'consciousness', and 'consciousness' cannot be described other than using the words such as 'awareness', 'I-ness', etc. which are just synonyms for 'consciousness'.

Thus, knowing and consciousness are the most elementary ideas, and everything develops as a type, aspect, or part of this knowledge. That simplicity is indicated by the fact that you can never describe knowledge or consciousness without using these words. All your descriptions would use these words, besides other words, and that would be a *complex* description because you haven't been able to describe it simply—i.e. by removing or reducing the number of words. You only have more words, including the word that you were trying to reduce or explain, so your explanation is necessarily more complex. Simplicity would be if we accepted 'knowledge' and 'consciousness' as fundamental words that cannot be simplified further. In other words, they are the simplest atomic ideas, that must be used *as is*.

Sāñkhya philosophy describes a hierarchy of types using a relation of simplicity and complexity. The sense of seeing is simple, the seeing of color is more complex, and the seeing of the color red is even more complex. This is because 'seeing' involves just one word, 'seeing color' involves two words, and 'seeing color red' involves three words. Moreover, even if we try to describe 'seeing' in terms of other theories, we ultimately will find that we are invoking more types of seeing—e.g. color, shape, size, etc.—because whatever properties we use in describing this seeing also need to be seen.

Thus, the simplest idea is consciousness, the consciousness of seeing is more complex, the consciousness of seeing color is even more complex, and so forth. Hence, simplicity is not the *smallest thing*. It is the *fewest words*. If small things—e.g. quarks—require many more words to be described, then they are complex. Conversely, since consciousness requires one word—which cannot be reduced to any other word without using that word (or a synonym)—hence, the concept is simple. It is in fact the most abstract and pervasive idea; therefore, it follows that the simplest is the *biggest*.

This constitutes the inversion of the physical hierarchy of complexity in which the smallest is the simplest and the biggest is the most complex. The semantic hierarchy of simple to complex is useful when we talk about knowledge or theories, and it represents the simplest ideas. Hence, when we say that the axioms, principles, or laws of nature must be simple, we are referring to the ideas that cannot be restated in fewer words. When we say that knowledge is a simple idea, we are saying that even if we know electrons and protons, they are subclasses of 'knowing'. The principles of knowing that we are discussing in this book, namely, consistency, completeness, simplicity, parsimony, necessity, sufficiency, empiricism, rationalism, operationality, instrumentality, stability, and originality, are the simplest ideas. We can try to reduce these ideas to more fundamental ideas, but we will find that we will either use synonyms of this idea (along with other ideas), or we will fail to explain what we mean by all these ideas. When an idea cannot be explained in terms of simpler ideas, then it is itself the simplest idea.

Therefore, by 'simplicity' I mean semantic simplicity. But it can also be converted into a *quantitative simplicity* as we can talk about *fewer words*. On the other hand, when we try for physical simplicity, then we use many more words, and simplicity now begins to contradict parsimony. In short, we can never satisfy the twin criteria for simplicity and parsimony if we stay within the physical worldview. This is achievable only with semanticism, where the atoms of reality are the axioms of the theory by which we describe it.

Knowledge is Beauty

In Vedic philosophy, God is described as *beauty*; not someone who is *beautiful*, but as beauty itself. His beauty exceeds that of everything else, and everything else demonstrates beauty partially. As we have discussed, beauty is that symmetry by knowing which everything else is known. Then, we also discussed that this symmetry must itself be simple and parsimonious. In short, there is order in nature, and the laws of this orderliness—which presents itself as repetition in space and time—must be few, and each of these laws must be simple. In this form, knowledge differs from beauty in the sense that knowledge is knowing the individual *things*, and beauty is knowing the *theory* by which that thing can be understood. If knowledge is knowing the individual bicycles, cars, trucks, and airplanes, then beauty is knowing the theory of motion that underlies each of these. In subsequent chapters we will see how this theory must be necessary and sufficient, rational and empirical, operational and instrumental, stable and novel. At this juncture, we can say that knowledge is *everything*, and beauty is the *theory* of everything. Knowledge of individual things exists as a potential, but there is a core entity within that knowledge of everything that converts that potentiality into a reality. That core entity, in Vedic philosophy, is called Bhagavan or God, who manifests that potentiality, whereby it also becomes all the reality.

This is a scientific notion of God as the laws of nature that not just govern nature, but also *produce* that nature from an unmanifest to a manifest state. In short, the laws of nature are *generative*. That generation requires the potentiality of everything, which is called knowledge, and then operating upon it with beauty, and the result is the manifestation. We will use the next chapter to discuss the nature of its manifestation—i.e. that it must be necessary and sufficient to validate both the knowledge and the beauty (and this property of God is called His 'renunciation' as it is originally His part, and yet, due to manifestation, it remains different from the whole—its source). Once we know the beauty in the manifested world, then we also know the mechanism by which the world is manifest, since it constitutes the *causality* or the primal *lawfulness* by which the world comes into manifestation.

This lawfulness, causality, or order in the created world can be further described to comprise three parts—*what* and *when* things happen, *how* and *where* things happen, and *who* and *why* things happen. These are said to be three modalities of the Absolute Truth, in which God is identified as the first modality of what and when things happen. The second modality of 'how' and 'where' represent God's feminine consort, that unites with God to produce the manifest world. Finally, the third modality of 'why' and 'who' represent the soul, that enters this creation to partake and enjoy in it.

In the case of God, the 'what' constitutes His knowledge of all that is possible, but He chooses to manifest it by His will, and therefore, two kinds of 'time' are produced—(a) the will is Causal Time, (b) the orderliness in nature is the effect of this causality, and because it is orderly, it constitutes beauty. In short, God's will is not random; it is also governed by a symmetry, an orderliness, which presents itself as periodicity in the will. However, this periodicity—which we can study as a 'law' of nature—is not a law that is 'imposed' upon God by an external condition. It is rather the nature of His beauty that creates the orderliness in creation. This beauty can be understood by us if we understand the order in nature, and by knowing the laws of nature, therefore, we are understanding the nature of God's beauty.

Vedic texts describe this beauty as God's masculine sexual attractiveness. Similarly, the beauty in God's consort is described as the feminine sexual attractiveness. And the beauty in the soul is said to be the attractiveness present in children—which is neither masculine nor feminine sexuality, and yet it is very attractive. As a result, God, His consort, and the soul can are called attractive in a masculine, feminine, and neutral sense, and the attraction determines the six types of causalities or orderliness in the manifested world. We can say that there are six primary causes—the what, the when, the where, the how, the who, and the why—which combine to produce reality, and each type of causality brings with it a beautifulness.

In the Absolute Truth, also known as Krishna, the feminine and the childish beauties are also present, along with the masculine beauty, and this makes Krishna attractive to everyone. However, these forms of beauty are visible to different individuals based on the type of attractiveness they hold. For instance, the individuals with feminine beauty see the masculine or childish aspect of Krishna. Those with the masculine beauty see either the feminine or the childish aspect of Krishna. And those with childish beauty see the masculine or feminine aspect of Krishna. Thus, Krishna remains all attractive, because His beauty combines everyone else's beauty. Even Krishna is attracted to Himself, and as a result, He remains independent.

4

Necessity and Sufficiency: The Principle of Renunciation

The Problems of Causality

All claims of knowledge or truth must pass the conditions of necessity and sufficiency, but these are not easily understood. So, let's start by understanding the problem involved in assessing necessity and sufficiency.

A condition is said to be sufficient to cause an effect if its mere presence assures us of the effect. Now, the problems are in deciding whether the condition merely *accompanies* the effect, or is also the *cause* of the effect. For example, someone can say that "being a king is a sufficient condition to being a male". This statement is generally accepted to be true, because the condition of sufficiency is interpreted to be that which accompanies the effect, even if it is not the cause of the effect. If we try to interpret it as causality, then being a king would be the cause of a person's masculinity, which means that masculinity must come after someone is appointed as a king, which is obviously false. Being a male is also necessary to being a king, since being male is part of the meaning of being a king, and this doesn't tell us how sufficiency is distinct from necessity. If we assign a more specific property to something, then the more general property is implied. In this case, being male is a more general property, and being king is more specific. If we say that someone is a king, then his being 'male' is implied by the semantics of the words, and doesn't constitute any causality. Therefore, I will argue that we must apply the more stringent criteria of causality to determine if something is sufficiently a cause, not just by accompanying the effect.

An example of sufficiency would be the claim: "fire is sufficient to heat a pot of water". Now, you can counterargue: What if the pot of water is placed in an air-conditioned room, which keeps cooling it such that the water never becomes hot? If the water doesn't become hot, then we cannot say that fire created an effect, and then it would not be a sufficient condition for the pot to get hotter. The problem is that if we argue in this manner, then nothing will ever be a sufficient condition for an effect, because there can always be contravening causes that undo the change. For example, someone can say: "Hearing the thunder is a sufficient condition to seeing the lightning". But this is claim is false for a blind person, or someone inside a dark room. Ultimately, by taking this approach, the only sufficient conditions would be those implied by semantics, in which case we would not be saying anything about the real world, just about the meaning of words. When sufficiency is implied by meanings, then necessity is also implied, and we would then not need two conditions, because one would suffice.

The correct statement in this case would be: "Fire is a sufficient but not *necessary* condition to heat a pot of water". Necessity in this case would mean two things. First, water can also be heated by sunlight or microwave radiation, so fire is not necessary to produce the effect of hot water. Second, while fire is sufficient to heat water, it is not necessary because other conditions—such as air conditioning of the pot—must also be *absent*. In one sense, the absence of something is a cause, because it contributes to the effect. But the absence is not an *active* cause, although it must be recognized. The problem is that there could be other similar contributing causes—e.g. blowing wind or the pouring of liquid nitrogen—that must be absent, so if we take into account their contribution (or lack thereof), then our statement about fire being a sufficient cause of the water heating up, would also remain incomplete. But this is the price we must pay to speak about sufficiency being a condition that causes an effect, rather than merely accompanying the effect. In one sense, it is better than the present condition of sufficiency (which can merely accompany the effect), because we are now talking about the real world rather than just the meaning of words. In another sense, the real-world causality is more complex than merely the meanings of words.

A Solution to the Problem

One approach to resolve these problems is to say that matter exists in a state of *potentiality*, such that water can potentially be hot or cold. These are additional attributes of water, and they can be attached to, or detached from it. When the property of heat is attached to water, in one sense, a potentiality that was previously hidden in water has become manifest. So, heat is not entirely something that comes from 'outside'—e.g. fire. It was also something that was potential inside water, and fire is just that agency that manifests the potentiality in water. In that process, fire itself changes its state, and what was previously manifest in fire—i.e. heat—now becomes unmanifest. So, fire is going from a state of manifested potentiality (heat) to a state of unmanifested potentiality (absence of heat), while water is going from a state of unmanifested potentiality (absence of heat) to a state of manifested potentiality (heat). These two changes are correlated and therefore we can say that fire is a sufficient cause of the water becoming hot. If, instead, another cause came around that produced the same effect, then we would be able to say that fire is not necessarily the cause of heat in water.

The term 'necessity' now means that heat must be transferred from fire to water, but that transfer is not necessary: the heat could also be transferred elsewhere. Similarly, heat must be received by water, but that reception is not necessary: the heat may not be received by water (because it is transferred to something else), or it may be transferred after being received (e.g. when the air conditioner cools the water just as fire is heating it up).

In all these ways, sufficiency means the existence of a *potentiality* in matter, and necessity means the conversion of this potentiality into a *reality*. If there is no potentiality, then the cause is insufficient; but even if there is potentiality, the conversion into reality is not necessary because the potentiality may not be used, used in other ways, or contravened by other potentialities. Thus, if the world is seen as a potentiality being converted to a reality, then the logical conditions of necessity and sufficiency are altered.

The problem of necessity needs even further considerations. Since water could be heated by microwave or sunlight instead of fire, how do we know which of these is indeed the case? In short, keeping aside the potentiality for the moment, how do we derive the causes from the effects? What signifying marks can exist in the effect that indicate their causes? This is the traditional domain of detective work; the detective sees the crime, but doesn't know the causes. From these effects, he must derive the causes, identify the culprits, and the methods used by them to commit a crime. In short, we assume that there are some markers left behind by the criminal, which can connect him to the crime. Quite often, crime analysts look into the past records—e.g. who was present in which place? —however, they are able to look into such records because they exist in the present. In short, we are looking at the present reality and interpreting it to derive some information. We are then using that information to interpret other records to understand what they mean. The detective doesn't go into the past to see what is actually happening. He or she rather infers the past from the present. The question is: How does the past exist in the present to be inferred from it? Ideally, in a physical universe, there should be no traces of the past.

Imagine for a moment that we are looking at a moving billiard ball. This ball could be moving because it was pushed by another ball, or by a cue. How do we know which of these caused the effect—without being present in the past? We are of course allowed to look at anything in the present. The answer has to come from the idea that the present states of the world somehow signify one out of the many possible pasts. In short, the past doesn't exist in the present physically but *symbolically*—we can *infer* the past from what we have at the present, but we cannot *perceive* the past.

If we cannot infer the past from the present, then we cannot establish necessity, and this is indeed the case for physicalist theories of nature. These theories remain indeterministic because the present is consistent with many futures, and the futures are consistent with many pasts. To overcome this indeterminism, we must be able to say that the future exists in the present as an *effect* that will come later, and the past exists in the present as the *cause* which is now gone. In short, if there is some heat in the fire, then it only exists as a potentiality. It must be combined with another cause—namely a goal—which causes this heat to be directed toward water (instead of other possible destinations), at a certain time (instead of any possible time). Similarly, when the effect has not been produced—e.g. the water is not hot—then we must be able to relate that effect to the causes such as fire heating the water and the air conditioner cooling the water at the same time.

This creates a problem because, in the selection of a destination, choice is involved. How can we build laws of nature if any cause can be used to produce any effect (given that these effects are changes in their potentialities)? To avoid this problem of causation, we must say that the sufficiency of the cause to produce an effect is not the necessity, and necessity requires another causal agency because sufficiency only says that something is possible, but not what is going to be real. This additional cause is said to be an *entitlement* to receive in Vedic philosophy, that is combined with a *desire* to consume that entitlement. Here is an example to illustrate this idea.

Suppose that there is a tasty plate of food in a restaurant, and you have the capacity to eat it. But does that mean that everyone is going to eat it? No. They have to pay for the plate of food first. Not everyone wants to eat the food, and not everyone who wants to eat the food has the money in their pocket to pay for it. They instead might eat home cooked meals and save their money, instead of eating in the restaurant. Why? The desire to eat is a cause that determines the goal—i.e. whether to eat. And the money in the pocket decides if they are entitled to fulfill the goal. Thus, the possibility cannot become a reality until these goals and entitlements are taken into account, and this is why sufficiency (i.e. my capacity to eat) is not necessity (i.e. that I will eat restaurant food). To convert the possibility into a reality, additional causes must be considered that produce a reality.

Therefore, when the world is described as a possibility, then two additional causal agents—my desire and my entitlement—become *necessary* to produce an effect. The entitlement is just like money—it must have been earned in the past due to some actions, and can be thought of as the reward or punishment for an action. The reward exists as a positive entitlement, which means that it is like money and we have a greater choice on how we want to spend it. The punishment exists as a negative entitlement, which means that it is like a debt and we have lesser choice on how we repay it. The 'greater' choice means that for a reward the choice is dominant and the entitlement is subordinate, and hence choice is the main cause of the effect. The 'lesser' choice means that for the debt, the entitlement is dominant and the choice is subordinate, and therefore the entitlement is the main cause of the effect. If the choices are used correctly, then good entitlements are produced, and if it is used incorrectly, then bad entitlements are created.

Thus, we can see how simple changes in the definitions of necessity and sufficiency create a drastic change in our concepts of causation. First, the world is described as a potentiality that becomes a reality. Second, to produce an effect from a cause, the effect and the cause must be paired, and that pairing requires two-way causation: an effect can potentially be caused by many causes, so one specific cause must be selected, and a cause can potentially cause many effects, so one specific effect must be selected. The forward causality from the cause to the effect is the selection of a goal. And the backward causation from the effect to the cause is the entitlement. We have choices to pick our goals, but they will be successful depending on the entitlement. A goal can be frustrated because there are contravening causes, that don't let the effect be created—e.g. an air conditioner that cools the water even as we are trying to heat the water using the fire. The energy in the fire is lost, and the goal of heating the water is not attained, and that is because there is backward causation due to the effects of entitlement.

The current discussion on necessity and sufficiency attributes sufficiency to mere accompaniment rather than to real causation. Likewise, the current discussion on necessity cannot determine which effect was produced by which cause, because it cannot act backwards to the goal, since reality is described physically, and a physical reality cannot have goals and entitlements. Therefore, I will use the modified notions of necessity and sufficiency that are based on possibilities, choices, and responsibilities, rather than the ideas of causation that are based on reality and physicality.

Implications for Knowledge

The conditions of necessity and sufficiency exert stringent requirements on the knowledge of the world. The requirement is that to know the truth is to know the sufficient and necessary cause of the world. A theory that says if X exists then Y will exist is not sufficient. It is also necessary to show that if Y exists, then X must be its cause. Thus, knowledge is adequate if we can show this bidirectional causation— (1) prove that the cause is sufficient to produce the world, and (2) the cause is necessary to produce the world. Any theory of causation which doesn't permit us to go back and forth from cause to effect, and from effect to cause, is not knowledge.

To prove such a theory, the world must also be necessary and sufficient. Sufficiency means that there must be as much information in the world that can verify a theory. And necessity means that there must be no more information in this world than is necessary to verify the theory. Thus, if X is the necessary amount of information to validate a theory, then the world should not be larger than X. And if X is the sufficient amount of information to validate a theory, then the world must not be smaller than X. In other words, the world must be exactly X—neither smaller than necessary to validate a theory, nor larger than sufficient to validate a theory.

The two conditions of necessity and sufficiency can also be understood in terms of two criteria for scientific knowledge—prediction and explanation. Since the cause is sufficient to cause an effect, if no other contravening causes are present, then, the cause can explain the effect. Likewise, since the cause is necessary to produce an effect, if no other contravening causes are present, then, the cause must predict the effect. The explanation would say that this effect is caused by a cause, as it could produce the effect. And the prediction would say that if the cause was present, then it must produce the effect, and no other effects. The cause to effect relation indicates that the cause is capable of producing an effect, and the effect to cause relationship indicates that it was this specific cause, and none other, that caused it.

Thus, necessity and sufficiency exert restrictions both on the theory that explains and predicts the information in this world, as well as on the information that is predicted and explained by the theory. Indeed, these two become mutually affirming ways of knowing reality. The theory is necessary and sufficient to cause the information in the world, and the world is necessary and sufficient to validate the theory that caused its existence. If the theory was necessary and sufficient to produce the world, but there wasn't necessary and sufficient amount of information to validate the theory, then we could always doubt the theory: Yes, this theory explains and predicts the world, but there could be an alternative theory that also explains and predicts the world equally well. Such a world would not therefore lead to confirmation of the theory, as there could be lingering doubts about the theory. Likewise, if there was necessary and sufficient information to validate the theory, but the theory did not predict and explain all this information, then obviously we would not consider the theory adequate. In the former case, the theory is sufficient, but not necessarily true. In the latter case, the theory may be necessary, but not sufficiently explanatory; i.e. we will now need additional ideas (e.g. randomness) to explain the world.

This mutual relation between the theory and the world can be understood if we relate them as *truth* and *proof*. The truth must be sufficiently powerful to produce the proof, and must necessarily not produce anything other than the proof. And the proof must be sufficiently strong to affirm the truth, and must necessarily not affirm anything other than the truth.

In short, the truth is *generative*—it produces its own proof. And the proof is *generated*—it affirms that truth which has generated it. Since the truth generates the proof, therefore, we can say that the proof 'existed within' the truth, and was produced by that truth. And since the proof affirms the truth, therefore, we can say that the truth 'exists within' the proof, and can be known and affirmed by the very existence of the proof.

Recall from earlier chapters where we argued that a theory of reality must abide by the criteria of simplicity, parsimony, consistency, and completeness. But these criteria can be interpreted in two ways. First, we can talk about whether our description is simple, parsimonious, consistent, and complete, with regard to *one thing*—e.g. an apple. Second, we can also talk about whether our description is simple, parsimonious, consistent, and complete, with regard to *everything*—e.g. not just apples, but also elephants. We can have a consistent, complete, simple, and parsimonious description of an apple, and someone else can have a consistent, complete, simple, and parsimonious description of an elephant. In each individual case, we can satisfy these criteria, but someone can counterargue that the individual descriptions of apples and elephants are neither necessary nor sufficient; potentially, there can be alternative explanations that are also simple, parsimonious, consistent, and complete. How do we know that these are the only possible explanations? Unless we know that, we don't have the truth.

This leads to the insight that the *diversity* of numerous objects that we see in the world doesn't indicate their *truth*, because truth must be *fundamental*. Truth must be one, and that truth must explain the diversities—e.g. elephants and apples. As a result, we must draw a distinction between *fact* and *truth*: the existence of elephants and apples is a *fact*, but it is not the truth; the truth is that which stands apart from the facts, and explains them. Knowing the fact is knowledge, and knowing the truth is knowledge, and both kinds of knowing are important, because the truth constitutes the cause of the facts, and the facts constitute the tests of the truth. Something cannot be considered true if it has no proof. And the proof cannot exist unless there is truth. Thus, the truth must cause all proofs, and the proofs must all indicate the truth. Apples and elephants are now the proofs of truth, but they are not the truth, and yet, they can be explained by the truth, they must be caused by the truth, and they must also then indicate the truth. Thus, what we mean by facts is that a proof is produced by the truth.

For example, if the description of apples fails to explain the elephants, then by the criteria that the truth must be fundamental, a theory of apples that doesn't apply to elephants, cannot be truth, even though it may be a consistent, complete, simple, and parsimonious description *of the apple*. By the fact that the description doesn't apply to the elephant, and truth must apply to everything, it is *falsified*. Similarly, if the theory of apples works for the elephants, then the theory can be considered verified—for the elephant. In effect, every fact validates the truth, and no fact falsifies the truth. However, that truth cannot be any of these facts, but must stand apart from them.

Hierarchy in Necessity and Sufficiency

In ordinary experience, knowledge is produced as a result of the combination of a knower, a known, and the connection of knowing. Typically, these three aspects of knowledge remain separate in the material world. For example, the thing to be seen may exist, but you may not exist, so your knowledge of that thing would also not exist. Similarly, you may exist, but the thing to be seen may not, and then, the knowledge of that thing would not exist. Finally, both you and the thing to be seen may exist, but the connection between you and that thing may not exist, and then the knowledge of that thing would not exist. Therefore, you, the thing to be seen, and the connection between you and that thing are all necessary just as their combination is a necessary condition for the vision of that thing. Each of these necessary conditions (i.e., the knower, the known, and knowing) can be further divided into many subparts. For example, the necessity of your existence can be divided into—(a) you existing, (b) you being capable of seeing, (c) you having a desire to see—as opposed to being averse to the vision. Likewise, the necessity of the thing you see can also be divided into—(a) the thing existing, (b) the thing being capable of being seen—e.g. it is not air or space, and (c) the thing being visible—e.g. emitting light to be seen.

If you contrast these examples with the one about the fire being sufficient to heat water, then you can see that there are two ways in which the terms necessity and sufficiency can be employed. First, my existence, my capacity to see, and my desire to see are all necessary for me to see. But when we combine these three necessities, then we get a sufficiency—I am sufficiently capable of seeing. That doesn't mean that I will see a *specific* something. Similarly, the existence of something, that thing being capable of being seen, and that thing being visible are all necessary for us to see. But when we combine these three necessities, then we get a sufficiency—that thing is sufficiently capable of being seen. In short, some necessities within each thing combine to make them sufficiently capable of being seen or seeing. That doesn't entail a vision, but it is just the readiness for an observation. Second, once these sufficient conditions are met, then we can combine them again to produce an experience; however, that combination is necessary for the vision. Thus, the two ways in which we must use necessity and sufficiency are that some necessary conditions combine to produce a sufficient condition, and then some sufficient conditions combine to create a necessary condition. Necessity and sufficiency must keep alternating.

This can seem confusing but it doesn't have to be so if we try to *negate* the seeing, and ask: Why did we not see? There are many answers to this question, ranging from the object to be seen not being available, to the conditions not being right to see, to we ourselves not being available for seeing. Let's just focus on ourselves, for the moment. Why did I not see? There can be two answers: (1) I'm blind and not capable of seeing, and (2) I'm not blind but I was sleeping, I had closed my eyes, or I wasn't willing, etc. These two types of conditions exist within me, but they exist as a *possibility* and a *choice*. The possibility can be called a sufficient condition *if it exists*. And a possibility can be called a necessary condition *if it doesn't exist*. Thus, for a person who is capable of seeing, his eyes are sufficient conditions to see. But for blind person, his eyes are the necessary conditions for seeing. This is a matter of perspective and contextuality, and not universally known.

If the eyes are capable of seeing, and the ability to see combines with the desire to see, then the preliminary preparation for seeing has been achieved—I am now ready to see. And this preparation basically means that some sufficient condition (namely, that I have working eyes) and some necessary condition (namely, that I am willing to see) have combined to produce another sufficient condition—namely that I'm now ready to see with my eyes open, seeking something to see. This state of seeking is also a possibility and hence a sufficient condition to see. It must now combine with more such sufficient conditions—by a necessary condition—to see.

In simple terms, all that exists as a possibility constitutes a sufficient condition, and when a choice acts upon the possibility, that constitutes a necessary condition. If that possibility itself doesn't exist, then it constitutes a necessary condition. Thus, the absence of possibility creates a necessary condition, and the presence of possibility must be combined by another necessary condition—i.e. a choice—to produce a sufficient condition.

The essence of this doctrine of experience is that a pure possibility becomes a reality through *many levels* of choices, whereby a pure possibility is converted into something that is closer to reality by a choice through stages. This 'closer to reality' is still a possibility, and so it constitutes a sufficient condition, and the choice that brings it even closer to reality is a necessary condition. Thus, we see a succession of possibilities and choices which can be called the sufficient and necessary conditions, but if something is closer to reality, and yet not a reality, then it can be called a sufficient condition from the perspective of the *next* state, and a necessary condition from the perspective of the *previous* state. Context decides which name is used.

The Nature of Consciousness

Now we can easily understand the Vedic philosophical description of cause and effect. The essence of that description is that potentiality exists in three forms, which are called *sat*, *chit*, and *ananda*. The *sat* is the potentiality for relations. The *chit* is the potentiality for cognition, or something to be a knower or known. And *ananda* is the potentiality for emotion such as a desire to connect some knower with some known through a relation. A soul is said to be these three potentialities and each of them is sufficient in creating an experience. Each soul has these three potentialities, so the necessary conditions of having these potentialities is already satisfied. Therefore, the next necessary condition—namely, the combination of these three potentialities—is essential to produce an experience. Each of these three potentialities can become the dominant reason for producing an experience.

For instance, sometimes we are driven toward a known due to an emotion (e.g. desire), and this emotion is then the dominant cause of the combination. In that sense, we can say that it is necessary. However, just the emotion alone doesn't make me capable of seeing. I must also have the senses for seeing, and I must be prepared to interact with the thing that I want to see. These too are necessary conditions for seeing. When I'm prepared to interact, when I'm prepared to open my eyes, and when I desire to see, then these three aspects (which constitute the three sufficient conditions of seeing) have combined by a necessary condition—i.e. the choice to see—to produce another sufficient condition: I'm now ready to see.

Similarly, there must be something that exists as a potential; that thing must be prepared to be seen; and that thing must be ready to enter into a relation with an observer. These are three sufficient conditions, that can combine by a necessary condition (which we can call the choice to be seen), to become another sufficient condition—namely, that the thing can now be seen. Similarly, due to the combination of a desire to see a specific thing, due to the entitlement to see that thing, and the possibility of a relation with that thing—by a choice—another sufficient condition of a relationship between a knower and a known is produced. Now we have three sufficient conditions—the knower is prepared to see, the known is prepared to be seen, and there is a relationship that is available for the vision to occur.

If these three sufficient conditions combine—i.e. we choose to fulfill our desire of seeing, utilize our entitlement of seeing, through a specific relation of seeing—that choice produces an experience or knowledge.

In this way, three sufficient conditions combine within an observer (by a choice—the necessary condition) to produce another sufficient condition: the observer is ready to see. Likewise, three sufficient conditions combine within an observed (by a choice—the necessary condition) to produce another sufficient condition: the observed is ready to be seen. Similarly, three sufficient conditions combine within a relation (by a choice—the necessary condition) to produce another sufficient condition: the relation is ready. Finally, these three sufficient conditions combine (by a choice—the necessary condition) to produce the effect of vision, knowledge, or experience.

Thus, it is hard to characterize the nature of necessary and sufficient conditions, because some sufficient conditions combine by a necessary condition to create another sufficient condition, and then some necessary conditions combine by some sufficient conditions to produce another necessary condition. In simple terms, if I am seeing an apple, then there are potentialities that have combined within me to create me as a potential knower. Similarly, there are potentialities that have combined in an apple to create it as a potential known. And there are potentialities that have combined to create a relation between the knower and the known. And these potentialities themselves combine to create the experience of seeing an apple. The alternating combination of necessary conditions to produce a sufficient condition, and the combination of sufficient conditions to create a necessary condition, produces a hierarchy, in which each thing is a sufficient condition if we consider it a part of a larger necessary condition, and a necessary condition if we consider it the whole caused by partial sufficient conditions.

The primordial nature of consciousness is self-awareness in which the potentialities of relation, cognition, and emotion combine with each other to create self-awareness: the knower, the known, and the knowing are the same individual, and therefore we can say that the knower knows himself through his own power of knowing, creating the knowledge of the self.

When this idea is extended, the original consciousness—God—is also the same three potentialities, but in His case, He is the complete knower, the complete known, and the complete relation between the knower and the known. His potentialities to be the knower, the known, and knowing constitute the sufficient conditions for everything that comes subsequently. Similarly, the combination of these potentialities—i.e. the knowledge that is produced from the combination of the knower, the known, and knowing—constitutes the necessary condition. Thus, as aspects of His person, He is the sufficient condition. But as the combination of these aspects to create knowledge, which form His experience, He is the necessary condition.

When this necessary and sufficient condition expands—as the proofs of the truth—then the collection of all the proofs are necessary and sufficient to prove the truth. That is, there are only as many theorems or statements about the truth as are necessary and sufficient to prove the truth. Any more statements, and these statements would produce redundancy in the theorems, and no logical system should have redundancies. Likewise, any fewer statements, and some aspect of the truth would be left unproven. Again, a logical system should not have any claim that is left unproven. Therefore, the original truth is necessary and sufficient, and the proofs produced from this truth are necessary and sufficient proofs of the truth.

Knowledge is Renunciation

The expansion of the truth into the proof is called God's *renunciation*. God is the full truth, and the world is the expansion of this truth. The expansion, however, is also a partial truth, in the sense that it exists, it has a meaning (namely, that it refers to the original truth), it can be proved (from the original truth), and that it can lead to more proofs which can also be called truths in the same way. To distinguish the original truth from the proofs which have expanded from this truth, we can use the terms Absolute and Relative Truths. The Absolute Truth has no proof—it is the *axiom* of the logical system. But all the Relative Truths have a proof—from the Absolute Truth. These Relative Truths can be called 'truths' because they too can expand into a proof, and this hierarchical expansion of the truth into the proof constructs a tree-like structure in which the Absolute Truth expands into some proofs, which then expand into more proofs, thus diversifying the primal Absolute Truth into innumerable Relative Truths.

This overturns the classical definition of proof and truth. In the classical definition, the axiom is the 'atom' of the logical system, from which new proofs are constructed by *combination* of the atoms. In the new definition, the axiom is the 'whole' truth in the logical system, from which new proofs are constructed by the *division* of the whole into its constituent parts. The root of the tree is therefore the whole, and the trunks, branches, and leaves of the tree are the parts, and the parts expand from the whole. In the classical definition, the successive proofs are 'constructed' from the combination of the axioms, but in the new definition, the successive proofs must already exist as the 'possibilities' within the whole truth, which are then converted into a reality, whereby they can be said to have 'manifested'. When they were mere possibilities, we could say that they are 'unmanifest'.

As we discussed earlier in the part about Gödel's Incompleteness, there is no axiom system that can prove all the truths about numbers. These numbers, as we saw, can denote any arbitrary statement. Therefore, if we picked some axioms, then we could potentially generate some statements, but not other statements. To generate those statements, we would have to add some more axioms. The problem is that in order to prove some statements, we would have to add some axioms that in turn contradict the previously added statements, such that the total system would become self-contradictory. To recover consistency, we need some axioms that are consistent, and yet capable of producing all the provable statements. This requires us to traverse the path from the leaves to the branches to the trunks to the root of the tree. In this process, mutually contradictory ideas would be reconciled as *aspects* of the whole truth, like 'head' and 'tail' are both aspects of a 'coin'.

This introduces the necessity to think of the Absolute Truth in terms of a *form* with many *aspects*. Just like a coin has two aspects, a cube has six faces, similarly, the Absolute Truth has infinite aspects. Hence, the Absolute Truth is called is called Bhagavan, and the infinite aspects of the Absolute Truth are called Brahman which are called 'rays' emanating from Bhagavan. These 'rays' are the aspects of Bhagavan, and they are *parts* of Bhagavan, quite like head and tail are aspects and parts of the coin. When Bhagavan expands into these aspects, the world is produced from Himself. The Brahman can be called the proofs of Bhagavan, just as they are themselves truths. We can also say that all the truths combined together is the whole truth, but this claim is generally not made because Brahman is not the original truth. Therefore, Bhagavan is also called Param-Brahman or the Supreme Truth, from which the partial or relative truths have expanded or emanated.

The emanation is not a *creation*, because the partial truth also exists eternally as an aspect of the Absolute Truth and is simply *manifested* from Him. Thus, all the statements of this world—which we can call the theorems or proofs—have an eternal existence. As most mathematicians believe, they exist eternally as a Platonic reality, but that existence is not always *manifest*—i.e. we may not know about that theorem or proof. Therefore, even Brahman is eternal, however, it is not the original truth, because it can be unmanifest. In that unmanifest state, it exists, but it remains unknown. Manifestation is coming into knowing of something that exists eternally.

God's renunciation is the emanation of Brahman from Himself, by which He reveals His nature as varied aspects of His eternal existence. And yet, just as the truth can exist even if the proof is not known, similarly, He as the truth exists independent of Brahman. The latter, however, has no existence apart from the Absolute Truth. Thus, Bhagavan 'renounces' Brahman, but Brahman cannot renounce Bhagavan. In simple terms, the truth can exist if even if not proven, but the proof cannot exist without a truth, because the very existence of the proof indicates the existence of truth.

5

Empirical and Rational: The Principle of Power

A Brief History of Rationalism

Rationalists believe that all new knowledge can be acquired by reason alone. It was historically demonstrated by Descartes in his complex and circuitous reasoning to establish his own existence, the existence of God and the reality of the world. Descartes is today not remembered for his reasons for believing in God but for the mind-body dualism and the method of doubt that he introduced in philosophy. This method, also often called the "critical attitude", has become a defining trait for all modern philosophy. Philosophy today is defined by its critical attitude to experience, knowledge, not only in the analytic systems but also in continental philosophy. Here we will concentrate on how Descartes uses it to establish rationalism.

All of us know we have illusions. The world appears colored when seen through tainted glasses. Rail tracks appear to converge at a distance. Some people are color blind, everyone sees mirages in deserts. How do we know, Descartes asked, that we are not hallucinating? Sense experience, though vital for daily transactions, is fraught with problems and cannot provide grounds for certain knowledge; it is only reason that can give certainty. The certainty of mathematical truths, for example, is not derived from experience; it is necessitated by reason. The claim that the sum of all the angles in a triangle is 180 degrees is not the result of confirming this feature about triangles in individual triangles but how things must be on any plane surface. Mathematical knowledge is independent of experience; what is true about it today must always be true and there can never be any doubt about proven mathematical statements. Therefore, reason is the standard for truth.

But does mathematics acquaint us with the world? As Leibniz would later point out, propositions can be either analytic or synthetic. Only synthetic statements are about the world, analytic statements do not tell us anything about the world. The statement "All Bachelors are unmarried men", for instance, is an analytic statement. It relies, for its truth, not on the situation in the world—facts so to speak—but on the meaning of the word 'bachelor'. Synthetic statements, on the other hand, are about matters of fact in the world, such as the color of the table in front of me, and they can be known only through experience. Mathematics, in this view, is analytic because the truth of mathematical statements is proved using mathematical axioms and the principles of mathematical inference. A follower of this view might further claim that having the sum of angles to be 180 degrees, is part of what we 'mean' by triangle. In making a claim that "the sum of all angles in a plane triangle is 180 degrees" we are not saying anything apart from what is already assumed in the axioms; the extent to which mathematics explains the world is due to the fact that such knowledge about the world is already incorporated into the axioms of mathematics. It follows that mathematics does not present new features about the world, or how the world is itself. It only reiterates more explicitly what is assumed in the axioms.

This argument is impressive and is often forwarded, even today, against most forms of rationalistic attempts at knowledge, so it is important to better understand the issues here. The first of these is the belief that the world presents us with novelty every instant and this is the reason why any claim about the world must be synthetic. The mathematics-is-analytic view, however, claims that there is no novelty in a mathematical claim; what was present in axioms is reiterated in the conclusions. The situation becomes even more paradoxical when mathematics finds application in the world. Take for example, the classical physics worldview where, given some initial conditions, the future behavior of a system is well-defined if we incorporate the initial conditions into the axioms of a mathematical theory. This means that the mathematical formalism of a classical theory plus some initial conditions form an analytic system. If we knew all the initial conditions at any moment in time, we could construct a completely analytic account of the world. The problem reduces to knowing all the axioms to be used by reason.

Of course, you might say: How do we know the initial conditions other than by observation? And the rationalist answers: *We* might know them by observation, but we are not running the world. It is God who has decided the initial conditions, and He must have a *sufficient* reason for deciding one set of initial conditions over another (i.e. God is also a rational being). We might sometimes condemn or regret what goes around in the world, but if we knew the alternative to that we would understand God's benevolent nature. Therefore, the world is completely rational, and if we knew God's mind, then we will also know the sufficient reason for choosing some initial conditions, and then the world would be completely rational. It just seems that the universe is not rational because we don't know God's mind.

Indeed, Leibniz (Newton's contemporary and co-discoverer of calculus), seems to have recognized the difficulties with his own analytic/synthetic distinction; for, having made one of the most important distinctions in the history of philosophy, he goes on to obliterate it by saying that even synthetic statements are analytic. The analytic/synthetic distinction, Leibniz says, is between our and God's knowledge, and not within knowledge itself. To the extent our knowledge comes closer to God's knowledge, that knowledge would be analytic, because it will also have a *sufficient reason.*

The Cartesian solution to the analytic/synthetic problem is different. Descartes makes a connection between mathematics and the world through the notion of substance. He claims that the idea of causality is not derived from experience but ever present in us. Indeed, causality is not about how things are in the world, but the very notion of rationality—i.e. that every effect must have a cause. If effects were produced without a cause, then we could say that the world is irrational. Experience simply confirms to us that the world is rational, but the rationality of the world is innate in us. Now, if you ask: Why should the world be rational, if in principle it could be irrational? Descartes now invokes another idea, that of *perfection*. He says we have the idea of a creator God who is a perfect being. Such a being must exist because a being that exists is more perfect than one that does not. A perfect being would not want to deceive us by creating an illusory world, because, again, an illusory world would be a less perfect creation. Also, a being who exists only to deceive us would be imperfect. Similarly, the world is working according to God's plan, which is a rational plan, because rationality is more perfect than irrationality. And we have these ideas about perfection, rationality, causality innate in us, so we don't have to know them by observation; however, if we like, we can *confirm* them by observation.

The Cartesian idea of perfection is essential even for us, as I have discussed earlier. The skeptic can say: Well, the idea of perfection is just our idea, and we have no way of knowing that it indeed exists or is true. That skepticism, however, doesn't work all the way, because in an imperfect world, we should not mind being tortured, face injustices, or not receive returns for our efforts. But we do. We don't like torture, injustice, or being cheated. An unfair world is acceptable if it is unfair *in our favor*. Against us, unfairness is not acceptable. That means even the skeptic aspires for perfection, although he may not accept that just for the sake of argument. Now, Descartes appeals to that perfection, and says: The world need not be fair, just, or righteous, but we *want* it to be that way, so we must say that it is the work of a creator. If the world is accidentally created, there is no reason for it to be just, righteous, or fair. So, perfection leads us to the idea of God. The difference between the Cartesian argument and Vedic philosophy is a subtle one: God is not just; God is *justice*—the very idea of things being just.

Once it is established that God will not deceive us, then the reality of the world is established by reason. Since we say that a perfect world is also rational, therefore, the rationality of this real world is established by reason. In short, we derive everything from a simple idea of *perfection.* We might raise the question: Why do we live in a perfect world, when we could potentially be living in an imperfect world? The answer to that question, it would seem, is uninteresting, because whether such a world exists or not is unverifiable. Then, you might argue that we have suffering all around us, and the world doesn't seem to be as good as it can be. How can you claim that it is perfect? And the answer to that problem is that things are never so bad that they cannot get worse! The world could be worse, but it is not, and there is a reason for that. It is God's plan and we may or may not know that plan, but any analysis would show that the plan is perfect. Thus, the combination of the arguments from Descartes and Leibniz prove to be formidable.

Now Descartes says that the knowledge of the world is possible if we apply mathematical truths to the innate idea of substance, since we will see mathematically conforming objects in the world. When this *a priori* truth is applied to substance (which is different from the mind in Cartesian metaphysics) we arrive at a knowledge of the world (which would otherwise be *a posteriori*). A knowledge of mathematical truths is thus knowledge of the world also because objects like tables, chairs etc., conform to mathematics. Mathematics in turn relies on self-evident claims like "the shortest line connecting two points is a straight line", or "two lines that are not parallel must intersect at some point", which can be grasped by pure intuition. By extending and combining these self-evident premises and then applying them to the idea of substance, we get a knowledge of the world. Mathematics is thus both about the world and independent of it. It relies on truths grasped by pure reason, but these truths also apply to the objects in the world.

Cartesian view has similarities to the Greek distinction between *form* and *substance*—the mind is the form, and the body is the substance. The substance is contingent and synthetic while the forms are analytic. But a closer inspection shows that the forms are not purely analytic, because the rules of idea-combining don't fully prescribe the results of such ideas. For example, one mathematician might use the same ideas and rules to propose one theorem, whereas another mathematician may propose a different theorem. All theorems don't appear simultaneously in everyone's mind. Moreover, we are not prevented from being irrational. We can make false claims, because if this falsity did not exist, then epistemology would also not need to exist because the distinction between true and false itself would not exist. So, the Cartesian view that mathematics determines the form of the world is false. Certainly, if we are rational, it restricts the possible forms. But we neither have to be rational, nor can rationality determine all forms. Rationality must therefore consider the existence of irrationality and conclude: *if* you are irrational or false, then these are the consequences. That position acknowledges meaning and choice, which become the synthetic sources of our actions—i.e. we can choose to do different things in the world—combined with the rational (i.e. analytic) consequences of those actions.

Prior to Descartes, mathematical knowledge was either about a world of things or about a Platonic world of ideas. If we claim that mathematics is derived from experience, then we face the objection that any knowledge derived from experience may be in error. If on the other hand, we say that mathematics is about a Platonic realm then we are at a loss about how to account for how mathematics describes the world. Descartes avoids both extremes and is a precursor to modern ideas on the nature of mathematics that position themselves between realism and idealism. Specifically, we saw, Descartes claims *a priori* knowledge of an *a posteriori* world, by positing innate, self-evident ideas and the applicability of reason upon these ideas. The trouble with the Cartesian view is that a mathematical world is not the rich world of everyday acquaintance: the forms of everyday world are not all geometrical and Descartes avoids both the route of experience and the world as it appears to us. He replaces it with a cold, dry substance with geometrical properties. Leibniz acknowledged the everyday world and he called statements that gave us knowledge of this world synthetic in contrast to mathematical statements that are analytic. However, his commitment to rationalism prevents him from using his own analytic/synthetic distinction to the extent that many subsequent philosophers did. Empiricists, as these philosophers were later called, were fundamentally opposed to the speculative and the a priori grounds on which rationalistic philosophers used to base their arguments. They believed reason cannot give new knowledge, it just reiterates what is already assumed in language. Experience, on the other hand, acquaints us with the world; the world as it exists is not evident to reason, but must be discovered by the perception of the five senses.

A Brief History of Empiricism

John Locke who formally launched empiricism believed that the mind of a child at birth is a blank slate. Subsequently, all knowledge is acquired through experience—specifically sense-data of the five senses: ears, nose, eye, skin and tongue. Locke believed that sensations create impressions on the mind and cause what he called simple ideas. Sour, hot, yellow, pungent, etc., are some examples. Thereupon, we operate with reason on these simple ideas, combine them into complexes and give them sophisticated names. The idea of an apple, for example, is the product of combining the simple ideas resulting from the sensations of red, round and sweet. More sophisticated ideas like justice or beauty are abstractions obtained by operating with reason upon the simpler ideas and experiences. These ideas then give us the empirical foundation for making moral and/or aesthetic judgements.

The world, however, as it exists has little to do with our ideas and sensations. It comprises of what Locke called primary properties. These are features of the world as it exists independent of being known by any subject. Length, mass, temperature etc., for example, are features of the world as it exists by itself. The secondary properties in contrast, such as color, form, taste etc., are contingent on the kind of psycho-physical apparatus we possess. A scientific description of the world, Locke believed, must be occupied with the use of primary properties; secondary properties are manifestations of the primary properties and come about through elementary physical interactions in the world. In Locke's view, the ideal of knowledge is that which grasps the world as it exists independent of being known. True knowledge is a passive recognition of the above-said types of observations and therefore, it is necessary to get rid of personal prejudices, beliefs, and all other forms of subjective influences in the search of objective knowledge.

Locke was opposed to rationalism, yet he retained some of the ideas of Cartesian metaphysics. For example, the idea of substance is necessary in Locke's philosophy. Locke believed that knowledge is a passive recognition of primary properties. But what were these properties *of*? With tongue-in-cheek Locke replied: 'material substance'. The substance is the material carrier of primary properties, yet it causes subjective experiences, although the two are otherwise fundamentally different. The distinction between appearance and reality, originally introduced by Descartes, now became ensconced in empiricism. Science ever since has been treading on this path. Scientists believe that our subjective experiences supervene on primary properties. In other words, primary properties cause, through a complex process, our experiences. The primary properties exist objectively whereas the secondary properties are the subjective appearances of the primary properties.

Now, it might strike some that even our knowledge of primary properties is possible only through experiences (the so-called secondary properties) and at first sight this appears so commonplace to hardly deserve a second thought. But George Berkeley made this a crucial point of departure for a big philosophical leap by saying that primary properties are derived from secondary properties. In many ways Descartes is the founder of modern Western philosophy. But if there is anyone who has given modern philosophy a unique and distinct critical flavor, that is Berkeley. To me, he epitomizes the first significant attack on naive realism, or the idea that we know the world as it is, and his writing anticipated much scientific thought.

All of us who have undergone scientific education were led to believe in school days that primary properties like length, mass, temperature etc., are the properties of the world that endures without our intervention. The discovery of quantum theory, which in some interpretations suggests a dependence of experimental results on the conscious observer, came as a rude shock to my scientific sensibility. It meant that the 'objective' description of classical science is fundamentally flawed even at everyday levels and there is a need to revise this description. But I did not yet know there already existed challenges to the classical scientific view of the world articulated much before science grew to such prominence. The full magnitude of the problem with the classical description did not sink in until I read Berkeley.

Berkeley was not happy with Locke's distinction between primary and secondary properties. He said that all properties are derived from experience; the primary properties are obtained by objectivizing secondary properties (Berkeley did not use the term objectivizing, but in a modern scientific context his view effectively amounts to it). For example, the notion of temperature is obtained by objectivizing the sensation of touch, the notion of length by objectivizing the sensation of sight and so on. Secondary properties are fundamental, from these the primary properties are derived. Berkeley went on to proclaim his dictum: *esse es percipi*, or the essence of anything is in its being perceived. What this means is that it doesn't make sense to talk about a world independent of being known, unlike Locke who said that the world is primary properties and we could know them. Our knowledge is limited by our experiences and the world is only as it appears to us.

Locke in his distinction between appearance and reality had made reality primary and appearance ephemeral. Berkeley on the other hand makes appearance primary. The so-called reality is not evident in experience and is yet metaphysically postulated to exist. Such convenience, Berkeley said, is philosophically reprehensible on the grounds that Occam has taught us not to multiply entities beyond necessity. By all counts, a belief in a metaphysical substance is superfluous and we must therefore give it up. But if there is no substance, how does the world persist when no one is observing it? Remember that according to Berkeley the essence of a thing is its being observed? Does it mean that when I go out of my room and no one else is observing, all its contents disappear? Berkeley says that when no one is observing the world, God is still observing it, and thus the world persists even without us. We observe finite portions, but God observes the whole world, and the world's essence is that God observes it. The world is God's vision.

But, if the essence of the world is in being observed, then why are we not solipsistically confined to our experiences? Conventionally, this is the 'other minds' problem: the claim that because the world is only my percepts, therefore, I can never believe in the existence of other people. As far as I can tell, I'm the only perceiver who has such experiences. But Berkeley avoids this extreme. He gets rid of material substance, but he retains a spiritual substance as the knower and experiencer. Although the different spiritual substances do not know each other via experience, they can communicate through inter-subjectively agreed upon words that consistently relate them to experiences. But in going from one consciousness to another, the words must transcend my consciousness. That transcendence is itself what we mean by objectivity. However, for Berkeley, this objectivity is only outside our minds. It is in fact within God's mind, and therefore, all the observers are somehow parts of God. When we speak words, they leave by consciousness, but not God's consciousness, and they enter someone else's consciousness without leaving God's consciousness. Therefore, God is the 'space' in which everything exists, and this is the spiritual substance.

For Locke, communication is possible because of material substance that forms the common reference point for all individuals to confirm and verify. Berkeley replaces the material substance with language, but language would itself not solve the problem of objectivity if there were no spiritual substance. Therefore, the main difference between Locke and Berkeley is that the substance that transcends us is called 'material' vs. 'spiritual'.

The importance of Berkeley's idea lies in his attack on commonsense, everyday realism. Modern philosophy marks a break from the obvious or apparent. Classical philosophy took the apparent to be reality. (The notable exception was Socrates who claimed that the world we see is shadows on a cave's wall, which could be cast by dancers behind the cave men.) Modern philosophy pursues a critical attitude toward the reality of the perceived world. It considers appearances necessarily a product of the way we perceive the world, of our cultural, historical conditioning and the psycho-physical apparatus we use to perceive and conceive the world. The appearance vs. reality distinction is such a fundamental foundation of epistemology that to imbibe it is vital to understanding the debate about knowledge and the influence that has had on modern thinking. And yet, it can prove elusive for a lot of newcomers to philosophy. It was certainly difficult for me.

To explicate this more clearly, I will here give an example from the writing of Ernst Mach who in modern times was one of the predecessors to empiricism's most radical incarnation, called *positivism*. Mach took the instance of a glass rod dipped in a glass jar being looked at from the sides. The glass rod, we can guess, appears bent where the rod meets the surface of water. Now, many would say that the glass rod is actually straight, but it appears bent to us (the Lockean way of thinking about it). Indeed, this is how mostly everyone is taught to think about this phenomenon in school. We are told that the bentness is an illusion caused by the refraction of light. The rod is straight, but the light from the rod bends at the surface of water and when this light is used to construct an image of the rod on the retina, we find the rod bent, although it was light that underwent distortion. But this is not how Mach saw it. He says that to believe that the glass rod is straight is to have a metaphysical belief unjustified based upon the experience of the rod itself. Experiences acquaint us with the world; even the refraction is only our experience. However, with theoretical constructs like electromagnetic waves (of which visible light is a special case) we're able to acquire a picture of the causal nature of things. Based on this causal picture we can believe that the rod is straight, and light underwent distortion, but this is a conceptual construction of the world and not how the world is.

The world is in the ultimate sense a metaphysical belief and the appearance vs. reality distinction is a logical one only. Even to say that there is an unknown or unknowable reality is to make a metaphysical assertion for which we have no empirical grounds for belief. Positivists, amongst whom Mach was an important founding leader, claim that the meaning of a statement is the method of its confirmation. Assertions that cannot be confirmed via experience simply do not have any meaning. To the idea of God, a positivist (with the glint of mischief in his eyes) would say, "Do you mean to say that if I was to do such-and-such then I would see such-and-such? No? Then what exactly do you mean by the word God?" It should be obvious that many ideas cannot be explained by pointing to sense-experience and even positivists recognized this quite clearly. The point of introducing apparently innocuous but frustrating arguments was to eliminate the use of ideas and words that positivists did not like. Because assertions about reality can never be confirmed or denied in experience, they are not true or false in positivism; they are meaningless—in the literal sense of the word.

Positivism was not just an attack on metaphysics, it also influenced science. Einstein's theory of relativity, for instance, had precursors in Mach's discussion on mechanics. Mach argued that the classical distinction between stationary and moving frames or inertial and gravitational masses is not evident in experience and to use them is to have metaphysical beliefs. In retrospect, these are the distinctions that Einstein outmoded. In fact, moved by Mach's ideas, Einstein during his early days was a positivist. It is only later, when he grappled with the problems of atomic theory, that he revised his position and accepted a creative role in ordering our experiences.

But I have jumped quite a bit. The extent to which positivism went would not have been possible without another of early empiricists—David Hume—who radicalized Berkeley's empiricism and pitch-forked the analytic/synthetic distinction into great prominence. The analytic statements, as we saw, rely on their meaning upon the way a sentence is constituted. This, Hume claimed, means that their truth is known *a priori*. In other words, there is no need to look at the world to decide if an analytic statement is true. They are either tautologies and hence vacuous or self-contradictory and hence pointless. In either case they are not useful sources of knowledge about the world. The truth of synthetic statements on the other hand can be decided only by examining the world because they are *a posteriori*. All analytic statements are *a priori*, and all synthetic statements are *a posteriori*.

Now, having denounced reason as epistemologically sterile, one might expect Hume to go on and sing paeans for empiricism. But he does quite the opposite. Experience acquaints us with the world, Hume said, but this is not enough to give us the kind of knowledge of the world our scientific enterprise claims to achieve. The notion of causality, for example, cannot be analytic since any causal claim should rely on the situation in the world. Yet, nowhere in our experiences can we find the experience of cause. What we mean by causality (say in the case of one billiard ball hitting another and causing it to move) is spatial proximity and the temporal succession of experiences. By causality we have come to associate an inductive notion of succession of experiences. Given A we expect B. And there is no guarantee that this succession is necessary. With causality we must associate necessity but there is nothing in our experience that corresponds to necessity. In simple words, we have seen the sun rising for so many days but that does not guarantee that it will rise tomorrow. There are no *a priori* reasons to believe in causes since causality must be a matter of how things are in the world, but there is nothing in the world (at least not that we can perceive) that can make us believe that there must be such a thing as necessary causality.

At this juncture, we can note the difference of opinion between Hume and Leibniz. The latter claimed that the world existed in a certain way because there was *sufficient reason* for it to be so. This sufficient reason was rationality in God's mind. The problem is that by that logic we can rationalize anything and everything as a reason in God's mind, but that neither gives us the capacity to predict what will happen, nor explain why it happened. Indeed, God would now be the sole causal explanation for everything, because whatever occurs does so due to reasons in God's mind. Hume counters that idea to say that scientific explanations must also be *natural* and when we seek that naturality we find that there is none. Now, one could go back to the position of Leibniz and say that the world is governed only by God's mind, but that would undermine science itself. Whether Hume was trying to undercut science in order to establish religion isn't clear. What is obvious is that he was undercutting science. His argument about necessity not being seen in the world stands till today.

We might today laugh at the idea that the sun may not rise tomorrow, but it is no laughing matter. It was an even more serious matter at that time, since science was nascent. Science had to prove that it was epistemologically superior. Science had to show that it was discovering reality—the kind of things that are unknown and inaccessible by reason or revelation. In this scenario, Hume dealt a critical blow to science. His critique of causality meant that ultimately causes are not part of the world but something that we impose on it. Indeed, Hume believed that there was no reason to postulate an order in the world, and even if it existed, it could not be known.

It would be fair to say that if Hume had his way, all of philosophy and perhaps even science would have met a premature end. But Kant, who in his own words, was "shaken from his dogmatic slumber" by Hume's attack on science, set about writing its defense. Science was important for Kant; he came to philosophy from mathematics and physics and much of the writing in his magnum opus *The Critique of Pure Reason* is influenced by the ideas that form the backbone of Newtonian physics. Kant's work has given him a permanent place in epistemology; he is credited with a revolution in philosophy much like what Copernicus ushered in cosmology. Prior to Copernicus, the universe was believed to be geocentric. Copernicus turned it around and made it heliocentric. Kant is also credited with a similar revolution. Prior to Kant our knowledge was believed to be about the world and therefore a justification was required that we were knowing the world. First Berkeley and then Hume's critique of causality dealt a blow to this belief. Either there was no world that existed all by itself (Berkeley) or if such a world existed, then its scientific causal description had elements of metaphysics in it (Hume). The scientific realism was therefore either entirely wrong (Berkeley thought everything was happening in the mind of God) or at any rate not much superior to that given by religion which also postulated metaphysical notions for a causal explanation of the world (Hume).

Kant's turnaround idea that reinstates the epistemologically superior status of science was to say that our knowledge is not about the world but about the 'irredeemable glasses' we use to perceive it. Geometry for instance is not about some space existing out there in the world but about the way we order experiences in consciousness. Similarly, time, causality, individuality, etc. are not a product of the world but the fundamental ways in which we perceive the world. These ways are hard-wired in our consciousness and we cannot but experience the world in this way. Science is not about the world and therefore does not involve metaphysical elements. Rather, its form is the result of the way we structure knowledge and experiences.

Kant's position in epistemology becomes clearer if we consider the position Einstein took regarding science; besides, it also brings out the limitations in Kant's view. It is therefore of value to consider the historical developments leading to and necessitating Einstein's view of science. Prior to physical theories like quantum mechanics and relativity, science entirely depended on classical notions like particles and waves, forces, energy, which were derived from everyday experience. The notion of a particle, for instance, was derived by logically extending the idea of large objects, smaller objects, and even smaller objects to a dimensionless point never actually seen in the world. Although a particle is a figment of imagination there are certain experiences to which that idea can be related and the role of a scientist in classical science was to look into the everyday world and come up with new concepts that might help order experiences. In this sense, almost all of knowledge was derived from experiences; even concepts that are used in ordering experiences were the product of everyday experience.

This notion of how scientific concepts are created is quite in line with Locke who believed that we obtain new ideas by combining sensations and operating upon them by reason. In this view, sense data is enough for science. Although concepts are required for ordering data, even these can be derived from experience and there is no need to introduce any other logical category besides sense-data (although Locke additionally required the notion of substance, it was not to arrive at knowledge but rather to assert its realist status). But what about concepts like quanta or metric, that are crucial to quantum theory and relativity? Surely these concepts have no counterpart in everyday experience! Einstein's reaction to this was to say that concepts are not got by looking into the world but are freely created by us. To order experiences we need not investigate the everyday world; indeed, as science progresses, we might not find the required concepts in the world of everyday experience. Concepts are logically independent of data that science tries to explain and predict. In *Physics and Reality*, Einstein writes, "Physics is developing a logical system of thinking whose foundations cannot be obtained by extraction from past experience according to some inductive methods, but come only by free fantasy." By concepts we create order amongst experiences and discover the laws in nature and concepts are logically distinct from sense data. It is for this reason that even if some concepts do not have counterparts in everyday intuitions, it is not a bad thing for science. A scientist can have creative ways of ordering experiences and if freely created concepts help in seeing the world in a new way that is good enough if the theories in which such concepts are used are predictively successful.

Concepts of science, Einstein believed, are like tokens we get when we hang our coat at a party. The value of the token is that when we go out of the party hall, we can get back our coat in exchange for the token. The token and the coat have no fundamental relation to each other. Similarly, the concepts of science have no relation with the world, but they are useful as book-keeping devices. We throw in some tokens and we get back some coats and concepts like energy, momentum etc., are the tokens to ensure that the totality of these observations can be obtained in exchange for tokens.

But what do these concepts describe? What are they about? Kant's answer is that categories describe the mind, but for Einstein concepts don't describe anything, they are not about anything. Concepts are free creations and if concepts are useful in making predictions, they are logically real, i.e., concepts become real in a theoretical context after the theory is successful. Realism in both everyday as well as philosophical notions posits the existence of a reality independent of observation. However, most of the standard philosophical thought today, like Einstein, regards that such concepts have a pragmatic, heuristic significance only and the theories in which they appear are instruments by which we model reality. The success of their predictions is the sole means by which we can evaluate a theory, or their concepts and all such successful theories and concepts are real in this pragmatic sense although they may not have any counterpart in everyday experience. Einstein's view amounts to a revision of the epistemological status of scientific concepts: concepts are *good* or *bad*, not *true* or *false*. Successful concepts are good, unsuccessful ones bad; concepts do not pertain to the reality in an external world and hence they can never be considered true or false.

The importance of Einstein's idea is in reinstating the logically independent status of concepts in science, something that Kant did before Einstein in philosophy. Kant believed that our knowledge is not about the world but about the way we order experiences. Einstein also holds similar views, although he does not believe that concepts are about anything. In Einstein's view, science is not about the world. All knowledge is a free creation, but it helps us in coordinating experiences. The value of knowledge is that given certain experiences, through freely created concepts, we can predict certain other experiences and that is all science is about. Einstein's difference with Kant is twofold. One, that at Kant's time relativity and quantum theory were unknown and therefore Kant believed that classical ideas about space and time were the fixed ways of knowing the world. Einstein's extension is that concepts are free creations and new concepts can be invented by creative scientists to order new phenomena in new kinds of ways. Two, Kant thought concepts portray structures of the mind, Einstein does not. These distinctions are found on a difference between Kantian categories and Einstein's concepts. For Kant, categories are things in terms of which we experience, for Einstein they are the things that order experiences. Einstein's concepts create knowledge, Kantian categories constitute it.

Kant's ideas are set with some grave problems. Of particularly deep importance is the age-old distinction between appearance and reality. In Kant's philosophy it is described using the words *phenomena* and *noumena*. Kant believed that what we know is in the realm of phenomena; it is by no means reality. Experience cannot lead us to knowledge of the world as it exists, it can only lead us to know the world as it appears to us. Prior to Kant the appearance/reality distinction was based on the possibility of error. We have illusions and make perceptual errors. And hence, there must be a fundamental difference between how the world appears and how it is all by itself. But, in Kant, this distinction is introduced by the possibility of knowledge. Knowledge arises because we organize it in a certain way that conforms to our understanding. Bare sense-data wouldn't make any sense without the categories that constitute it into a world. Kant's solution therefore introduces a basic limitation to knowledge. Prior to Kant, there was hope of eliminating perceptual errors by repeated observation although as Descartes would have said, even then we could be wrong each time. In Kant, however, there is another limitation to knowledge in addition to perceptual errors. This is that the world needs to be organized to become knowable, and our knowledge is conditioned in the attempt to know.

The phenomena/noumena distinction is so disconcerting that Kant felt a need to justify the existence of noumena by means other than experiences. In his *Critique of Practical Reason* Kant writes that the existence of the world is not evident in experience but can be asserted by a faith in the goodness of moral life. Life would be senseless if we were only confined to our own minds. So, it makes sense to believe in the existence of the world simply on the grounds that this would lead to a more meaningful and happy life.

Kant's suggestion proved quite notorious. It led many generations of subsequent philosophers into the search for the noumena along quite different lines than the critical route Kant himself had set. The reason is not far to see in Kant himself. Kant says that we cannot know the noumena and yet does not refrain from talking about it. It was Schopenhauer who brought out Kant's dilemma more clearly, and he puts it in a much better light than Kant himself. The noumena, Schopenhauer says is "one", although this one is not the kind of "one" we get from counting things. By one he means an undifferentiable something. Counting depends upon our ability to make spatial-temporal distinctions, which are possible only in the realm of phenomena. By making such distinctions we create "objective" reality. In the noumena, however, no such distinctions can be made because they inherently depend on our ability to make spatial-temporal relations. Yet, this indistinguishability gives us a reason why moral action is compatible with selfishness. Because the world is one, whatever we do to others would get back to us, indeed, the self/other distinction is also one that can be made in the realm of phenomena alone. One must therefore indulge only in good acts because what we do to others, we do to ourselves too. Schopenhauer rationalizes the uncritical aspects of Kant's philosophy. He brings out Kant's presuppositions and is one of the many subsequent philosophers who were deeply influenced by Kant but chose to traverse directions quite differently from Kant himself. Schopenhauer had little regard for what otherwise went on in philosophy, but he was quite impressed by the Upanishads that posit an undifferentiated reality as the source of the phenomenal universe. He saw a parallel between the Upanishads and the view he was advocating.

Schopenhauer's work gives us a glimpse into the nature of philosophy after Kant. Hegel, Nietzsche, Kierkegaard, and many others, like Schopenhauer, had gone along quite different lines from the general direction that Kant himself took. By the time early 20th century language analysis made its appearance, philosophy was almost entirely occupied with uncritical speculation triggered by Kant's noumena. The language analysts found this trend so disgusting that they decided to even forego Kant and begin all their discussion from where Hume had left it. Their work is so clearly innocent of Kant that one sometimes wonders how they could afford to ignore someone who is regarded as the greatest philosopher the West has ever seen.

But the reason for this willful error is not far to find. Kant had created a room for metaphysical speculation, and there was no stopping people who wanted to talk about it. The analytic philosophers therefore decided they did not want to allow any such nuisance. In positivism and other allied trends, even to say that the world cannot be known is to make a metaphysical statement. It implicitly assumes that the world exists for which there are no empirical reasons. Positivism, in creating a radical empiricism, rejects all obsessions with reality. The meaning of a statement is the method of its confirmation. This practically means that a statement must prescribe how it can be confirmed or denied. For example, the meaning of the claim that there is a wall in front of me is that if I was to have the experience of walking towards it, then I should have the experience of being hit on my head.

20th century philosophy of science, taking a cue from this, rejects all obsessions with reality although in a sense opposite to positivism. In positivism, all concepts that do not have some counterpart in experience are vacuous. In positivism, all scientific 'reality' is reducible to sense experiences and we need not postulate anything apart from experience; all claims that suggest the existence of a reality are vacuous. In Einstein's view, concepts do not pertain to a reality and all attempts to relate concepts with reality are needless. However, that doesn't mean that we are not free to create such concepts at will. Ironically, Einsteinian anti-metaphysicalism survived at the cost of positivism, which initially pioneered the drive against metaphysics.

It was realized that concepts cannot always be reduced to experiences; of great importance was Quine's critique of positivism aptly summarized in the claim "data underdetermines theory". We have seen the thrust of this argument while discussing Einstein's position, which treats concepts logically independent and over and beyond sense-data. The fact that successful concepts like quanta or metric do not have counterparts in experience reinforces the belief that future concepts may not come from experiences of the five senses but might need to be freely created.

Subsequent philosophy further reinforces this view, and we shall discuss it again in a later chapter.

There have been two major modifications to empiricism from the time of Hume. Hume believed that no amount of repeated experimentation could give us certainty about our empirical knowledge, because it is always possible that in the future our experiments may give quite different results or some other data or experience leads us to radically revise our notions about the cause underlying the experiences. In modern terms, Hume's problem is the problem of induction. The first reply to Hume's challenge was given by Kant who said that the certainty lied not in the world but in the way we ordered the world and there were fixed, unchanging ways to do it. Knowledge is not about an unchanging world but about our unchanging ways of knowing it. We have already seen how Einstein modifies this position. Einstein claims that concepts are convenient tools to let us order experiences about the world and this is all science needs to do. If someday, scientific predictions were to turn out to be wrong (as Hume might object) we could conveniently revise our concepts as there was anyway nothing sacred about them. The new notions would then continue until we found sustainable objections to their usefulness, and science is thus an ongoing process. Einstein's view makes an important difference. Science in this view is not about the world (the classical view) nor is it about the mind that orders experiences (Kant) but about some middle ground we call order. Science discovers order amidst experiences and describes this order. What is unchanging and certain is not the world or the mind but the 'universal' laws of nature that are produced by a combination of data and concepts.

The other answer to Hume's challenge is Popper's philosophy of science. In response to Hume's attack that we could never be certain that our theories were right, Popper would say, "But we could be sure that they were wrong!" What he means is that a theory can never be verified but it can always be falsified. Given a useful theory, we can only assert that it has not yet been disproved. While we cannot know what is true by this method, we can always know what is false. A truly scientific theory should be in principle falsifiable, that is, it should allow means by which we could test its validity. If a theory does not allow such means to test its correctness, it is not a scientific theory. Consider Darwinian theory for example. The "survival of the fittest", is a vacuous proposal in falsificationism. The fittest means that which will survive; what will survive is called the fittest. There are no objective criteria by which to verify this principle, as it does not make a prediction: it does not tell us which species will survive and which will not. It circularly assumes the surviving and the fittest species to be one and the same. As a theory therefore, "survival of the fittest" cannot be falsified. This naturally means, according to Popper, that the theory is not scientific.

This is where empiricism stands today. There hasn't been much advance on this front since Kant although positivism and later Einstein and Popper did modify its position. While theories in pragmatism, such as Conventionalism, Instrumentalism, and Operationalism have asserted a logical independence of scientific entities from both the world and experience, they depend on the free creation of ideas and in this sense, they do not substantially overshoot Einstein's view that combines the best out of an empirical approach to science with a rationalist construal for scientific entities.

The problem with empiricism is that any inductively true conception of knowledge cannot assert the reality of its concepts. This was shown first by Hume in his critique of causality and then by Kant in his distinction between phenomena and noumena. Hume shows that the necessity associated with any causal claim is nowhere evident in experience and therefore causality is not a feature of the world. Kant reiterates Hume's belief but adds that causality is one of the fundamental ways in which we order experiences. Causality is not a feature of the world but of our cognitive apparatus, and science describes not the world as such, but the way we perceive or conceive it. Put together, Hume and Kant suggest an ideality of our physical conceptions. Our concepts are logically independent of the world although they find use in ordering phenomena. This was not so bad because Kantian ways of thinking were the ways in which classical science operated. Once science started departing from everyday modes of thinking, its conceptions came in stark contrast with the world as it was commonsensically thought.

Presuppositions of Epistemology

Having discussed the histories of rationalism and empiricism, let us discuss some of the problems in these doctrines. The most fundamental issue in these ideologies is that they don't relate the problem of knowledge to the problem of moral action, and the suffering that ensues from immoral action. Greek philosophy had identified three divisions of philosophy called *logos, ethos,* and *pathos.* Logos pertained to the nature of the truth; ethos to the nature of the right; and pathos to the nature of the good. At the dawn of Western Enlightenment, these questions were disconnected. The question of the good was a private matter. The question of the right was to be collectively decided by the people and their government. And the nature of the truth had to be determined by science. By that segregation of concerns, truth was disconnected from social and private lives, and science was disconnected from your political and religious views. Ever since, the modern world lives under the shadow of incessant conflicts between these domains.

We suppose that our politics doesn't determine our science and philosophy, but that is not true. We suppose that our religious preferences don't decide the nature of the truth, but that is also false. The fact is that truth leads us to right action, and right action leads us to the good. We do things because we want to be happy. But to achieve that we must be righteous or moral. This means that there must be objective judgments about right and good, and these must emerge from our understanding of the truth.

This separation of truth, right, and good, which is the hallmark of modern Western thinking is rejected in Vedic philosophy. The Absolute Truth is described as three fundamental ideas—*sat, chit,* and *ānanda.* The *chit* pertains to the truth, the *sat* to the right, and *ānanda* to the good. These are discernable traits of God, but they are not separable. In short, everything in this world—which has expanded from the Absolute Truth—must have components of truth, right, and good. The concern with truth leads to the idea that the world presents us with some meanings, which can be true or false, and the intellect judges the truth. The concern with righteous action leads us to the idea that the world presents us with opportunities for action, the actions can be right or wrong, and the moral sense judges the rightness. The concern with goodness leads to the idea that we desire happiness, and we create our goals based on what we consider to be our happiness.

Righteousness means that our happiness cannot be disconnected from the happiness of others, and truth is the method of attaining that happiness. Thus, the soul is said to fall into the material world when he disconnects his happiness from those of the others; in short, he develops a selfish attitude. Under this selfishness, the soul indulges in immoral and unethical actions, hoping to gain his preferred type of happiness, but that only leads to suffering. However, due to his selfish attitude, the soul refuses to see what might be good for everyone, and why our happiness depends on morality.

Thus, the truth is believed to be *universal*, but morality and happiness are defined to be *personal*. Whatever is personal is our choice, but whatever is universal cannot be chosen. By this disconnection between truth, right, and good, an 'objective' criterion for truth is constructed, that is devoid of a purpose of life (happiness), and righteousness that fulfills this purpose.

If we must study knowledge, then we must study it considering truth, right, and good. To acquire knowledge, or the universal truth, we must also seek the universal right, and the universal good. When these concerns are disconnected, then the truth is also reviled, and then we are not trying to know what is factually true but trying to know what we *want to be true*.

Western philosophy is the presentation not of that which is true, but of that which we *want to be true*. The essence of this wanting is that the quest for truth must be disconnected from the problem of sin and evil in Christianity. In religious philosophies, the soul enters the world because of sin and evil, which lead to misreading the situation, and then to mistakes in actions. The exercise of Western philosophy is meant to never talk about the problems in the soul. The exercise assumes that we can know the world without any change to ourselves. While religion would say that perfection will be attained if you change yourself, science will claim that perfection can be attained without any change to you. Indeed, that perfection is just within our reach, and we need to decide which method is best suited for achieving it. Even the cynics who attack the idea of knowledge, do not relate it to any shortcoming in the observer. If at all these shortcomings exist, they are permanent, and the blame for their existence certainly doesn't rest with us.

For example, the mind is a blank slate in Locke's philosophy, the mind is imbued with perfect intuitive ideas in Kant's philosophy, and the mind is not deluded by an evil demon in the case of Descartes. On the contrary, according to Berkeley, the essence of the world is its perception by us (and God maintains the world while we are not perceiving it—again so that we can perceive it when we want), everything happens due to a sufficient reason in the case of Leibniz, so the world works rationally and can be known by us, and we are free to create our understanding of the world in Einstein's philosophy. Each of these philosophies describes either a virtue in us or a virtue in the world that enables our knowledge. God facilitates our knowing in Berkeley's case, at zero cost to us. Then there is the cynic—Hume—who attacks the idea of reality and causality, and claims that there is no certainty, which can be interpreted to mean that *after* we rejected the certainty of religion, we must also reject the certainties of science. Now, the world is nothing but a collection of unpredictable and inexplicable sensations.

In all such ways, philosophy and science have moved to undercut the basic premise of religion, namely, that there is something wrong with *us*. That we are ignorant or that we are suffering because we have some faults, which could potentially be overcome if we were rid of these problems. Even as philosophers and scientists have opportunistically used sufficient reason in God's divine plan, persistence by God's observation, appealing to His rational and benevolent nature, there hasn't been a single acknowledgement of the problem within us. God, if He exists, facilitates our knowledge of the world, helping us control nature. But if He doesn't exist, then we are free to create theories of nature, testing them against the criteria we set for correctness, and changing them when they don't work for our own needs.

If we were to psychoanalyze all these philosophies, they come across as speculations of an infantile and entitled view of the present existence. We *deserve* to exist, God facilitates our right to exist and know, and if He doesn't, then we are free anyway. Children think in this way. Namely, that the parents exist to serve us; they are responsible to facilitate our knowledge, because we are pure and beautiful. If parents don't exist, then we are free to do as we please, because we came out of nothing and remain answerable to no one. Under no circumstance are we responsible for our actions, there is certainly nothing wrong with us, and hence the problem of knowledge involves no corrections to our current state of consciousness or methods of knowing. This is a radical rejection of the fundamental problem of suffering, ignorance, and sinfulness, with each causing the other in religions, and replacing them with a supposed paradise of knowledge and freedom. The paradise may be created and maintained by God, but it is a paradise. If this world is itself the paradise of knowledge and freedom, then another world is not needed. Let it exist, if someone wants to believe in its existence. What difference does that belief make if we are already living in a paradise?

This is the fundamental point of departure between Western and Vedic philosophy. The soul falls into this world due to rebellion against God (like Christianity). To help him enjoy the world in a limited way under this rebellious attitude, the consciousness of the soul is covered by ignorance—the ignorance is that the soul cannot see the true nature of reality because he doesn't want to see the truth. He wants to believe that he is a beautiful child in a paradise, roaming around the world with wonder at nature's creation, free to do as he pleases, without any consequence or responsibility.

This covering is like Kantian goggles through which the world is seen, but the property of these goggles is that they obfuscate the truth. If reality were truly seen, then the soul would realize that it is a proof of the truth, that it emerged from the truth, and that it exists to validate that truth. Suffering is then the inevitable consequence of that proof—it denies us the right to enjoy with the assumption that God doesn't exist, or that God exists solely for our enjoyment. In short, the child cannot remain entitled. The child must become cognizant, recognize the flaw in his perceptual apparatus, understand that it is unable to see the cause of his suffering unless he removes the goggles, and go on suffering if the goggles are retained.

Like Leibniz, we can say that God has sufficient reason to do everything rationally. Like Descartes, we can say God is not trying to delude us into a false idea. Like Locke, we can say that originally consciousness is pure and capable of seeing everything perfectly. Like Berkeley, we can say that God maintains the world by His will even if we don't recognize His existence. Like Hume, we can say that we have no understanding of how the world is working—i.e. that God maintains the world that leads to suffering. And like Einstein, we can say that we are free to change the goggles by which we see the world. All these are not mutually contradictory ideas, but they are all imperfect and incomplete unless we recognize that freedom comes with responsibility. Speculation on the nature of reality—as Einstein claims—is not a route to knowledge. Indeed, it has a cost, namely, that unless we see the nature of truth, we remain ignorant that the world exists to prove the Absolute Truth, and that ignorance will perpetuate the suffering of frustrated desires that presuppose that we are independent of God. Accepting that God maintains the world, and everything exists inside the 'spiritual substance', won't solve the problem of the existence of ignorance, because God's benevolence is also that He allows us to live in ignorance—because we desire it. God facilitates a limited kind of enjoyment, that is constantly mixed with suffering, because we choose to remain ignorant. Contrary to the idea that there is no intelligent demon deluding us, because there is God enlightening us, there is indeed a demon—our desire—that deludes us. We choose to surrender to that demon, and be deluded by its machinations, because we refuse to accept that there is something wrong within us.

Thus, Vedic texts describe three fundamental problems in our current existence. First, the soul's entitlement to be independent of God. The soul thinks: if God exists, then He exists to serve us; otherwise He doesn't exist, and we are free. Second, as a corollary of independence, we think that there is nothing wrong with us, that we are not covered by ignorance. Vedic texts describe how God facilitates an illusion by creating an illusory covering of our pure cognitive abilities. This is because if we know the truth, then we cannot enjoy our deluded aspirations; we will realize that we are not truth; we are the proofs of the truth, and our life must be lived to prove that truth. Third, as evidence that our delusion is not the truth, and the world is not a paradise, the world creates a problem of suffering. We think we can solve this problem by knowledge, but since knowledge is never acquired if we are averse to the truth, therefore, there is also no cessation of suffering. Driven by the problem of suffering, we are forced to reexamine our desires for independence, purify our desires, and change the goggles of vision.

Western empiricism and rationalism are a victim of the first problem of rebellion, which then leads us to believe that we are either free or already in paradise. However, that conclusion contradicts the observed fact that we don't get perfect knowledge, without that knowledge we aren't able to solve the problems of life, and as a result we go on suffering, although we tend to believe that there is 'progress' in our knowledge and lessening of the suffering, when the fact is that the problems don't go away; they change *form*. In short, one problem is replaced by another, but due to the delusion, we either don't see the problem (it remains invisible to us), or we recognize its existence, but we think that we are eventually going to solve that problem.

Innate to Western philosophy is the idea that time is *linear* and *progressive* rather than *cyclical* and *repetitive*. This idea underlies all philosophy and science, and leads to the belief that we are progressing along a straight line where all the problems would eventually be solved rather than going in a circle where one problem replaces another problem, and the problems are never solved; they are only substituted by a different set of problems. Thus, all philosophers of epistemology eventually provide a method to solve a problem that creates a problem that did not previously exist. Thus, each philosopher can say something to overcome the problems of other philosophers, but they don't recognize the problems in their own philosophy. This is also a form of ignorance—when you see one thing, then you don't see the other things. You can see a problem and its solution, but you don't see the problems that you are creating because of adopting that solution.

The Process of Perception

Commensurate with this philosophical attitude, Vedic philosophy describes a model of perception in which our minds are not blank slates but *sieves* through which we see the world, and the world is *filtered* in our perception according to the forms of the 'holes' in the sieve. These 'holes' are the concepts, categories, and ideas in terms of which we filter, categorize, and organize the world. To correctly see the world, the holes in the sieve must conform to the forms of things as they truly exist. Unless this correction is made, we must face one of the following two problems: (1) if the world doesn't fit the form of the holes in the sieve, then some features of the world would be discarded to force-fit the world into our present modes of thinking, and our knowledge will remain incomplete, and (2) if we recognize the incompatibility between the holes in our sieve and the reality of the world, but only make minor changes to the sieve to solve the incompatibility in one situation, then we will encounter contradictions between the sieve holes and reality in other situations. This is the general problem of inconsistency vs. incompleteness: either the world is inconsistent with our sieves, or if the sieves are changed arbitrarily to fit the world in one situation, then that sieve contradicts the reality in other situations. The process of knowledge therefore requires us to correct the nature of filters by which we categorize, classify, organize, and structure the world in our consciousness. Kant's idea that we see the world through some goggles is correct. However, the supposition that our goggles are already perfectly suited to see the world is false. We can see the world perfectly; but we have chosen not to see it perfectly. Unless we reject our perverted desires, we cannot find the truth because we will keep filtering the truth by the sieves of our deluded aspirations, or trying to force-fit it into those deluded aspirations, but always failing to do so.

The sieve through which we filter the world is called *māyā* in Vedic philosophy. These sieves must exist for us to see anything. If the sieve ceases to exist, then we stop seeing the distinctions in the world and thereby we fail to classify, categorize, organize, and structure the world in our experience. This existence, which is devoid of categorization, is sometimes called *Brahman*, or the undifferentiated state of existence. It is not that the reality is undifferentiated or "one". It is that we have removed the goggles by which we classify this reality into categories and organize it into experience. The undifferentiated experience is therefore free of the *illusions* of this world, which arise because the holes in sieves don't have the correct form. But it is also the *ignorance* of the nature of reality. Notably, therefore, ignorance can exist, even when the illusions don't exist. That is, we may not know the truth (ignorance) even when we don't accept falsity as the truth (illusion).

Vedic philosophy describes the nature of *māyā* in both cognitive and emotive ways. The emotive sense—or what we *want* to see—is more fundamental. When the soul falls into the world, then it wants to enjoy in a specific manner, and it wishes to see only those things that will help it enjoy, while the rest must be ignored. Quite specifically, all that we dislike, and which leads to suffering and pain must be ignored and rejected. Over time, as these desires are fulfilled, the form of the sieve becomes cognitive—we don't have to actively seek some things, and we don't have to actively reject other things. These filters of vision become our automatic habits of perceptual filtering and we stop seeing those things even if they are present.

The vision of modern science, for example, which reduces all sense perceptions to primary properties, is one such filter. Under this filter, we fail to recognize the reality of the 'secondary' properties; we rather say that these properties are *generated* or caused by the 'primary' properties. The nomenclature of primary and secondary betrays that bias in our perception—we think that what we see is an illusion created by the 'primary' properties.

Each of us, therefore, carries a different set of filters, by which we consider some idea to be more fundamental or 'primary' and other ideas to be 'secondary'. If the filters are removed, then we cannot see anything. Therefore, the filters must be *purified*, corrected, or reformed for correct perception. This purification simply means reinstating those filters that will help us see the world consistently and completely, simply and parsimoniously, necessarily and sufficiently. The principles of sufficient reason can now be reinstated, and we can see *how* things are working due to a good reason. Unless we change the filters, we will either not know why something happens (e.g. describe the world as probabilities, if we describe it at all), or describe the world contrary to the observations (i.e. as a false theory). In the former case, the theory would be incomplete, and in the latter, inconsistent. Even if the theories are consistent and complete, they could be overly complicated and superfluous, or not have sufficient reason to justify their existence—i.e. not be necessary and sufficient justifications of the world.

Given this description of experience, the fundamental process of epistemology is not expanding the realm of observations and/or theories that describe them. The fundamental process is purification of the consciousness. When consciousness is purified of the incorrect filters, then every experience is understood perfectly, because it is classified, categorized, and organized in a way that is consistent, complete, simple, parsimonious, necessary and sufficient. At that point, we can say that by reason and experience we can know the world, and by that knowing, we can know the Absolute Truth, because the perceptual apparatus is appropriate for knowing. If the perceptual apparatus is flawed, then no amount of perception or reasoning can help. Each such perception and reasoning will create confusion because it either fails to explain through reason all that we can perceive or predicts something based on false rationality that we do not actually perceive.

Problems in Rationalism

With this philosophical background about the origins of material experience, and why illusion exists due to the filters of experience we have chosen, we can understand some specific problems in each philosophy.

Let's begin with rationalism. When Descartes says that the forms of mathematics apply to the substance to create the world, he assumes that the world is *physical.* To explicate the problem, we can use the analogy of sentences. Each sentence is written using some ink, which we can call 'substance'. (Vedic philosophy doesn't agree with the idea that ink is a 'substance' but let's use the example anyway. We shall return to correct this later once we show the problems even with this assumption.) For the sentence to be meaningful, it must follow some logical rules, in some perfect language like mathematics; we can call these rules the 'grammar' of the language. However, the combination of grammar and ink doesn't produce sentences; we also need some words which are representations of meanings, and to read the words, we must *interpret* their meaning. This interpretation then requires the mind, but it also requires an objective sentence, which was previously produced by some mind. That mind can be deluded or ignorant, and false statements can be produced by such a mind. God facilitates this process of delusion, but the soul is the cause of the delusions. Therefore, God is also in control of the delusion, but God is acting on behalf of the soul, rather than forcing the soul to be under delusion. Thus, there is sufficient reason underlying each sentence, even though they are false, and that reason is that we want to be deluded. The sufficient reason is not God; the sufficient reason is the desire in the soul. The rules of grammar allow us to produce what *we* consider truthful, even though it is false. Thus, the existence of the rules doesn't preclude the falsities, and we can see this problem only when we describe the world as sentences, not as physical objects. If we treat the world physically, then there are only substances and rules, and everything that exists is also true according to the application of rules. This idea that rules determine the truth becomes the basis of later problems.

All Western rationalism is built upon a physical ideology in which the world is *things* rather than *meanings*. This simplifies the ontology to rules and substances and eliminates concepts from the world. Whatever concepts exist in our mind are primitive self-evident axioms (such as the shortest path between two points is a straight line). We can agree that there are some primitive self-evident axioms in us. However, the *choice* of combining these axioms also exists. And this choice is not predetermined by the rules. We can perfectly follow all the rules of grammar, and yet say something that is either meaningless, or meaningful in a context, or only to a person. The rules of mathematics can describe which words can be combined to denote meaning, but these rules are the grammar of language. These rules don't fix the words that we use in the language, and since we choose those words, therefore, there is choice in formulating the sentence. That choice exists objectively as the chosen words, and subjectively as the meaning we will to communicate. Therefore, the mind is not merely mathematical rules. It is also meanings that can be combined by our choices. We can also choose to not follow the rules, not produce something meaningful, etc. In such cases, for the principle of sufficient reason to hold, we need new kinds of rules that connect choices to the consequences of irresponsible choices.

Thus, we must distinguish between two kinds of rules. First, a sentence encodes an objective meaning that existed in the mind of the speaker and can be decoded from the sentence if we know enough about the time, place, and person who spoke or authored the sentence. The objectivity of such meaning depends on individual choices to combine words and grammar, which doesn't violate the laws of nature. Second, as a consequence of this objective meaning, in a given time, place, and by a person's choices, a consequence of that choice must be produced which cannot be optional, because then there would never be a 'sufficient reason' for anything. However, these rules pertain to meanings and choices, and not to matter itself.

Hidden in Cartesian reasoning is the elimination of the subject from the study of the world, which Descartes calls the mind-body duality. This separation is further based on the idea that the world is physical. While ideas about God's rationality and benevolence are used, they don't amount to much except to justify the existence of a world governed by rationality. But since the mind is separated from matter, therefore, the choices of the mind effected into matter are not associated with any laws. All the laws are then reduced to mathematical formulae which abide regardless of choice. This entire conception of laws and reality, and the doctrine of knowledge upon which it is based, is false in Vedic philosophy. Even the idea that there is a 'substance' upon which mathematical laws apply is also false because even sense perceived properties such as color, taste, smell, etc. are concepts, and hence they are all *forms*. We don't have to just sense yellow; we can also think about it, and it can exist objectively. The conceptual reality therefore is neither mind, nor sensation, nor body, but it can exist as either of these.

The mind and body are defined in Vedic philosophy relative to the filters of perception. In different species, these filters exist differently—sometimes they are more abstract ideas and sometimes they are more contingent ideas. Accordingly, some species have a bigger body, and some have a smaller body. The variations in their forms depends on how they perceive the world. Thus, there is no absolute designation for 'mind' and 'body'. These are relative to the one's filters of perception. Hence, a different species of life is defined as the soul wearing a different set of goggles to see the world differently. Each pair of goggles is limited in some way or another. Humans are more intelligent than animals, because our goggles include sophisticated ideas like knowledge, beauty, wealth, heroism, power, and detachment. We can think of all these things and see them in the world. The animals cannot see these things because they don't have the goggles to see them. Thus, based on the type of goggles, the soul sees something different, and these goggles constitute the 'mind'. The body is the object we see ourselves as; based on what we want to see, we become the type of object that we want to see. The interaction between the body and the mind is like that between the goggles and the objects that pass through these goggles.

There is thus a difference between mind and body—there are like sockets and balls (that can fit into the sockets). But both balls and sockets are *forms* and not substances. Their interaction involves the consistency, completeness, simplicity, parsimony, necessity, sufficiency, etc. of the forms. There is hence no mind-body interaction problem, because the interaction is between two kinds of forms—one form is like a socket, and the other one is like a ball that can fit into the socket. The mind and body can thus be compatible—when the balls and sockets fit. They can be incompatible—when balls and sockets do not fit. Accordingly, sometimes we understand the world, and sometimes we don't. Sometimes we enjoy the world, and sometimes we don't. Ignorance and suffering are hence related to the problem of knowledge, and they cannot be separated from our perceptual biases.

Problems in Empiricism

The notion of the mind as a blank slate is probably naivete at its worst, because it doesn't explain why every person is different in what they find interesting, likable, their mental and intellectual capacities, how they feel under different situations, etc. Even twins, who have the same genetic material, and nearly identical upbringing, turn out to be completely different. How do we explain this difference other than by saying that this difference preexists in each person and it filters the world into our perception, such that no two people look at the world in the same way, even if they are exposed to the same situation and reality? Moreover, unless we possess the concepts, we cannot classify and categorize things into groups and label them by the same words. We must share the concepts about color, shape, size, etc. such that we can classify yellow different from blue, triangles different from squares, bright different from darkness, big different from small, etc. If some of these categories are missing—e.g. some people lack empathy, some people find mathematics difficult, some people cannot relate to other people—then we cannot put sensations into different buckets, and without those buckets, which must be preexisting in us, there is no knowledge.

Berkeley's *esse es percepi* is correct to an extent that the forms of the world must be like the forms of our perception otherwise we cannot perceive the world. However, that doesn't entail the absence of an objective reality. If God perceives everything like Berkeley claims, and maintains the world by this perception, then God must also experience the suffering and pain that we are undergoing, and then God must be suffering or enjoying just like we are. Indeed, God must be suffering the pain of every single individual, even when that suffering is entailed by their bad choices. This idea about one person suffering because of the choices of the others is completely contrary to the principles of responsibility for a person's choices. Therefore, it is rejected in Vedic philosophy. The world is objective, and it exists independent of us. Therefore, it doesn't exist inside our minds, and it is for this reason that two people can talk about the same thing in different ways, because those ways of perception are in our minds, but the thing being perceived is not. If everything is in our mind, then how can there be any notion of truth? Everything would be true because it is in our mind.

Kant's philosophy about the ideas used in perception is correct—these ideas exist as filters of perception. However, no two people have the same filters. The evolution of science shows that these filters evolve with time, as we begin to describe the world in different ways. So, while the filters enable knowledge, they are not always the grounds for certainty, unless we reach a point whether the filters stop evolving, and that can happen only when we obtain the perfect truth. Thereafter, everything is seen perfectly, and there is no need to revise that conception of reality because it is always consistent, complete, simple, parsimonious, necessary, sufficient, empirical, and rational. Ideas evolve only when the theories using them fail to explain the world. Therefore, the perfect filters are eternal, and the false filters are temporary. Since everyone has varying degrees of true and false filters, hence, (1) the filters are not universal, and (2) the filters are not necessarily knowledge. They will become knowledge if consciousness is purified.

Hume's critique of causality is partially true because things may not happen just the way they have always happened because we can use our free will to change the world. Does that mean there is no causation? No. There is causation, but it is the causation of meaning and choice. The effect of an interaction is due to the nature of meaning, but the cause of the interaction is a choice. These choices have consequences, which then limit and change our interactions, and sometimes force some interactions, so, conditioned by the effects of past actions, we cannot always exhibit free will. But that doesn't entail that free will is itself absent. The critique of causality should simply say that the necessity associated with the events is false; some things may not happen tomorrow. But the necessity must be associated with the consequences of choices, and this necessity is established not by observation but by fact that there will be no morality if this necessity was absent. In a world that enables choices, rationality means consequences of choices. Society cannot be organized without moral principles, and society will create whimsical rules and regulations unless there exists a natural morality.

A deeper problem in Western philosophy is that it hasn't been able to explain *sufficient reason* as morality. Yes, things happen for a reason, but what is that reason? Can we explain why one man is rich and another man is poor by any reason? Can we explain why someone is healthy while someone else is sick? Can we explain why someone is enjoying and another person is suffering? Sufficient reason entails the ability to explain these things. So, Leibniz is right in saying that there is always a rational criterion for why things happen. But unless we spell out that rational criterion, and reconcile it with the rest of the worldview, 'sufficient reason' is not meaningful.

The Necessity of an Alternative

Even if we disagree with Vedic philosophical ideas about how truth can be discovered, or how the mind works to create perception, we can prove that the rational-empirical method of discovery alone cannot lead to the complete truth. The empirical reason is that we never have all the data to validate a theory. But if we had enough data, then we would not have the time and capacity to process this data to determine the nature of reality.

For example, to collect and store all the data, we must be present across space and time, and to record and store this data, we will need another universe—as big as this universe—for each moment of time. As time passes, this universe evolves, and we will need another universe to store all the data emerging from the present universe, until we finish collecting all the data to begin its analysis. Thus, if this universe exists for M moments in time, then we need M universes to just record the data of the present universe.

Then, if we start analyzing this data to arrive at a theory of nature, we find that each event has at least two interpretations— (1) it is the fundamental event in terms of which all reality can be modeled, and (2) it is not the fundamental event, and it must be modeled based on some other event. If a universe comprises N events, then checking each of the N theories (that claim that the event is fundamental) against the N-1 other events (that are considered non-fundamental) would require a universe of size N(N-1). The N in this case is all the data in the M universes. Its analysis requires a universe of size M (M -1) universes. If we add the M universes used to store the data, then the number of universes needed for analyzing one universe is M2. This holds true even for smaller parts of the universe. For any data of size M, we need M2 size to complete the rational-empirical process. This rapid growth entails that we cannot analyze enough to know anything.

Since the empirical-rational process can never be completed, the empirical-rational process cannot be used for discovery because as more and more data is collected, the costs of analyzing this data increase quadratically. Any process whose cost grows so rapidly is bound to fail eventually.

Thus, we have two alternatives. One, we can say that the process of rational-empirical discovery is so hard that it can never be completed, so there are practical limits to pursuing this type of knowledge. Two, we can say that there are other methods of discovery that are simpler. The method of purifying our consciousness arises due to this conclusion. Note that even if we were to complete the rational-empirical process, we would still have to change our worldview, although the process would be very slow. The demands upon changing ourselves therefore don't go away in the rational-empirical system; we still need to keep changing our ways of thinking to accept new ways of thinking and then to change them again to overcome their problems. The process of changing our consciousness is therefore unavoidable, even if we use the rational-empirical process. The difference is simply whether we bring this change *voluntarily* or we are *forced* to bring a change. The voluntary process is fast and easy, whereas the forced process is hard and long. In fact, the forced process is so long that it can never be completed, unless we adopt some measure of the voluntary change.

The process of voluntary change is also not easy if we pursue this process but keep resisting the change. The change, if it must occur, must occur in our *choice* of the filters. That choice is free and can be completed in a moment. Hence, perfect knowledge can also be acquired in a moment—if we know what that perfection is, and if we choose it. The problem is always that we don't want that perfection immediately, unless it is forced upon us. This makes the process as hard as we resist, and as easy as we wish. Since the process can be very easy, therefore, the process itself is easy. However, our resistance to accept that process of purification makes it harder.

Knowledge is Power

The combination of empirical and rational knowledge gives us the power to control the world, and it is therefore called God's *power*. This power is manifest through our mind, intellect, the senses of knowing, and the senses of action. The essence of this power is the ability to realize what previously lies as *potentiality*. Recall that, in the previous chapter, we discussed the nature of God's renunciation, and described it as the production of Brahman, or all that is potential or possible. Our minds can perceive this possibility, our intellects can formulate a plan to achieve a certain possibility (more on this topic in the next chapter, where I will discuss how we arrive at the path to attain a possibility), and then our senses act to convert that possibility into a reality. An apple may exist, but we might not see or taste it. Therefore, when we perceive the apple, then our senses of knowing are converting that possibility into an experience. Hence, our senses and mind are required in converting something manifest into our experience. Similarly, the apple may not exist, and in order to taste it, we have to grow it first. Our senses of actions are needed to plant the apple tree, water it, nourish it, protect it from pests, and then harvest the apple for consumption.

Our power to know and control the world manifests in some specific forms, such as seeing, tasting, touching, smelling, hearing, holding, walking, pushing, talking, procreation, etc. These modalities of power are consistent and complete, in the sense that they can be employed without producing a contradiction, and there is no aspect of reality that is left unknowable by these methods. All these modalities are necessary and sufficient in the sense that if we did not have some of these modalities, then we would not know some aspect of reality, and by these modalities we can know everything. These are simple and parsimonious, in the sense that if we tried to reduce them to anything simpler, then we would use the same modalities, along with the other modalities, and the result would not be simpler; likewise, if we tried to describe the world in terms of fewer modalities, then the result would also become more complicated than if we used all the modalities. But even if we *can* know the world consistently, completely, simply, parsimoniously, necessarily, and sufficiently, this possibility is not automatically a reality. We still need the modalities in terms of which we must know the world, and control the world, to produce what we can be knowing.

Therefore, it is not enough to say that consistent, complete, parsimonious, simple, necessary, and sufficient knowledge of the world is possible. We must also say that this knowledge is possible using the five senses of knowledge, the five senses of action, a mind that gives meaning to the world, and an intellect that judges if this meaning is true. In other words, after describing the properties of knowledge, we must describe the modes of knowing, the properties of the knower, and their methods of knowing. This constitutes the 'power' by which we become capable of knowledge. The methods of knowing and acting, the mind, and the intellect constitute the *aspects* of this power of knowing by which the knower accumulates an understanding of the world, and can use that to control the known, create the things that are known, and transform one known into another (without disregarding the fact that after a transformation, the previous knowns become a possibility that can potentially be known after an inverse transform).

If the theorems exist as proofs of the knowledge, then the senses of knowing and acting, the mind and the intellect by which we know constitute the methods by which these theorems are known and created. As we have discussed before, the world comprises the knower, the known, and their relation. The proofs are the known, and the senses, mind, and the intellect are the knowers. However, the qualities by which the senses, the mind, and the intellect know must also be present in the known, otherwise, they could not be known, created, or controlled. Therefore, the power of knowing and control exist as potentiality by which the world is known and controlled in the proofs—e.g. that the proofs must be visible to our eyes—and it must exist in the knower as the capacity to know and create such proofs. This is an additional requirement beyond the abstract notion of knowledge. By this requirement, we can say that the knowledge exists as the power to be known and used in the world, and as the power to know and act in the knower.

6

Operationality and Instrumentality: The Principle of Wealth

The Problem of Realism

Western philosophy has a long tradition of skepticism regarding any claims about knowing the nature of reality. It began in Greek times, when Socrates described our experiences as shadows on the wall cast by something behind the scenes that we could not see. We can compare this idea to watching a movie. The naïve interpretation of sitting in a movie theatre is that there are real people, real voices, and real actions. But, of course, the fact is that what we see are mere images projected upon a screen. Now, you could argue: Even if these are images projected on a screen, they are recordings of actual actors and actions performed in the past. But then, what about animated movies? They too have live characters which did not exist anywhere outside an artist's sketch board, and more often now, outside an animating computer. There are an increasing number of arguments today that claim that we might be living in virtual reality, which casts images on our senses although the reality that casts the image is nothing like what we see. This deep suspicion about our ability to trust our sense perceptions undermines all empiricism, because, for all we know, when we make a measurement, the process of measurement may just be a movie being projected, and the reality that produces such images is nothing like the measurement.

The images we see on a computer screen are good examples of such illusions. The screensaver on your computer may show a lovely landscape, but all that you have underlying that landscape is a set of bits—1s and 0s stored in a file. There is no landscape; the reality that projects this landscape is completely unlike what you perceive by your senses. If such things are indeed possible, then how can we insist on knowing some reality because the images we see are compatible both with a real landscape and a file?

This problem has prompted philosophers to provide *pragmatic* definitions of all concepts, that only talk about sense experience, rather than about reality. For example, when you say that you see a landscape, there is no assurance that there is indeed a landscape. Your observation doesn't translate into a reality. It only remains a vision. So, the claim that a 'landscape exists' is just a claim about your ability to see something, not a claim about how things are in reality, or what the real causes of that perception are. Therefore, the pragmatism would say that we should stop this obsession with trying to know the nature of reality or truth. We must content ourselves with what we can see, because we can never know the nature of truth. Whatever we see is all that we can pragmatically say is our idea of the truth.

A pragmatical scientist goes even further. He says: even if you see color, taste, smell, etc. we must reduce these properties to some *measurement* procedures. For example, the idea color must be reduced to the measurement of frequency—as even the empiricist would agree. A pragmatist would further say that there isn't anything real about a 'frequency'—i.e., it is not a real property of nature, and even if we use this property in a scientific theory, we are not staking a claim that there is indeed such a thing as 'frequency'. All that we are saying is that we are performing a procedure of measurement, which we have chosen to call 'frequency', and this property has no realist connotations other than the empirical observations made in an experiment. Effectively, we don't say that primary properties are real (as an empiricist would say). We certainly don't say that secondary properties are real. We just say that by a primary property *we mean* such and such measurement procedure. What is that procedure? There is an arbitrary measuring instrument that we have chosen—which we can call the 'frequency measurement apparatus'. This instrument gives pointer or meter readings. And we interpret these readings as values of frequency. That's all that frequency *means*. There is nothing objective or real called 'frequency' in the world 'out there'.

This claim about reducing secondary properties to primary properties (which even empiricists agree upon), and then reducing the primary properties to some actions and observations (which are secondary properties) doesn't ultimately solve any problem, because we are still using the same number of secondary properties; we have added some primary properties, whose meaning we are trying to define and reduce to some secondary properties. Effectively, we already had all the words that denoted the secondary properties. Then we added some words that denoted primary properties. Now we have even more words that map primary properties to secondary properties. Meanwhile, we have also rejected any claim to objective reality.

To understand this problem, we must realize that to cognize any perception, we must possess all the *concepts* in terms of which we cognize. These concepts cannot be primary properties, because we are claiming that they cannot be real. We have already rejected the reality of secondary properties in empiricism. And yet, we perceive everything in terms of these secondary properties—a child is not *taught* how to taste, touch, smell, etc. This is ingrained and inborn. In short, all these secondary properties are *a priori*.

For example, if you see yellow color, and you cognize it as yellow, then 'yellow' doesn't just refer to something in the external world; it also refers to the concept you use to cognize. This just means that even if we try to give a pragmatic definition to 'yellow', in terms of what we observe, we will automatically assume the preexistence of some properties in terms of which we can perceive the color 'yellow'. For instance, even if you decided to reduce color to a frequency, and then present this frequency as length on scale that represents frequency, you will still need to be able to read the markings on that frequency scale. These markings may be black or white lines, accompanies by squiggles that represent numbers. There must be a pointer which will have its own color and shape, and you must know how to perceive and cognize that color and shape to identify the pointer. Thus, the observation of frequency—which you think reduces color to a frequency—itself requires the perception of color, shape, size, numbers, position, etc. You previously had a single property of 'color' which is now defined in terms of multiple properties—shape, size, position, number, and color, so you haven't achieved any simplification in this process. Indeed, by defining one concept in terms of other concepts, we have complicated the narrative more than if we did not have this process of reduction to begin with.

Now the persistent pragmatist may argue: Let's grant that all the perceptual properties are indeed irreducible. What about more abstract concepts such as tables and chairs? Surely, we must be able to reduce these concepts to perceptions (which, we can grant, seem to be irreducible). The problem is if you try to carry out this reduction, then you end up with literally infinite definitions of tables and chairs. Some of these are square, others are round. Some of them are white, others are black. Some of the chairs have backrests and hand rests, others do not. Some tables have 4 legs, others can have 6, 8, 10, or any other number of legs. Whatever definition of a table or chair that you come up with, will work in some cases, and not in other cases. Now, you can argue that this is because chairs and tables are often defined in terms of how we *use* them, and each type of table is meant to be used for a different kind of purpose. So, instead of defining chairs and tables in terms of how they look, we should define them in terms of how we use them. For example, if you can sit on anything, then you can call it a chair. The problem is that you can also sit on a bed or a table. Likewise, whatever we defined as a chair or table based on its looks, can also be used as ladder or a bed—you can, for instance, sleep on a chair. Therefore, the conclusion is that neither observed properties nor uses of things truly define what we mean by a concept like a chair or a table. Then what does?

To understand this problem, we can think about Heisenberg's Uncertainty principle in atomic theory. It says that two properties of a particle—namely, position and momentum—cannot be measured at once with infinite accuracy. If position is certain, then the momentum is completely uncertain, and vice versa. This principle can be adapted to the two ways in which we understand the world through the senses of knowledge and action; the senses of knowledge tell us how a thing *looks,* and the senses of action tell us how we *use* it. If we try to define a chair by its usage—e.g. as something that we sit upon—then the looks of that thing are highly uncertain. It can look like a chair, a table, a bed, a floor, a mat, etc. Conversely, if we try to define a chair by how it looks—e.g. something that has 4 legs and a cushion on top—then its usage is highly uncertain. For instance, we can also use this chair as a ladder, as a table, or as a weapon. If you insist upon using precise definitions of how a thing looks and is used as the definition of a chair, then lots of things that don't look like the specific thing you have in mind (and which would be considered chairs otherwise) will fall outside your definition, and your definition of a chair would become too narrow. Likewise, if you allow lots of looks and ways of using in your definition of chair, then your definition would become too broad, and lots of things that should not be called chairs would be included into your classification. The point is that we cannot reduce concepts like tables and chairs to sense perceptions of the senses of knowledge and action; we have to accept that these concepts are a unique type of reality that cannot be reduced to percepts.

Thus, we arrive at the following two conclusions. First, that percepts cannot be reduced to fewer percepts because in such reductions we keep using percepts, and the best-case scenario is that we reduce one percept to another percept, and the worst-case scenario is that a single percept would be reduced to many percepts. We can in principle reduce all perceptions to numbers, which can be uttered as tones or sounds, but by this reduction we will still get words such as 'frequency', 'temperature', 'mass', 'momentum', etc. which are not numbers. These properties will then become pure concepts like tables and chairs. Second, we cannot reduce concepts like table and chair, or any other abstract concept to any sense perception. If we try to perform this reduction, then either our definition will be too broad or too narrow. In the former case, we will admit too many entities to which the concept cannot be applied. And in the latter case, we will not apply the concept to many entities where the concept must indeed be applied.

In this regard we can note that such attempts at reduction were made in 20th century language philosophy, and they failed miserably. That failure indicates the impossibility of reducing our language to fewer words. All the words in our language—if they are not perfect synonyms—are therefore important, and they exist because they capture ideas that are not represented by other words. Language is not an accident of human egregiousness at using concepts. Language is simply a reflection of how broad we are able to think. We can certainly limit our language, but in that process, we will not *reduce* the concepts; we will simply eliminate some reality from our discourse. Those concepts that are left out will either never be understood in our limited language, or they would be understood partially and incorrectly.

The Work of an Evil Genius

Once we realize that our language and concepts cannot be reduced (unless there are numerous perfect synonyms) then we have addressed the first part of the pragmatic concern, which tries to reduce the reality to fewer concepts. This attempt is futile. Now, we can come to the second part of the problem, which is whether what we perceive and conceive is actually real in just the way we think it is. To recall our virtual reality example, we could be living in a simulated reality, and using a variety of words, which are then produced by something that is completely unlike that description. For instance, people and things in virtual reality can just be computer bits. How do we know what reality is, based upon our perception and reasoning?

You could say that we can employ repeated experimentation to confirm if things are just the way they are. But such experiments will work perfectly well in virtual reality as well, without telling us about the reality. No amount of reasoning about the real causation can tell us what the real cause is. This validates the basic premise underlying pragmatism, namely, that when we cannot know for sure the nature of reality, then we should adopt a pragmatic attitude and restrict ourselves to *descriptions* rather than claims of *reality*.

The pragmatic approach will tell us that if we have the experience of bringing into contact a thermometer with a hot object, and then we have the experience of observing a meter reading, then all we can claim is that we found a meter reading. There is no evidence to suggest that this meter reading wasn't produced by a virtual reality system in which the entire process of measurement was just an appearance. Therefore, we cannot claim that there is a real hot object, a real thermometer, which measures a real property called temperature, producing a real reading of the temperature. For all we know, these are just appearances created by a virtual reality system.

Similarly, we can say that if we have the experience of performing a state preparation, and then an experience of an observation, then our scientific theories can predict the connection between state preparation and observation. Such theories may also use some *models* of reality—e.g. a space and time with material particles and waves, with some properties etc., but none of the explanatory framework presents us with the truth or reality. For all we know, a virtual reality system is creating the succession of experiences using a computer program, and we are thinking that it is really happening. Since we cannot know what the truth is, therefore, all our models of behavior are simply the tools and methods to predict, not truth or reality.

The fundamental problem of rationalism and empiricism is that it doesn't tell us if our model is indeed reality, *even if it works*. In short, we must completely reject *correspondence realism*, or the idea that reality corresponds to our theory even if our theory works. A correspondence between scientific concepts and the world has commonly been held in science. For example, in mechanics or electrodynamics, after the theories were successful, it was believed that the world is comprised of particles or waves. Of course, there is no basis in assuming that just because it works, it is also real. Therefore, pragmatism argues that we should give up our obsession with truth and reality. We should rather just focus upon formulating predictive theories.

This is not such a straightforward problem, however. What happens, for instance, if we reject the pursuit of reality and truth, and say that it is entirely possible that our experience is produced by an evil genius? Since we cannot know reality, we also cannot know that our experience is not produced by an evil genius. Now this is a serious problem because if the world is indeed produced by the evil genius, then nature may not be rational in the way we think it is. In fact, it may not work consistently at all times. Certainly, it may behave differently in different places or situations. All that we formulate in terms of laws would therefore fall victim to the problem of evil genius that Descartes was trying to solve by a 'good God' argument. In that case, whatever time and energy we are spending in trying to understand the world is a veritable waste of time. As a concrete example, many of our theories are currently incomplete, and some of these theories are mutually contradictory. It is only owing to correspondence realism that we even try to reconcile their contradictions and arrive at a better theory. If we truly believed that our experience is the creation of a virtual reality system, then it would be far easier to say that whatever we are seeing doesn't deserve to be understood, because it is indeed not rational. It is rather the work of a creative evil genius who is deluding us with incoherent observations which make us believe that we don't understand nature, when our very premise that nature can be understood, and that there is a reality, is itself false.

Pragmatism now becomes the hellhole into which we can sink and stop our attempts at knowledge, because we have stopped believing in the existence of a correspondence realism, or that a working theory indicates the existence of a reality. Of course, a pragmatist can still argue: In so far as the laws of nature *seem* to work, even if they are the works of an evil genius, we can still accept this work and try to understand how our experiences are created and use them to improve the conditions of our living. Moreover, while the laws of nature are not guaranteed to work forever (because the evil genius may change his mind, and alter the virtual reality program that produces our experiences), we can stop our endeavors at such improvement if the laws stop working, and nature appears to be totally random. In so far as there appears to be repeatability and predictability in nature, there is no harm in pragmatically continuing to acquire knowledge if it works.

But this argument is really weak. It doesn't tell us how much we should try to solve a problem. If we have failed for 25 years to solve a problem, should we say that it is because of the evil genius has created an unsolvable problem? Or should we say that the problem is really not understood? Moreover, whatever works today may not work tomorrow, and even if it works tomorrow, who is to say that how we *think* it works is indeed real?

The Work of a Good Genius

Vedic philosophy provides an answer to this problem, and the answer is that the laws of nature are not physical; they are rather the laws of choice and responsibility. For example, we get our daily bread because we have performed good deeds in the past that entitle us to some food. This entitlement comes to us as the opportunities to consume food. The results of this food consumption depend on the meanings, but the access to that consumption depends on our past choices. If we change our choices, then the effects of consumption will not change, however, we will get opportunities to consume different (better or worse) kinds of choices. The consequences resulting from the change in choices are pragmatically available to us. So, we can practically change our actions and see the results. These changes would indicate that there is another class of laws—the laws of choice and morality—that improve our life if we act morally and worsen it if we act immorally. The existence of morality indicates that even if there were a genius controlling our lives, that genius is *good* rather than *evil.* The purpose of this control, and the troubles in trying to understand reality, become easy if we understand that the laws of nature are not just based on meanings but also based on choices. By altering our choices, we see a different reality.

In Vedic philosophy, the world we are perceiving is indeed different from reality. Reality is like the symbols of meaning, and our experiences are like the sensations and concepts encoded as meaning in the symbols. Just like a computer picture is different from the information bits stored in the computer, similarly, reality is the symbols that encode sensations and concepts, and our experience is the experience of these sensations and concepts. Given a certain reality, and our senses, the laws of nature are universally true, and can be described if we describe the nature of meanings.

However, quite apart from these meanings is the question of who gets to access which type of meaning. Not everyone has access to the same kind of body, lifestyle, education, or prosperity. This access to different kinds of reality is due to our past actions, but it is delivered only at certain times, and that temporal control of what happens when to whom is attributed to God. Hence, there is a genius in control of our experiences. However, the laws of choice and responsibility reward moral action and punish immoral actions. Therefore, the genius in control of our experiences prefers morality over immorality. Even as the laws of nature are universal, they don't *act* the same on everyone; therefore, by changing our actions and choices, we can know that nature rewards moral activity just as it punishes immoral actions.

That is a pragmatic test we can perform, and if we do, then we find that the laws of morality are not *blind.* For instance, an immoral action performed inadvertently, unconsciously, under ignorance, or under force of circumstances, invites a smaller punishment than an action that is performed consciously and deliberately. For the laws to be based on a person's intentions, and be adapted according to circumstances, the laws must be cognizant of our intentions. Similarly, the rewards and punishments are delivered according to our nature. If we dislike something, getting those things would not be rewards, and if we like something, then getting those things would not be punishment. Thus, the punishment and rewards are adapted according to our nature, and if our nature changes (after some reward and punishment is determined), then the rewards and punishments are also adapted. Again, the laws are not blind; they are cognizant of our personal likes. Finally, the Vedic texts state that the good or bad consequences of moral action end if one becomes a devotee of God, since then the purpose of reward and punishment—i.e. correction of our nature—has been achieved.

If we combine all these tests and assess their results, then we can conclude three things: (1) the laws are not blind, (2) they are not the work of an evil genius, and (3) they are the works of a good genius who frees a person from these consequences of their actions once the goal has been achieved.

In short, the laws are based on intentions (as the rewards and punishments depend on intentions), and they aim to correct our intentions in relation to God. The laws can still be interpreted impersonally even if we just say that the laws are not blind. We might just say that the laws happen to be what they are; they just act on deeper levels of reality (i.e. our intentions) than before. The laws seem somewhat less impersonal, when we understand that these laws encourage morality, and one could argue that they cannot be the work of an evil genius; they might as well be the works of a good genius. But it is entirely possible that the good genius may have designed the laws once and doesn't interfere with the world thereafter. The laws however become the works of a good genius if we realize that if the soul is trying to reach God, then God constantly provides inner inspiration and guidance to deal with the circumstances. These inspirations are also part of our experience, but they don't exist for everyone. Most people feel unhappy when facing difficult situations, and they struggle with their problems. The devotee of God, however, receives guidance and inspiration on how to deal with the situation. Again, this is not an imaginary idea; we can experience it. When such experiences are obtained, then we get confirmation that the laws are the works of a good genius. This is also practical experience and testable by individuals; by performing such tests, we understand how our minds can become our enemies if a person is ignorant or opposed to God, but the same mind becomes our best friend if a person is trying to reach God.

This confirmation destroys the aforesaid doubts. As we have noted, we can analyze and determine that the senses and the mind don't reduce to each other, or to something else, so experience is itself not an illusion. This experience could still be caused by an arbitrary material reality, or an evil genius, but by practical testing, we find that this is not the case. We also find that the laws of nature are not blind, because they act based on our mental state. Finally, we find that we are guided toward our goal from within, which means that certain goals—if they are directed toward God—are assisted *as if* the universe is conspiring for us to attain that goal, and that assistance brings us to the confirmation that reality is the work of a good genius.

Thus, contrary to the arguments from pragmatism, where we cannot know the nature of reality because the experiences can be interpreted in various ways, the short answer is that experiences lead us to a rational conclusion in which the skepticism and doubts are gradually destroyed.

What is Operationalism?

With this background about how the problem of interpretation is resolved in Vedic philosophy, we can now turn to how pragmatism has been used in Western philosophy, especially in the philosophy of science.

Pragmatism began as an approach to knowledge due to the failure of empiricism and rationalism in determining the nature of truth. As we noted in the previous chapter, there is never enough data to validate a theory because we cannot observe everything across all space and time, and whatever data exists, can be interpreted in more than one way. Willard Quine therefore argued that "data underdetermines theory" indicating that there is always more than one way to interpret the data. Of course, if there is sufficient data, then we can eliminate the false propositions. The universe, as we saw earlier, has necessary and sufficient data to eliminate false ideas. However, because we can only observe one thing at a time, ignorance about the nature of reality requires M2 time to correctly interpret the data of M time. The empirical-rational method of theory confirmation is therefore logically impossible. Now the pragmatist argues that there is no way to know the truth, because correspondence realism requires blind faith in the existence of a reality, which may not be true. We can, however, make theories about the world, and if they seem to work, then we can pragmatically and tentatively use these theories until we find that they do not work. At that point, we can again pragmatically create new theories that seem to work tentatively.

To support this pragmatic attitude, two approaches were needed. The first approach, which eventually fails, requires us to reduce the meaning of all concepts—such as position, momentum, energy, speed, temperature, etc. to a *method* of measurement. Note that the problem of realism is worsened when we say that there are innumerable concepts, because these concepts are then denoted by different words, and different languages then understand these concepts differently: some languages might not have the words for some ideas, others may have words for subdivisions of an idea, and yet others may combine multiple ideas into one. The proliferation of concepts, and the question of realism that it leads to, would be considerably simplified if we were able to reduce numerous words into fewer words. This was the goal of *logical positivism* for the concepts of ordinary language, and it was the goal of Operationalism for the words (such as position, momentum, mass, energy, etc.) employed in science. Founded by P. W. Bridgman, Operationalism claimed that we must not think of physical properties as realities in themselves. For example, we should not assume that time moves uniformly for all observers, unless we have a *procedure* of measurement that validates the claim. This is because the word 'time' has no meaning other than a process of measurement carried out by the use of measuring instruments.

Similarly, there is no meaning to words such as 'pressure' and 'temperature', other than what is indicated by the pressure and temperature *gauges*. Bridgman was studying high-pressure physics, and he had to constantly come up with instruments that allowed him to measure higher pressures. In this process, the old pressure gauges proved useless, and since the property of 'pressure' at a higher value required a different gauge, therefore, Bridgman concluded that there was no meaning to 'pressure' except what a gauge told him. More often than not, a higher-pressure gauge won't work at lower pressure, and vice versa. Therefore, typically one would use a lower-pressure gauge to measure at the higher-end of its pressure spectrum, while using a higher-pressure gauge at the lower end of the spectrum to determine if these scales were aligned correctly in their numerical output. But there was no way to know that outside these areas of mutual correspondence, the scales were measuring pressure uniformly, and hence indicating a real property. The property of 'pressure' for Bridgman was no more than the gauge itself.

This argument can be extended by a philosopher to say that we have no way of knowing the meaning of 'color' other than what we see by our eyes. We cannot say that there is some objective property of 'color' independent of our sensual apparatus. This argument is correct, and as we have discussed earlier, if our senses are distorted, incapable of knowing something, or they filter what we can see, then there is no way to know what the reality is. That reality is simply what we perceive by our senses. But that doesn't necessarily entail that if *I* don't have the ability to measure a property, the property itself doesn't exist. However, pragmatism makes that argument. It says: If I cannot measure a property, how do I know that it exists? The converse argument is that *even if* you measure the property, you still cannot know if what caused the observation was indeed the property. Therefore, if we cannot make the argument that a property exists when we don't measure it, we must also make the argument that the property cannot be known to exist even if we measure it. Operationalism doesn't make this argument, so its argument is one-sided, and that one-sided argument leads us to claim that properties are defined by our senses, when the correct conclusion is that our *knowledge* of the property is defined by our senses.

The fact is that we can never deny the reality of the world, if we have to do science. We can say that a given property is defined by a measurement procedure, which is just like saying that color is defined by our eyes. But after we make a measurement, we allow the reality to evolve on its own, and then make another measurement. Science is the correlation between two or more such measurements, but what happens in between the measurements? Obviously, when we are not observing the world, then something must exist. Otherwise, we cannot rationally explain the consistency of observations or why the experiments are repeatable. What exists is being modeled by our theories, and that model may not be correct, but the incorrectness of the model doesn't make the reality itself absent. Therefore, realism must always be assumed in science because without it there is no causality; without causality there is no necessity and sufficiency, and without these we cannot use logic and mathematics to predict a measurement from another measurement. However, that realism doesn't pertain to properties like pressure and temperature. From an operational standpoint, even the idea that we measure 'pressure' in relation to a gauge is false because the measured and measuring systems are our perception. For all we know, an evil genius could be creating these sensations in us, and the reality may be quite different. Moreover, due to the dependence of observation on our senses, we cannot say that 'pressure' is even a real property; as we saw above, what we mean by 'pressure' is just some sensations of color, touch, sound, shape, etc. And, no property can be reduced to another property, so they are all valid and irreducible properties. As a result, the only reality we can claim pertains to the sense perceptions and conceptions by which we order the world, not to the world that supposedly exists 'behind' these perceptions and conceptions.

Thus, the argument of Operationalism that properties are defined in relation to measuring instruments is false; they are defined in relation to our senses, and our idea that there is a measuring instrument that objectively measures the properties of the world is equally as false as the notion that there is an objective property that exists independent of the instrument. The argument that makes the property not objective without an instrument, also makes the instrument not objective without the senses to perceive it. So, whatever we call 'pressure' or 'temperature' is meaningless. We just have the sensation of using an instrument followed by the sensation of a value indicated by an instrument, and these are simply relationships between the sensations, which equally well do not tell us whether there is an instrument.

However, since we cannot do science without assuming a reality, therefore, we must assume a reality, although the best reality that we can assume is that of the secondary properties. If we cannot assert the realism of secondary properties, then we certainly cannot assert the realism of anything else. But even if we can assert the realism of secondary properties, we may still not be able to assert the realism of other properties. This takes us back to Berkeley's idea that the essence of the world is in it being perceived.

You can argue that many people have the same experience, but the pragmatist might say: How do we know that those people exist? They are as much 'behind' our sensations as anything else that we know by appearances. Likewise, you could argue that there is an evil genius at work, but that evil genius is also independent of us, and hence real. Thus, Operationalism's attack on realism undercuts itself, and reifies all secondary properties.

What is Instrumentalism?

Once the argument of Operationalism is refuted in this way, then we have a more sophisticated argument called Instrumentalism, which says that theories of nature are simply *our models*. We cannot hold correspondence realism about these theories. These theories simply connect some perceptions that we call 'state preparation' to other perceptions that we can call 'observation', and the theory is a model that predicts which state preparation leads to which observation. However, there is no guarantee that the model will always work, or that the model is true. It is just a model; it works today so we use it; if it stops working then we will change it. And after we change the model, which then works better than the previous model, we still have no right to claim that the new model is true or real. It is just a *better model*.

Operationalism and Instrumentalism seem rather similar, but there is an important difference: Operationalism is about the *properties* (such as position, momentum, energy, etc.) whereas Instrumentalism is about the *theories* (such as classical mechanics, quantum mechanics, general relativity, etc.). A theory is used to make predictions and provide explanations, so it is a mental construct, which is then applied back to the world (even though that application may be partially true, or wholly false). The properties on the other hand, pertain to the actions and observations of the senses. In simple words, properties are sensual while the theories are mental constructs.

Empiricism and rationalism are still necessary because (a) we must know what we are seeing, and (b) we must be able to build a rational model of that seeing. The correctness of our vision and the logical coherence of the theoretical model don't guarantee their reality, because there are other potential explanations that can explain the phenomena equally well. That doesn't mean we are free to not even observe, or use distorted senses to perceive, or use theories that are logically contradictory and not well-reasoned. It just means that even with these precautions we are not guaranteed to know the nature of reality. Now, we must explore other methods by which we can know. And that method, as we have discussed, is that our rational theories themselves will lead us to conclusions about reality.

Knowledge by Theory Building

The way rational theories lead to the conclusion about reality is that among all the theories available, we pick that theory which is consistent, complete, simple and parsimonious. Here, I will focus on simplicity and parsimony. Let's understand how this principle leads to the idea that the world is indeed the objectification of sense perceptions. There are two reasons for this: (1) we cannot reduce one percept or concept to another (unless the words have the same meaning), and (2) the percepts by which we know the world are also the *simplest* and most *parsimonious* description of reality. If we try alternatives, then, in terms of operations, we will still need the same number of sensations or properties, and in terms of concepts, we will still require the same number of ideas. All that a scientific theory can do is change the names of these properties to something else, and that description can be a 'translation' of the world from one language to another.

Even as we cannot see behind the curtain, we can apply the criterion of *beauty* to say that because this description is the simplest and the most parsimonious therefore it is also true. Thus, rationalism says that there is a predictive model that connects sensations. The criteria of simplicity and parsimony says that the simplest and most parsimonious explanation is real.

Similarly, if the laws of choice and consequence are considered, the agency that adjudicates the morality of choices may not be known, but this much can be known: (a) that there is a moral law, because our opportunities expand and contract as a result of our choices, and (b) the agency that adjudicates the morality of choices is familiar with our intentions and delivers results accordingly, (c) when we act in a perfectly moral way, then true freedom is obtained because then the person who makes such choices is no longer forced by consequences of previous actions, (d) since the agency that adjudicates is aware of our intentions, namely, that we desire happiness, and delivers the freedom if we are moral, therefore, the agency governing this law has a *purpose*—namely, to make a person conscious of morality.

We can postulate impersonal laws of nature that determine the consequences based on our intentions. But we cannot have an impersonal law when the law has a purpose. Then we have to say that the agency that adjudicates this law must be a person, a Supreme Person, who is not only conscious and aware of our actions that are visible to everyone, but also of our intentions that are only known to us. That ability to know what nobody else knows, to adjudicate the moral laws across all persons, and to drive each person toward a morally responsible life, entails that the agency cannot be impersonal. Of course, this is still not the *perception* of that person. It is simply a rational conclusion from our own theory formation. We can still say that it is just our model, but now, there is no other *rational model* of this observation. We can try to conjure alternative models of morality, but we cannot sustain them. For example, we could argue that whatever we called a moral consequence was simply an accident of nature, and no such consequences exist. But that is not a rational argument, because by the same measure, no empirical verification of any state preparation and measurement can also lead to the conclusion that the model of nature is empirically verified.

So, arriving at the correct model necessitates that we be *rational* in our methods. Of course, rationality is not guaranteed, and if we are irrational, then it is impossible to arrive at any model of actions and perceptions.

Thus, what I'm claiming is that if we are rational, and prepared to perform the same kinds of tests that we perform in other pragmatic theories, then, we can also show—through rationality—that nature is moral, that it leads a person to permanent happiness, and the righteousness and goodness of these laws entail (in our model) that there is a Supreme Person. This Supreme Person is in the *model* and not a sense perception. Or, we can say that God is just a scientific concept at this point, used in a theory. If we don't use this concept, then we cannot make the observed predictions. Thus, without looking behind the curtain to see who or what causes the pictures on the screen, we can know that there is a Supreme Person.

Pragmatism and Knowledge

There is, however, still a problem. The principles of simplicity and parsimony are useful if we have two models—one that is simpler than the other. What if the simpler model is unknown, and we have a theory that is complicated, although because it is the only theory we have, we cannot compare it to another theory to decide if it is indeed the simplest theory.

Now, the difference of pragmatism can be introduced, namely, that we don't use science to understand reality, but to *create a reality*. What kind of reality will we create? Well, we can develop *technology* by which our lives can be altered for the better. This technology can be mundane—e.g. medicine, architecture, food quality, etc. And this technology can be esoteric—e.g. getting access to better opportunities. Pragmatism is just the idea that if we aren't sure if what we know is also reality, then we can use it to solve the problems of our day-to-day life. If the theory does solve those problems perfectly, then the theory can be called real and true. On the other hand, if the theory doesn't solve the problem, or doesn't solve the problem perfectly (e.g. creates new problems while solving a problem) then it is not true.

As an example, modern science has created many technologies that help us in day to day life. However, this technology is not perfect. We noted one example of this imperfection while discussing computers: the computers cannot know what a program will do, before it does it. An important area of shortfall is that the computer remains vulnerable to malicious programs. Similarly, another kind of technology is medicine. Each drug that cures a problem produces numerous side-effects, which may be equally harmful as the original illness. In some cases, people die as a reaction to cures, although the original illness would not have killed them. So, again, technology has problems. The perfect model of nature will not produce such problems; it will only solve these problems. Perfect technology will not create side effects; it has benefits, but no disadvantages. Hence, pragmatism exerts very strong conditions on any claims of truth and knowledge.

Today we claim that our theories about atoms and space-time have been tested to the accuracy of 1 part in a million or a billion. So, we claim that these theories are true. But in real life, the technology built using these theories has numerous faults, which should not exist if the theory were perfect. If we had never built this technology, and we remained content with the confirmation of theories, then we would say that these theories are true because they have been tested so accurately. But because we use these theories to develop technology, which doesn't work as well as we will like it to, therefore, we can say that these theories are not perfect. The pragmatic criteria of usefulness without harm goes beyond empirical/rational criteria.

Therefore, we can say that the basic difference between empiricism/rationalism and pragmatism is that in the former case we are studying the nature of reality that we did not create, and in the latter case we are creating the reality that is useful for us based on the study of reality that we did not create. Empiricism and rationalism are useful for the explanation of experience, and pragmatism is the use of that knowledge to create new experience. Such creation is very important when we start talking about transcendental experiences, for example, God. Since we might not have the direct experience of God, in knowing that reality, we are going to create a new experience. So, how do we know that our theory of reality will lead to God-experience? Can we prove that this theory leads to other kinds of new experiences, before we say that it leads to God-experience? This question exerts demands on the application of knowledge to our present life. To know if our ideas are true, we must be able to produce that experience which would otherwise be impossible. Then as we undergo a new experience, we might find further problems, which the theory must be able to solve.

The Least Action Principle

Pragmatism changes how we think of reality not as causes and effects, but as *costs* and *benefits.* A cause-effect theory can be deterministic, but a cost-benefit theory must have choices. The choices pertain to which costs must be incurred for which benefits. As a result, both costs and benefits exist as possibilities, and their selection involves choices. Likewise, pragmatism is driven toward the solution of problems, which means that we must choose which problems we want to solve. The building of technology requires investments of time, effort, money, etc. This technology then has to be tested and verified, which also requires similar investments. All such investments must then collectively be cheaper than the benefits we get from technology. For instance, if airplanes were so expensive that it would be cheaper to walk to your destination, then we would not consider it a technology.

Thus, pragmatism is the simple criterion of minimizing the costs and maximizing the benefits, and knowledge is that which achieves this. In short, knowledge is pragmatically defined as that which solves problems at a cost that is lower than the benefits accrued by solving the problem. If the costs of solving the problem are equal or higher than the benefits of solving the problem, then the method of solving it would not be considered 'knowledge'. We would all say: there has to be a better solution, and we must find it; until we find it, we can assume that we don't know a good solution. In short, not having a solution that is lower cost than the problem it solves becomes the mark of ignorance. Knowledge is what makes the solution *useful*—with usefulness being defined as costs lower than the benefits.

In physics, this idea is called 'least action'. What is it? It represents the minimization of a quantity called 'action'—which we can approximate to 'costs'. Of course, classical physics assumes that there is no choice, so things will happen automatically, and we try to find the lowest cost method. But with pragmatism, things will not happen unless the cost is lowered. Thus, we will not build a technology if we know that the cost-benefit analysis shows a negative result. A positive result of the cost-benefit analysis is key to deciding which technology is chosen, if anything at all. If all alternatives are more expensive than the problem, then we live with the problem.

Costs can be of two kinds—overt and covert. The overt cost of a thing is what it takes to produce it. And the covert cost of that thing is the side-effect of using, consuming, or employing that thing. In this world, everything must have an overt cost. For example, if you produce a machine, you must employ some labor, consume some materials, etc. These are the overt costs. But there can also be covert costs, for example, air, water, and sound pollution, physical and mental health risks, etc. The ideal technology is that which has an overt cost, but no covert costs. And our ability to produce that ideal technology without covert costs also defines perfect knowledge. Perfect knowledge must also minimize the overt costs. Thus, that which has high overt and covert costs cannot be considered the truth. Even if something 'works', the methodology which has high overt and covert costs must be equated to ignorance; there is something that we don't know which makes the technology expensive, and its consumption brings problems.

Thus, by definition, perfect knowledge is that which has minimum overt costs, and zero covert costs. It takes very little effort, produces great benefits, and has no adverse side effects. The answer to 'big questions' that lead us toward transcendence constitutes this kind of knowledge. Yes, it takes some effort, but that is miniscule compared to the benefits. More importantly, answers to these questions—if they are knowledge—must have no adverse side effects. In short, it is net gain from effort to knowledge, and there are no losses. Pragmatism thus enhances the definition of knowledge from technology that helps us simplify some problems but creates other problems to technology that lowers the costs, increases the benefits, and has no adverse side effects. Everything that has an adverse side effect can be quickly be rejected as ignorance. Moreover, we can then talk about the technology or practice, that delivers the same results with lowest costs.

The Vedic texts thus describe many paths to understanding God. These are called *karma-yoga*, *jnana-yoga*, *dhyāna-yoga* and *bhakti-yoga*. None of these processes have a covert cost—i.e. there are no hidden adverse side effects if they are practiced correctly. But, some of them have a higher overt cost. Of course, the benefits far outstrip even the overt costs. Therefore, all the methods are good when we compare the efforts expended to the benefits obtained. And yet, the process of *bhakti-yoga* has the least overt cost, and it is therefore said to be the best. This recommendation doesn't entail that the other paths are 'bad' because— (1) none of them have covert costs, and (2) all of them can deliver a result that outstrips the costs. But the cost to benefit ratio is smallest for the process of *bhakti-yoga*, and hence, it is the best. These paths are just examples of how pragmatic concerns play even into spiritual pursuits—we pick that path that works, and that which is the easiest.

Similar types of pragmatic principles can be applied for every other area of life—e.g. economics, profession, health, social organization, etc. In each case, we can evaluate the lowest cost for the greatest benefit, in addition to the elimination of covert costs. Those 'solutions' that have high covert costs are ultimately rejected, but only after they have caused a lot of damage. They are sometimes also presented as low overt cost options, because the knowledge needed to produce them hasn't been acquired. Thus, substandard ideas, technologies, methods are subsidized to attract people toward false promises. When these promises remain unfulfilled, then the solutions are rejected, but similar ones are proposed again. The larger issue in using pragmatism is that we don't apply pragmatism correctly. We just apply it selectively, not knowing the complete costs of using a method.

Defining Pragmatic Knowledge

With this background we are now equipped to redefine Operationalism and Instrumentalism. Operationalism means that we can *operationalize* ideas into technology that becomes a substitute for our doing those things. This is different from rationalism and empiricism in the sense that we are not merely understanding the nature of reality but creating a reality that does some work on our behalf, under our control, proving that we truly know. Instrumentalism means that whatever work is done by the reality that we produce is useful, and *instrumental* in solving the day-to-day problems. In short, the operational technology is an instrument within our control. Just like we use instruments, such as screwdrivers, saws, and hammers, to simplify those tasks which would otherwise be very hard by our hands, similarly, technology becomes an instrument in our hands—an extension of our bodies, that performs actions that are not effectively done by our bodies.

The technology and its usefulness are the pragmatic applications of knowledge, and they confirm that there is some truth in the theories based on which this technology has been built. To be perfectly true, such technology must also be immaculate—i.e. it must not create additional problems even as it is employed to solve the old ones. In so far as that isn't the case, pragmatism tells us that we don't have the perfect theory. Therefore, the search for a better theory goes on, because this search will solve some real-world problems, not just give us an insight into reality. Therefore, we can retain the distinction between Operationality and Instrumentality in a sense that science itself doesn't endorse. Now, the word 'operational' denotes technology, and it is 'instrumental' in solving the pragmatic problems.

There are many things that we can create that others can use. But they don't necessarily solve a problem. These things are operational, but not instrumental in our lives. An example of operational things that are not useful is the toys and gadgets that people create for fun, killing time, or just because they can. Endless varieties in fashion clothing, unnecessary luxuries that complicate life, or pointless songs, movies, and games that people use for entertainment, are also operational, but not instrumental in solving problems. Sure, when we acquire fashion accessories, read fairytales about romantic love, gadgets for entertainment, etc. there is something we know. We can also use these things. But knowing them doesn't constitute knowledge, because according to pragmatism, there is cost involved in producing them, but no value in using them. If at all, they worsen our problems by wasting our time, dulling our minds, and making us spend money on things that don't add value. Conversely, an example of something that is instrumental but not operational is goals and visions about the future of the world that can never be operationalized because they are irrational utopia that cannot become reality. Sure, we can think about all the ways in which our lives could be better—e.g. a tree that gives all kinds of fruits in all seasons, a genie in a bottle that fulfills whatever we desire, or a magic wand that can do the unthinkable. But these things cannot be realized, so dreaming about them is not knowledge. If such visions were realizable, and they could solve real problems, then such goals could be worthy. But because they are useless, they remain pure visions, without a workable reality.

Both extremes—one that can solve a problem but cannot be made to work, or that which works but cannot solve a problem—should be rejected as not being 'knowledge'. Whatever doesn't solve a worthy problem is not worthy of being called 'knowledge'. Likewise, whatever only seems like a good idea, but can never be implemented, cannot be called knowledge.

Mathematicians often create exotic theories about hypothetical objects. In mathematics, it is possible to produce anything theoretically just by making the right assumptions. If these assumptions could come true, then we could solve all our problems. But it is impossible to convert these theories into reality because the axioms underlying these theories contradict the axioms upon which the world of real things is working. Thus, fanciful mathematics that cannot be realized is not 'knowledge'. Since such theories fail to solve useful, relevant problems, therefore, they are not 'knowledge'.

In Vedic philosophy, the space of all the things that we can desire is 1000 times bigger than the things that can be rationally construed. Similarly, the space of rationality is 1000 times larger than the space of useful things. Likewise, the space of all meaningful things is 1000 times bigger than the space of things which can be practically realized. Pragmatism demands that things that we can desire, which are rational, that are meaningful, but which cannot be realized, do not constitute knowledge.

Yes, we can think of them, they can be dreamlands in which our problems do not exist, but such dreaming is not a solution to a problem, so they do not constitute knowledge.

By the standards of usefulness, and value for every cost, pragmatism requires us to reject such ideas and theories that seem perfect, but are ultimately useless. A good modern example of such a theory is String Theory. It states that everything is comprised of strings. Now, we can imagine these strings vibrating in dozens of dimensions, because the space of desires, rationality, and meaningfulness is considerably larger than the space of sense perceivable reality. Physicists know that String Theory is only viable in ten dimensions; in other dimensions, it produces contradictions. Since our world is only three-dimensional, a 10-dimensional theory is useless. String Theory is also known to be untestable in any foreseeable future, which is why it is impractical. Nevertheless, many physicists insist that it is a good theory because it exists in the realm of possibilities—like a genie in a bottle that can answer all our problems, although the genie is also unreal.

Pragmatism is based on the hierarchy of desires, beliefs, meanings, and sensations—and because successive domains get smaller, therefore, what is rational is smaller than what is likable, what is meaningful is smaller than what is rational, and what we can practically use by the senses is smaller than all that can be meaningful. Pragmatism is ultimately the criterion that knowledge must deliver happiness. To achieve happiness, we must be free of miseries. These miseries can exist in our body, or our mind, so, pragmatic usefulness is not merely physical technology; it also includes that knowledge which destroys suffering. By that measure, ultimate knowledge is that which ultimately solves all the problems of our lives; everything else may be partially and relatively useful, but it cannot be considered the ultimate truth.

Knowledge is Wealth

God is defined in Vedic philosophy as the controller of the world, or what we normally call 'omnipotent'. However, this omnipotence is not understood properly if we think of God as doing every small thing in the world, such as making the planets go round and round, making the fuel burn in engine cars, etc. God's omnipotence is that He creates subordinate controllers who perform the work on God's behalf, quite like cars and airplanes substitute our flying, washing machines and vacuum cleaners substitute our cleaning, and cookers and ovens substitute our lighting of fires. The possession of these amenities, which do things on our behalf is called 'wealth': we are rich if we possess the amenities that simplify our lives. Even the money we possess is merely a token of the amenities that we can acquire. With money, we can purchase the labor of workers who can do things on our behalf, so that labor, and the money by which it is purchased, is also wealth. In simple terms, everything that relieves us of labor is called wealth. If some wealth makes us perform more labor, then it cannot be called wealth.

Thus, God's wealth is that He has got nothing to do. He simply has to will, and everything is automatically done by delegated labor, technology, or instruments that perform the tasks that God would otherwise have performed, to fulfill His will. His effort is in creating those instruments of His will that will then perform the tasks on His behalf. Of course, in one sense, even these instruments are part of God, so we can say that ultimately it is God who is acting. In another sense, we can say that it is God's will that is acting through the instruments. The possession of all these instruments that offload the work from God, and fulfill His will then constitute His 'wealth'. Since this wealth is created by knowledge, therefore, we can say that by acquiring the knowledge of science, we can produce technology, and by that technology we can reduce our work, by offloading our work to it. The possession of wealth also means that we can hire other people to work for us. God is therefore the creator of workers who do the activities for Him.

Everything in this world can be an instrument of God's will, therefore, everything is at least potentially God's wealth. In so far as we might claim that God doesn't exist, or that we must 'prove' His existence, the problem is that He has delegated this proof to a number of subordinate workers. In Vedic philosophy, these workers are called the 'demigods' (*deva*) who control various aspects of our lives (and sometimes makes people think that the Vedic tradition is polytheistic). The fact is that a wealthy man would not be considered wealthy if we he was doing everything by himself. A wealthy man delegates work to other workers; so, if God is wealthy, then He must delegate. His power is that He can do everything by Himself, and we discussed the nature of this power in the last chapter—God has the senses of knowing and action, the mind and the intellect to do everything by Himself. But if He was doing everything by Himself, He would be omnipotent, and yet poor, as He would be busy managing the affairs of the material manifestation. Therefore, apart from His power—the capacity to do everything by Himself—He is also wealth, namely, that He delegates it to others.

The nature of this delegation is that the delegates are working, so they are *operational*. And their actions are doing the work that God would have otherwise done, so they are *instrumental* in fulfilling His will. Thus, God produces the type of workers that are both operational and instrumental. Since God is knowledge, this criterion applies to all forms of knowledge. Everything that we know must be operationalized and used as an instrument to fulfill a will. In Vedic philosophy, since we are also operational, and we must be instrumental in God's will, hence, all we do must also be a work performed as an instrument of God's will—as if God is doing it Himself.

7

Stability and Originality: The Principle of Heroism

Is Knowledge Finite or Infinite?

One of the central questions that surrounds the quest for knowledge is whether it comes to an end. Is perfection something that has an end, when it has been completely attained? If knowledge is finite, then one could argue that it is within our reach, and it can be attained. On the other hand, if perfection is infinite, then it cannot be attained, and there would be no point in trying to attain it. This presents us with a simple paradox. If knowledge is finite, then the final truth is attained, and thereafter, there is nothing left to know. What would life be after that perfection has been attained? Certainly, it would seem boring because there are no problems left to be solved, no questions remaining unanswered, and nothing that deserves our attention. Conversely, if knowledge is infinite, then life could be eternally exciting as new things are constantly being discovered, however, it will also mean that we are eternally ignorant, because there will always be something that we do not know. This frames a question about knowledge: Does perfect knowledge mean something attainable, and thereafter, there is nothing left to know? Or, is knowledge infinite, such that we never truly know, and thus, nobody can call themselves knowledgeable, as everyone is ignorant?

To resolve this paradox, let us think of Newton's three laws of motion. Newton's theory is certainly finite knowledge, that comes to an end if we know the laws. But in terms of applications, it probably has no end, because we can use Newton's three laws to create many kinds of cycles, cars, airplanes, trains, and many other things. In one sense, complete knowledge of Newton's laws is finite, and one who knows these laws can be said to possess complete knowledge, after which nothing needs to be known (assuming that these laws were indeed the only laws). In another sense, even if we know the laws, we can never know all the possible applications of these laws. We can instead keep discovering new things that were previously unknown, refining those things which we were aware of, and thereby expanding the variety of the world through various kinds of combinations.

Novelty and stability are thus not contradictory ideas. If the laws of motion are perfect knowledge, then there is nothing more left to be known after we know the laws. However, that doesn't entail an end to the novelty, as we can keep applying these laws in new ways. The truth of the laws of motion would entail a stability in our knowledge. But the inventiveness of the human mind would entail a constant expansion of its applications.

Thus, we can say that the laws of motion constitute finite knowledge that ends when we perfectly understand the laws. Similarly, we can say that the applications of the laws constitute infinite knowledge that never comes to an end, because we never know all the possible applications of the laws. Due to constant new discoveries, life doesn't become boring—and freedom from boredom is achieved due to ever-expanding novelties. However, due to the perfection of knowing the laws of nature, life is also not the fear of failure, just because we don't know if our knowledge will become ignorance in the future. Perfect knowledge is that which can solve all problems. There is one answer, but there are potentially infinite questions, and the answer can be adapted to suit those questions to answer unanswered questions.

Kuhn's Scientific Revolutions

Novelty and stability become contradictory ideas when the laws of nature are not known. Then, we formulate some laws, and they seem to work fine, at least for some time. Using those laws, some workable technology is produced, although this technology has many unsolved problems. Then, as these problems accumulate, and exceptions to the laws are widely understood, then we grow more and more disenchanted with the current laws, and begin seeking alternatives. The problem is that an alternative that fundamentally alters our understanding and approach to things would also make the previous type of thinking false. Those who have grown up thinking in the previous way, find it increasingly hard to think in a new way. After all, they will argue: The previous ways of thinking have produced so many benefits! How can we give up the previous thinking as if it were totally false? They would claim: The answer must be an incremental addition to the previous way of thinking, something that we missed all along, and that addition would make the thinking perfect, and solve all the unaddressed issues.

The desire for stability then leads to incrementalism, in which the fundamental ideas about our subject of study remain unchanged. For example, in the case of physics, we would not change basic ideas about space, time, matter, and force, but we would be prepared to add yet another type of force to the existing list of forces. Since particle physics already describes many kinds of particles, there is no harm in adding a few more particles, and incremental physics would keep searching for new particles. We might then also apply criteria for beauty and try to build more symmetric versions of atomic physics, that postulate heretofore unknown particles. If some forces are only attractive, while other forces have both attractive and repulsive versions, then we might postulate new theories that describe both attractive and repulsive versions. If some fundamental constants of nature have remained unexplained, then we might seek their explanation. If there are too many constants, then we might try to reduce them to fewer numbers. In short, there would be no fundamental changes to our way of thinking, however, the theory can be made more symmetric, and thus more beautiful.

However, if there are serious issues in the previous way of thinking, then this incrementalism proves to be self-defeating, as breakthroughs are not achieved, and even as we keep expanding its applications, and claim that it works for even more cases than before, the problems encountered in the process also keep mounting. The incremental progress also slows due to the unsolved problems and it becomes harder to produce new things that solve more problems than the problems they create. Indeed, under a pragmatic view of science, the costs of inventing new things constantly mount, while the benefits of investments into knowing those things keep declining.

This is a phase of *stagnation* where we are unable to change the thinking as we stand to lose a lot—all that we have invented in the past would seem to be based on a false way of thinking. At the same time, we are also unable to solve the new problems cheaply and effectively. In this phase of stagnation, internal conflicts erupt within the establishment of knowledge. The new guard argues that the current approaches are not working, and we must change our approach. But the old guard says that this approach has already led to successes, and we should continue on the same path, just because it has been fruitful in the past. The problem is also that the new guard isn't afforded the time and resources to develop an alternative to a point that it becomes a viable substitute for the old approach. Thus, the claims of the old guard—i.e., that there are no other alternatives—become a self-fulfilling prophecy. The old guard continues to suppress the arguments of the critics, because the critics can only point out a problem, although they cannot provide a solution, and they don't get the time and resources to build one.

As time passes, a new approach is eventually found—often outside the mainstream—and all those who previously agreed with the problems, but did not have an alternative approach or the courage to bring about a change, jump onto the new bandwagon, almost totally abandoning the old ideas. This change is called a 'disruption'. Once a disruption occurs, all that was described in one way is now described differently. There is rapid reformulation of the previous answers using new concepts, to *explain* and demonstrate its usefulness: it is important to show that the new ideas also solve the old problems, although using a different set of concepts. Meanwhile, the new thinking also leads to new discoveries and new technologies, which overcome the problems of the previous thinking and technology. Whatever seemed an expensive and error-prone solution to the problems is rejected, and a cheaper and error-free solution is found. Certain problems that were unsolvable earlier are now also solved. These achievements then establish the new thinking on solid grounds, and a *paradigm shift* has occurred.

If the new paradigm is imperfect, then as time passes, it will also produce unsolvable problems, and the solutions to problems that it indeed solves will either be expensive, unsatisfactory, or both. However, there will be ardent patrons of this approach who will resist the changes to it, and the cycle of resistance, stagnation, and disruption will repeat. Thus, if the new paradigm is imperfect, then it is forced to undergo a disruption, and this process continues indefinitely until the perfect paradigm is discovered.

Thomas Kuhn described this process of slow incremental progress interspersed by radical disruptions in thinking in his milestone book *The Structure of Scientific Revolutions*. In this book, Kuhn notes two kinds of scientific progresses—one that moves incrementally, adding and enhancing the established ideas, and the other that disrupts the established ideas by replacing them with new ideas. This disruption is not easily adopted, because the new ideas have to be proven to be at least as good as the established ideas, and then solve the problems that could not be solved using the old ideas. Kuhn distinguishes these as "normal science" and "revolutionary science".

Kuhn also talked about what he called *exemplars* of each model, the perfect embodiment that leads to the intuitions underlying the paradigm, and which then become the basis *in terms of which* we think of the other things. For example, the exemplar of electromagnetic theory was water waves or vibrations in musical instruments; the exemplar for Newton's gravitational theory was the collision of moving objects, such as billiard balls; the exemplar for thermodynamics was the vibrating lid of a pot in which water was being boiled, etc. Each of these exemplars gave us different ways of thinking about the world. It is important to identify an exemplar before a paradigm shift can occur, because these exemplars give others intuitive ways to think about the world. The problem is that if the exemplar doesn't sufficiently capture all the properties of reality, then it might succeed initially, but it becomes a hindrance eventually. A good example of such problems emerges in quantum mechanics, where the existing exemplars of waves and particles produce a hindrance in thinking about the world—how can the same thing be alternately described in terms of two contradicting exemplars? The answer is that each of these exemplars is flawed, and a new exemplar is needed to explain the world adequately. That new exemplar will not be either of the previous exemplars but something completely different. And yet, it would explain all that the previous exemplars were successfully explaining.

Another important idea that Kuhn's theory illustrates is the *non-linear* nature of history. In a linear history, there is continuous forward progress with passing time; at no time is there faster or slower progress, because time moves uniformly. The non-linear description of history instead identifies time as periods of rapid progress followed by declining progress leading to stagnation, which are then followed by disruptions and rapid progress.

Christensen's Disruptive Innovation

A similar idea about the non-linearity of ideological changes was argued for in Clayton Christensen's book *The Innovator's Dilemma*. Christensen argues that technologies come and go in cycles, with each new cycle proposing a new problem and a solution, or a new way of solving an old problem. He called these new solutions 'disruptions' in the slow and incremental process of technological evolution where existing technologies are modified and enhanced to adapt to new problems instead of inviting disruptive innovation. This creates a tussle between the old and new approaches. The proponents of the older view argue that they have been able to solve many problems in the past with their present approach, and the new problem therefore doesn't require a radically new solution; the incremental approach will work as well. The proponents of the newer view, on the other hand, argue that the new problem is indeed unique and requires a completely different approach.

Due to this tussle between the new and old approaches, the new approach is adopted slowly at the beginning. In this phase, the innovators try to match the powers of the new innovation with that of the old innovation. Once this match is achieved, then the new approach becomes a viable alternative, and it competes in the market. The new approach begins winning slowly because it has some advantages over the previous approach. Then follows a rapid phase of disruption—akin to Kuhn's 'paradigm shift'—in which the old is replaced by the new. As this replacement occurs, all those who previously supported the older approach begin lagging behind, as they have not invested their time and energy into new innovations. In some cases, if the new approach is disruptive, then the old guard may be completely overwhelmed by the change, and consigned to the dustbin of history, where the lack of their foresightedness is now cited as a lesson to be learnt by future generations, to remain ever watchful in their approach. Christensen argues that large and stable societies, institutions, and organizations are prone to disruption by smaller and nimble societies, institutions, and organization since the large and stable societies tend to resist disruption for too long, unable to adapt to the changing circumstances. As a result, large organizations are prone to die as smaller organizations replace them.

Non-Linear Ideas of Change

Such models have now been proposed in many areas. For example, Hegelian theories of history talk about a dialectic in which a thesis leads to its antithesis, and for a while the thesis and antithesis struggle for domination. Since neither of them is fundamentally better, and they solve different kinds of problems, therefore, ultimately, they are merged into a synthesis. If a society or civilization is unable to perform this synthesis, then it dies because it is weakened by its inner contradictions arising due to the battle between the thesis and the antithesis. The proponents of this non-linear model of history argue that the history of civilizations shows how civilizations rise very slowly in the initial phase, then grow and expand very rapidly, then stagnate, before they are disrupted by other civilizations. In the growth phase, a society or civilization conquers or influences other societies, and brings them under its control. However, the roots of dissent and differences are sown in this phase of expansion. They remain suppressed for a while, but as the society grows, these problems start coming to the forefront, until they attain a dominant status, and they try to overthrow the previously dominant people. This inner struggle for one-upmanship then weakens the society from within, as warring factions try to gain greater control. Under this weakened state, the society is disrupted by another stronger civilization. That new civilization, however, must synthesize the ideas of the civilizations it conquers, otherwise a new seed of dissent would be sown for later.

A good example of this phenomenon is the slow acceptance of Christianity for the initial nearly 300 years. Following this, when the Roman emperor Constantine adopted Christianity, he synthesized ideas from Greeks, Egyptians, Jews, and Assyrians—as many as were needed to produce a unified empire. Using this synthesis, Christianity spread across Europe. However, the synthesis wasn't perfect, because the simplicity and godliness of Christianity were undermined by the special status of kings and priests, which had nothing to do with Christianity, but were needed for a synthesis. The philosophical and critical approach of Greeks was rejected, and replaced by a firm faith in the authority of Church. The society was no longer open to ideas, inquiry, and criticism, rationality and observation. It only permitted the extension of the dogmas that the Church wanted people to believe in. And this resulted in what people now call the "dark ages", which can be equated to the stage of stagnation, in terms of Kuhn's ideas. Following this long stagnation, came the next disruption, that of European Enlightenment which replaced the dogmas of Christianity with science.

This illustrates the idea that synthesis alone doesn't prevent disruption. The synthesis should be *better* than all the individual ideas put together. It must be more consistent, complete, simple, and parsimonious, necessary, sufficient, rational, empirical, operational, instrumental, novel, and stable. A mixture of random ideas may seem to create unity but that unity is not inherently better than the separated ideas. It also eventually fragments.

In biology, a similar type of rapid growth and decline has been shown to occur in the various stages of biological evolution. The Cambrian Explosion, for example, shows that entire ecosystems of living entities suddenly appear in geological history, which contradicts the idea that species evolve through gradual and incremental evolution. Similarly, large populations of species are suddenly destroyed due to some cataclysmic geological event. The extinction of dinosaurs is an often-cited example in this case. Large populations of species do not dwindle slowly before they become extinct. Rather, the entire population of a species suddenly disappears in geological records. This again contradicts the linear and gradual notions of evolution. If biological evolution was a reality, a species should not disappear suddenly. There must be at least some members of the species that evolve to adapt to the changing circumstances. Indeed, why geology should have sudden shifts is itself a broader question that remains unanswered. If nature is working according to laws that dictate incremental change, then such 'critical phenomena' where a small set of changes lead to a big outcome must not occur. Since they occur, therefore, scientists develop non-linear models of change. The conflicts between linear and non-linear models of change is therefore quite well-established across many domains of scientific inquiry today.

The non-linear model of change in ideas—as proposed by Kuhn and Christensen—thus fits quite well with other large-scale non-linear models of change. The highlight of non-linearity is that new ideas are not adopted in proportion to their value or merit. Rather, incremental ideas are adopted faster than their merit would indicate. And radical ideas are adopted slower than the merit they command. Kuhn had demonstrated this non-linearity in the case of the Copernican (heliocentric model of the solar system) revolution, where the idea of Copernicus was initially rejected even as it was mathematically simpler, because it went against the established notions of a geocentric solar system. Conversely, the models that added new epicycles to existing orbits were adopted faster, because they fitted right into the existing paradigm. Given the advances the existing approach had already made, the new approach was expected to meet the same standards before it was accepted. It took a while for Copernicus to complete the orbits for the planets and demonstrate their simplicity, before his approach was considered. In the same way, the initial adoptions of new technologies are very slow, and people challenge these new ideas and expect them to live up to the prowess of the established models. But once that threshold is met, the subsequent changes are very rapid, due to the higher benefits of the new approach. The same fate, however, awaits even the new approach after it has reached its full potential and an even newer approach comes along to disrupt it.

The proponents of disruptive ideas scoff at the inability of the people supporting old ideas to adapt to changes. They claim that their desire for stability undermines their capacity to see the value in the new ideas. This criticism is only partly true because we need both stability and novelty.

If the system was constantly disrupting itself, the resulting instability would cause so much turmoil in society, that nothing of value would be achieved. Most people would begin playing a waiting game to figure out who wins the battle of disruption, and that waiting game is another kind of stagnation, that will weaken both opposing parties. The necessity for stability therefore cannot be denied. Hence, neither the disruptive model, nor the linear model works well in all cases, and there is no good scientific theory at present that can explain the occurrence of both these phenomena through a single underlying mechanism. As far as necessities go, we can see that both types of approaches are needed, because each brings its own value.

Change and Imperfection

Of course, if perfect knowledge were already obtained, then disruptions would end, because we will not be hampered in our progress. Change may then still move non-linearly, not because there are unsolvable problems that stagnate progress, which then lead to disruptive solutions, but because we choose to create disruption only when new problems arise. These problems would arise occasionally when the environment that we do not control, or things that are outside of our control, change. They would not be facilitated or created by our actions, namely, imperfect solutions that need to be patched. A good example of changes caused by the environment, or things outside of our control, is the passing of days. We do different things at different times of day: for instance, we sleep in the night, work in the afternoon, and relax in the evenings. This is just because we don't control the rising and setting of the sun, and different activities are more suited for different times. Thus, if time causes cyclical changes in the environment, then we can also act cyclically, adapting to the changing circumstances. This non-linear change may seem just like the cyclical changes accompanying disruptions, but it is not. The adaptation to environmental change is forced on us but the imperfect solutions to problems lead to changes created by us.

When non-linearity is produced due to environmental changes, the cyclical phasing of progress and stagnation is different from the disruptive model of phasing in which rapid progress compensates for previous stagnation, and stagnation compensates for the previous rapid changes. In short, there can be cycles of activity that don't lead to *instability*. Such cycles can be achieved if perfect knowledge is attained, and we cyclically accelerate or decelerate the pragmatic applications of this knowledge. On the other hand, there can be cycles of activity that lead to *instability*. Such cycles are necessary when perfect theoretical knowledge itself doesn't exist, and we cyclically accelerate or decelerate to solve the problems created by our solutions.

This problem can be addressed if we correlate change to imperfection. Kuhn's and Christensen's books present non-linear but progressive models of change, and they give the impression of a history in which society moves toward increasing perfection. Every new solution, they claim, solves an existing problem. But the new solution is not without its demerits—i.e. it solves some problems, rather imperfectly, and it creates a new set of problems. Those new problems then create the necessity for another disruption, because the previous solution wasn't perfect. What Kuhn and Christensen don't recognize is that an imperfect new solution doesn't solve *all* the problems. In most cases, a new solution solves a *part* of the problem, leaving the other parts in the same situation. Then another solution is proposed to solve the remaining problems, but the solutions now *fork*—each improvement addresses parts of the full problem—as it is impossible to reconcile the solutions into a complete solution. This leads to another idea of progression—namely, that progress is obtained when greater cohesion is achieved in the solutions, and we are able to apply a single solution to all the problems.

This idea of progression is Hegelian because it progresses through greater unity. The contradictory solutions must be reconciled because the solutions initially forked from a larger problem, and contradictory solutions solved different aspects of the problem. These contradictory solutions to different parts of the problem can be compared to the head and tail of a coin, which seem opposites of each other, but they are aspects of a deeper reality called a 'coin'. If we understand the coin, then we can reconcile them into a single theory. These contradictory ideas can be called a thesis and its antithesis—like the two opposing faces of a coin—but they are not logically opposed *if* we consider the problem to which they are proposed. They do seem opposed *if* we consider the solutions, however. Therefore, to reconcile them, it is important to stop looking at the solutions, and go back to the problem, and rethink it. This rethinking the problem in a new way can then lead to a new solution in which the previous contradictory solutions are merely parts or aspects. Each solution only addresses the problem partially, so their combination is necessary. This trend can be explained through the examples of the historical evolution of scientific theories, as follows.

Before the dawn of Newton's theory of gravitation, terrestrial and celestial mechanics were modeled by different theories. It was obvious that pushes and pulls are necessary for terrestrial mechanics, but these pushes and pulls involved *contact* between the cause and the effect—we can imagine a man pushing or pulling a cart, as an example. This seemed to not work for celestial mechanics because there was nothing connecting the heavenly bodies. How could their motion be explained using push and pull, without a contact? Newton's innovation was the idea of *action at a distance*, in which we postulated that the force of gravity could pull objects even without a contact between them. And by this, he was able to reconcile celestial and terrestrial motions into a single theory of gravitation. The idea of the action at a distance initially faced a lot of resistance, but it was eventually accepted. In fact, so ubiquitous was the acceptance that it came be used as a template for all kinds of forces and motions; if you cannot explain some behavior of some object, then postulate a new kind of property and force, assume that it acts at a distance, and then you can postulate another force to go with it.

Indeed, this is how the phenomena of electricity was initially discovered. It was found that besides celestial and terrestrial gravitation, there was another kind of motion which could not be explained by an object's mass. To solve this problem, a new property—called 'charge'—was postulated, a new law of force was assumed, and the motions were thus explained. It was also found that moving charged particles create another kind of force, which was then called 'magnetism', and two diverse phenomena (i.e. electricity and magnetism) were unified into a single theory called 'electromagnetism'.

Even as the unification between celestial and terrestrial mechanics on one hand, and electricity and magnetism on the other, was occurring, these two theories remained disparate. Then two attempts to reconcile them were made in the early part of the 20th century, although both attempts have remained incomplete. Quantum mechanics reconciled mechanics and electromagnetism by postulating that atomic particles have two properties—mass and charge—and the charge in oppositely charged particles (protons and electrons) constitute the atoms such as Oxygen and Carbon. Since both particles have mass, their combination has the mass of their individual sums. Quantum mechanics, however, also indicates that this matter exists as *possibilities* of energy states, and if we perform a measurement, then only one possibility is visible at one time, quite like you might roll a dice and only one face turns up. The question is: What happens to the gravitational force? If it acts on this possibility, then it effectively performs a measurement, and all these possibilities must simultaneously be real, instead of being possibilities. On the other hand, if the gravitational force doesn't act simultaneously, then there must be yet another force that somehow makes them act occasional. Since neither alternative is proven by observation, therefore, the attempt at reconciling electromagnetism and gravitational theory is incomplete.

A similar type of incompleteness is known in General Relativity, which is an extension of classical gravitational theory using three key ideas: (1)

light has a constant speed for all observers, moving or stationary, (2) the gravitational force also doesn't travel at infinite speed; its speed is limited to the speed of light, and (3) the classical mechanical distinction between constant speed motion and accelerated motion is an artificial one; a man falling from a high building will feel weightless (until he hits the ground) *as if* he wasn't moving at all; as a result, there is no way for this falling man to know if he is stationary, moving at constant speed, or accelerating. This reconciliation is however partial because it doesn't take into account the idea that all the individual objects are mere possibilities. How can they exert a force—i.e. emit a particle—if they are possibilities? The mere act of exerting a force requires emitting a particle, and if particles are constantly being emitted, then the measured object is not in a state of possibility. Thus, gravitational theory becomes contradictory to the basic tenets of quantum theory.

The point is this: the claim that our theories or technologies get better with time is not an unqualified certainty. To the extent that we see some unification, we can say that some problems in the past theories have been resolved, and this constitutes 'progress'. Certainly, formulating these theories in a form acceptable to everyone requires some struggle before they are widely accepted, and the process of this struggle can be called 'discovery' or 'innovation'. But what happens if as a result of some unifications we arrive at an unsolvable problem of disunity between two partially complete, but mutually incompatible theories? The problem of the unification of General Relativity and Quantum Theory, for instance, is unresolved for over a century. To many people it seems obvious that both these theories are false because they are mutually incompatible. Therefore, they must be replaced by something completely different—e.g. String Theory (which replaces all particles and forces using strings in a 10-dimensional space-time). However, there is no empirical evidence suggesting that this is indeed the case.

We can call disruptions in science a 'paradigm shift' but that doesn't adequately distinguish between the two ways in which this shift or disruption can occur. First, we can produce another pair of theories that reconcile most part of the current theories, but in the process, they make new predictions that are only partially confirmed, thereby leading to another fork after the unification in which the new phenomena are described using a theory that is mutually incompatible with the previous one. Second, we can indeed get a new theory that addresses all the problems, explains all those anomalies that currently lie unexplained, and constitutes the basis of a new kind of thinking; however, it doesn't create any new unsolved problems. According to the model of 'paradigm shift' we can call both these theories disruptive but they are completely different in nature. In the first case, we are moving the problem from one set of theories to another—gaining some new insights, but never closing the gaps between the theories or between theory and observation. In the second case, we are solving the current problem in a totally satisfactory manner, without creating a yet another problem.

The phenomenology of 'disruption' is not specific enough to distinguish solutions that go in circles substituting one problem for another, and solutions that are factually progressive because the net result of using such solutions is that existing problems are solved, and new ones are not created. Therefore, instead of using the terms 'disruption' and 'paradigm change' we can use alternative terms—i.e. 'cyclical change' and 'progressive change'. Both types of changes can appear disruptive, because the criterion for disruption is that the status quo is altered, and the efforts are refocused.

In simple terms, we can say that there is a type of disruption that creates instability, and substitutes one problem with another. And there is a type of disruption that creates net stability, solves the problem, and creates no further problems. The former type of change can be called *cyclical* and the latter *progressive*. When net stability is created, then in one sense the quest for new knowledge ends—if the laws are indeed perfect. In another sense, it is just the beginning of new applications, technologies, and solutions that were previously impossible. As we have seen, the theory can be one, but its applications infinite. Therefore, the discovery of the perfect theory doesn't stagnate knowledge, and it doesn't disrupt knowledge repetitively. A perfect theory rather achieves novelty with stability while an imperfect theory only achieves novelty, disrupting old theories, but also creating instability.

Disruptions can lead us to perfection or imperfection. When the disruption is imperfect, it can seem to be an improvement over the immediate past, but if we observe the evolution over a period of time, then the change returns to the problem that it started out with—it moves cyclically. If the disruption is perfect, then it not only seems to be an improvement over the immediate past, but if we observe it over a longer period of time, it doesn't return to the same problem—it moves progressively. Change can therefore be good or bad, and disruptions are also good and bad; bad change moves cyclically and good change moves progressively or linearly forward.

This helps us see why there is adequate justification in trading off between novelty and stability—if the process is cyclical. We resist the change because we are *afraid* that it will lead to net disruption, the efforts expended in the past in making some progress would be lost, and we would have to start all over again. This sounds bad only because we are not sure that the disruption is perfect. If we saw it as the logically next step toward perfection, then we will not resist it. Disruptions therefore have to be forced by circumstances, evidence, or crises in existing theories. Such change is accepted unwillingly. Novelty, innovation, and disruption, therefore, appear to be contradictory to stability, constancy, and permanence. Just as we have previously seen contradictions between consistency and completeness, parsimony and simplicity, rationalism and empiricism, etc. similarly, we can see a contradiction between innovation and stability. We want innovation because it produces novelty, but we abhor the resulting instabilities. Disruption is welcome only if we are assured that the future is definitely better, and the pain of disruption is a one-time struggle for adaptation to novelty. When change becomes the constant, then instability becomes the norm. Then it is better to not have innovation if we want stability, but it is impossible to continue living with the current problem. Hence, there is a forward push to solve the current problems, and a backward push against the change.

The Criterion for Knowledge

We can now talk about the distinction between truth and reality vs. that which only seems to be true and real based upon pragmatic considerations. As we noted earlier, there are two kinds of pragmatism. Under the first one we say "truth also works", and under the second one we say that "whatever works is true". The difference between the two is that it is possible to have a partially working theory of a narrowly defined set of phenomena. However, such a theory brings many problems, but whatever criteria we used to narrow the phenomena to a smaller set doesn't truly exist in nature. Modern academia, for instance, draws artificial divisions between natural sciences, life sciences, and social sciences, when the fact is that our observations depend on our senses, which are studied under life sciences, and this life exists in a socio-economic environment, which are studied in social sciences. The kinds of boundaries that we draw in these sciences are not real. However, we strip the other kinds of realities in natural sciences for *simplification*. This simplification can sometimes be oversimplification such that the theory is missing important ideas that exist in reality, but not in our theories.

Thus, the claim that "whatever works is true" is false, because it works in a narrow sense, rather than completely. The theory that works perfectly would not produce new problems; it will only solve the problems. If we broaden the scope of our reality, and include other things that were previously excluded, then it is possible to rethink the problem in a new way. That broadening and rethinking is also pragmatic: we are still modeling nature according to what works. When broader considerations are brought into theory formation, then we are not excluding potential effects that were likely excluded when the focus was narrowed. This broadening also requires the development of empirical and rational abilities such that we are able to think of reality differently than what we have thought of in narrow terms.

For example, a physicist thinks of reality in terms of subatomic particles, a biologist in terms of bodies and minds, and a sociologist in terms of societies and markets. To broaden our focus, we must bring elements of reality from other domains into our theory formation. This addition of elements that seem obvious in other domains but unobvious in the present domain constitutes 'disruption'—it is not an incremental addition to previous ideas, but a total rethink of a broader problem. If that broader problem is solved, then the narrower problem will also be solved—although in a different way, and the confirmations of this new way of thinking would also be indicated by the types of phenomena we consider in other areas.

The conflict between novelty and stability is a byproduct of narrowing of focus in understanding reality, and disruptions, innovations, novelties are produced when we bring ideas from other domains into the present domain. To see why this is true, we must ask: Where do we get new ideas from? The answer is 'observation' and 'reason'—about another reality. There are factually no new ideas. All these ideas exist in some idea-domain. But we remain unaware of these models due to narrowing of focus by excluding other domains. A physicist for example, doesn't think of the world in terms of relations that alter the related entities—everybody else realizes that if you form a social connection, then the connection modifies each individual through that relation (for example, in a relation, a father behaves differently than an employee). A physicist doesn't think in terms of people who occasionally and selectively interact with other people, which can, for instance, help us see why a physical reality can exist without interactions. A physicist doesn't think that the world is like a work of art, music, literature, or poetry, such that there is an important role of *interpretation* rather than just *observation*. The interpreted meaning is not merely in our 'minds' but in the 'objects' themselves. Thus, if a physicist considered a broader set of realities, then he would be able to disrupt thinking in physics by saying: (1) matter also encodes meaning, (2) an object interacts selectively with other objects, based on previously created relationships, and (3) material objects also have a purpose that predisposes them to act in certain way, rather than other ways.

Narrowing and Broadening

Now, we can explain the process of evolution of knowledge in a new way: disruptions occur if the problem domains are *broadened* or *narrowed*. The disruption of classical physics occurred due to narrowing, when Newton decided to forego the question of the Unmoved Mover, which had troubled philosophers since Aristotle's time, and focused on 'changes to motion'. This allowed him to postulate what is now called 'inertial mass', and a 'force' which changes its state of motion. The problem seems suddenly easier because we stopped thinking about the broader problem of how the world came into existence, and focused on describing changes to a preexisting world. In the process of narrowing, philosophy and religion were disrupted, and were relegated to something that was *not* physics. In contrast, in Greek times, physics was a part of philosophy, and philosophers were trying to solve general problems and identify the 'big picture' of reality, morality, the goal of life, rather than narrow their focus on the theory of atoms.

Likewise, disruptions occur when we try to unify theories by broadening our problem domain. We have seen above how unification of previously disconnected domains of knowledge brings disruptions, when previously contradictory ideas are reconciled into a new coherent description. We have previously termed this type of disruption Hegelian as it takes a thesis and its antithesis (e.g. particles and waves) and puts them into a single theory.

There is however a fundamental difference between these two mechanisms—if the domain is broadened, then we obtain novelty along with greater stability, but if the domain is narrowed, then we obtain novelty at the cost of stability. The instability resulting from the narrowing of focus is due to the fact that a smaller domain is influenced by the larger domain, but due to our narrowed focus we either cannot see that influence, or we refuse to see its presence, and continue to model nature in a narrower sense.

The disruptions of modern science have arisen because our focus was narrowed, and we started seeing 'details' and ignoring the 'big picture'. Each academic domain in the modern era focuses on a narrow subject, such as physics, biology, economics, psychology, etc. There are further specializations within each such area, such that knowledge is compartmentalized into many subjects. But reality is not compartmentalized in this way. Just because we put atoms in a separate box than minds or societies, doesn't mean that the societies don't affect the mind, or the mind doesn't affect the atoms. Thus, compartmentalization of knowledge—which became very prominent in the 19th and 20th centuries—leads to a disruption because the old questions and problems are rejected, and new questions and problems are formulated. We then find narrower answers to these narrower questions, and that leads to pragmatic technology that works in so far as the questions being asked of that technology are narrow. The fact, however, is that we cannot stop asking broader questions, because the technology we use exists in a society, is used by some mind, for purposes that transcend the individual boundaries of the narrowly focused academic inquiries. As a result, we find problems in our theories and technologies, because reality, when it is narrowly modeled, is also modeled incorrectly. Now, we can patch the narrow models by adding bells and whistles, and that constitutes the work of incremental science. We get into a disruption when the focus is broadened. That broadened focus, however, requires a fundamentally different way of thinking, and unless that thinking exists, the focus is again narrowed.

A disruption is thus the result of a different compartmentalization of nature, and disruptions can arise either because of narrowing or broadening of focus. The disruption caused by the broadening is a *good* disruption because it increases the stability of our knowledge. On the other hand, the disruption caused by the narrowing of focus is a *bad* disruption as it increases the contradictions between the different compartments of knowledge, and the absence of coherence in our knowledge then leads to instabilities.

Thus, we can draw a simple conclusion, that true knowledge is that which views reality as a whole, rather than divided into many compartments, each of which pragmatically comes up with their own theories of nature that are then claimed to be true just because they 'work' in a narrower sense. The world is not working according to thousands of theories that we have been invented in different departments. The world is working according to a single theory. But we cannot understand the truth if we remain compartmentalized in our thinking. Whatever we consider 'progress' by narrowing of focus is not real progress, *unless* it enhances and complements the big picture, and reinforces its understanding within a newer compartment. The scientist or philosopher who can work within a compartment without losing sight of the big picture can bring the disruptions that will be lasting and stable. On the other hand, those who remain myopically focused on narrower topics may produce some stunning results in the short run, but their results and theories will be forgotten over time, and their ideas displaced by theories that follow them. When real progress arrives by the broadening of our focuses, the myopically focused philosophers and scientists will become the butt of jokes, as their ideas would be dismissed as being too narrow.

Knowledge is Victory

This leads us to the idea that truth *wins*. It wins over narrower ideas because it is broader and therefore more encompassing. And it wins over broader ideas because it is free from inner contradictions which weaken the broadness. Thus, whatever is not true is weaker than the truth, and a weakened idea can be easily replaced by a stronger idea. The truth in a broader worldview makes it more stable, while the falsity in the narrower worldview makes it unstable. The truth in the narrower idea makes it novel, while the falsity in the narrower idea makes it repetitive, or not novel. Thus, for example, when things are produced by mechanization, they remain repetitive and not unique, which makes them less attractive than if things were handcrafted. Conversely, when things are handcrafted, then they are unique, but they are also less stable and reliable. As a result, we either trade off uniqueness with stability, or vice versa. The truth is that which is both unique and stable. Its stability is that when the truth is applied, then the application becomes long-lasting and reliable. And its novelty is that with the application of truth, everything can be made unique, never seen previously.

The combination of uniqueness and stability leads to the victory of truth, because whatever is not unique is defeated by the uniqueness—it lacks the unique features of truth. Similarly, whatever is unique but not stable is defeated by the truth because it is weakened by its inner contradictions.

As the truth survives the test of competitiveness against the falsities, it is ever victorious. It lasts longer than all the falsities, and in the ultimate sense, truth is eternal because it always defeats a falsity. God is described in Vedic texts as that hero Who destroys ignorance, darkness, evil, and deceit by truthfulness, which then brings with it, power, wealth, beauty, and ultimately victory. We must remember that this is a battle between truth and falsity. Therefore, God's advent in this world is always associated with the destruction of evil and falsity, and the propagation of truthfulness.

When God disappears, we see false ideas in this world because of two reasons: (1) people want the falsity rather than the truth, and (2) knowers of the truth may not always exist, or may not be willing to share the truth. Due to these conditions, it might seem that the truth loses, but it is not the truth that is losing; it is the people who don't know the truth that are losing. Ultimately, everyone who knows the truth survives the onslaught against the lies; they accomplish the purpose of life, which is defeating their own ignorance and misunderstanding, and that enlightenment then liberates them from the cycle of ignorance, followed by misdeeds, followed by suffering. As knowledge is obtained, the misdeeds end, suffering is overcome, and whatever misdeeds or suffering could have occurred due to ignorance is destroyed. In this sense, the main battle of life is not with other people; it is a battle within us—it is the defeating of ignorance through knowledge.

Epilogue

At the beginning of the book, I had proposed to describe the twelve conditions of knowing, and their nature, and we have done that in the preceding chapters. Let us recapitulate and summarize that discussion:

- Due to the semantic nature of the world, our descriptions can comprise modalities such as individual, universal, and contextual; completeness is the ability to incorporate all these modes in our knowledge. If any of these modes is skipped, the result is the incompleteness of knowing.
- Consistency is the ability to not use these modes at once, because that would lead to a contradiction; in short, even though the potentiality for a mode exists, it may be hidden or subordinated in a particular context, and the presence of the opposites doesn't create a contradiction.
- The language in terms of which we describe this reality consistently and completely must comprise the fewest number of possible assumptions. This is the parsimony of the description and unless the description has been shrunk to the smallest possible description, it is not true.
- Each of the ideas used in this description must be simple in the sense they must use those words which must unavoidably be used, and not use those words which can be avoided. The word 'consciousness' must enter all such descriptions because it can never be avoided.
- The explanations must be sufficient in explaining all the reality of the world. Due to this sufficiency, we can consider the reality of the world as the *proof* of the *truth*—i.e. that which certifies the truth. If some part of the world is not explained, then the theory

is not sufficient.

- The explanations must be necessary for explaining all the data of the world. If it seems that there are more than one possible explanation of the same phenomena, then the previous criteria for simplicity and parsimony of explanations can be employed to eliminate alternatives.
- All the explanations must be rationally justified. Rationality means that there cannot be gaps in the reasoning. We cannot jump from one premise to another. Similarly, we cannot use randomness or probabilities in the explanation because they are lacking in sufficient reason.
- All the explanations must be confirmable by direct observation. There cannot be theories that postulate the existence of exotic entities whose existence is in principle unconfirmable. Direct observation includes both the effects and the causes by which these effects are produced.
- All knowledge must be capable of being put into practice. If something has no practical usefulness, or that it cannot be converted into some procedure, it is not knowledge. Proofs by contradiction cannot be considered truth; we must be able to prove things by actual construction.
- All that is put into practice must solve some problems of our lives. Every single problem must have a solution, and these solutions must not create new unsolvable problems. That 'knowledge' which creates new or unsolvable problems cannot be considered knowledge.
- The pursuit of knowledge must be exciting because there is always something new to be discovered. Due to this novelty, knowledge is infinite because it incorporates or includes something that previously seemed disconnected from it, and knowing never comes to an end.
- The pursuit of knowledge must yield greater stability even as novelty is being produced. Due to this stability, the ultimate truth is eternal, and eternally the supreme truth, because under its existence, nothing else comes close to disrupting its preeminent position or stature.

At the beginning of the book, I had also promised that these criteria for knowing are *reflexive*, in the sense that each of these properties of knowing can be applied back to the properties themselves, due to which we can say that knowing these 12 properties also constitute *knowledge*. If we show that because it satisfies these 12 conditions, it is knowledge, then we can say that it is the ultimate truth, because it applies to everything, including itself, whereas all other knowledge is not ultimate because it cannot be applied to everything else. Thus, reflexivity of knowledge is important to establishing that these 12 conditions of knowing constitute the Absolute Truth.

To see how these 12 principles apply to knowledge, we can apply them to each of the three components of knowledge—the knower, the known, and the relation between them. Now, you might say: We are introducing a division inside knowledge, so knowledge cannot be fundamental. But this problem goes away when the knower, known, and the knowing are identical—which happens in the case of self-awareness. Now, the knower uses the 12 principles to know—i.e. test if something is knowledge. The known is the same 12 principles of knowledge—i.e. something that we are trying to know. And the relation of knowing is the reflexive application of the principles of knowing to the object of that knowing. So, reflexivity can also be defined as the Absolute Truth trying to become self-aware, in the course of which it uses itself to understand itself, by a relation to the self.

To illustrate this idea, let us consider the knower, the known, and knowing separately in the case of one of the above conditions—observability. First, the term 'empirical' means the methods by which we know. This includes, the five senses of taste, touch, smell, sound, and sight. Second, 'empirical' means the objects that we know. For example, an apple has the properties of being red, round, and sweet, which are perceived by the senses. Third, the relation between the knower and the known is also empirical because we can perceive our distance to the object of knowing. Finally, our knowledge—produced as the combination of the knower, known, and knowing—is empirical, because we can confirm through empirical methods whether someone claiming to have seen an apple has actually seen it.

Thus, we can say that the senses are the causes of experience, the objects are the causes of experience, and the relations between the senses and objects are the causes of experience. Finally, empiricism is the way we know the nature of empiricism. If we did not have the senses to perceive, the objects could not be perceived, then we would not know about illusions, hallucinations, or misperceptions. If we did not have such things, then we would not know that the same reality upon repeated observations produces the same result (if the observation is performed correctly), and hence the method of induction could be used to overcome occasional misperceptions. Without empirical experience we would not know the difference between dreaming and waking, and hence not realize that science must be conducted during waking. Indeed, without the waking experience, science would not exist, since we would all be dreaming different things in the private world. Without waking, there would be no communication, and hence I could not tell you anything about myself, and you would have no way of knowing that we are all similar. Each one of would think that we are completely alone. Thus, empirical experience gives us the tools to understand empiricism.

Likewise, consistency is a property of the knower—i.e. the knower seeks consistency in the knowledge. Consistency is a property of the objects being known—i.e. if this consistency did not objectively exist, then the consistency in the knower would be false. Finally, consistency is about the relation between the knower and the known—i.e. the knower and the known are mutually consistent—everything the knower can know is available as a known, and everything that exists as a known, the knower can know. If our thoughts could not be consistent, then we could never understand anything. If the world was not consistent, then knowledge would comprise mutually incompatible ideas, and we could not believe in the truth of anything.

If the knower and the known were inconsistent, then our knowing could never be complete—there would be things that exist in the world but that which we cannot imagine or think of, and hence never understand. What we cannot understand cannot be true. Consistency is how we understand consistency—because we find harmony and agreement, and that makes our beliefs in each thing stronger, and by that strength we are able to say that when more people agree with each other, or when more ideas are mutually consistent, then there is a much higher likelihood of something being true. If consistency did not exist, then no two people could agree with each other. We would be always arguing and disagreeing, and as a result nobody could firm their faith in anything, owing to the incessant arguments. If we see that agreement strengthens our individual beliefs, then we also think that a collection of consistent ideas strengthens those ideas.

If necessity and sufficiency were not criteria for knowing, then anything could be the cause of anything, although that would not work to either rationally predict or explain anything. But who is to say that we must be able to predict and explain? Why can't the world simply be an unpredictable and inexplicable succession of events? Indeed, since there can be so many more unpredictable and inexplicable worlds, such worlds are more likely than the ones that are predictable and explainable. Therefore, we don't accidentally discover that the world has order. We *believe* that the world has order and we seek it in the chaos that surrounds us. We believe that things happen for a reason, and that reason must be necessary and sufficient to cause those things. In short, we wear the goggles of necessity and sufficiency and then we try to understand the world through these goggles. If the world doesn't fit our paradigms of necessity and sufficiency, we don't immediately give up and say: Look, there is no necessary and sufficient explanation! We rather say: There must be such an explanation, but we haven't yet found it.

Then as we seek it, and find some such explanation, then we use that finding to refine what we mean by necessity and sufficiency. For example, it is not sufficient to have separate necessary and sufficient theories of motion and light; it is also necessary to have a single theory for both phenomena. In other words, we are discovering the necessity and sufficiency of theories of nature because we *believe* that there is order in nature, and are going in search for it. We have no proof that the world is indeed logical, because logic is extremely restrictive and illogic is far more likely than logic. And yet, we assume and force logic on the world to find it and study it. In this way, we use necessity and sufficiency to study necessity and sufficiency.

If the criteria for knowledge were infinite, then we could never believe in anything, because we could not know what it means to know. Without the affirmation that we have satisfied the conditions of knowing, we could not believe in anything—there would always be lingering doubts about everything. Similarly, if the criteria for knowledge were not simple, then only a very few people could understand and know the truth.

Everyone else would either have to just accept the authority of others, or perhaps not even that, because they could not know if the authority could be trusted because the criteria for determining this trust would also be infinitely complex.

Thus, a person who could deal with this complexity would know, but everyone else would be in the dark, not even able to know from others. When we say that knowledge must be simple and parsimonious, we are asserting the capacity of each individual to know the whole truth. You don't need thousands of books, and a great mind to know the truth. Some philosophers and scientists can spend this time deciding what is *not* truth, but when they arrive at the truth, everyone can *understand* it—even if they haven't spent countless hours thinking about it, or don't have the intellect for it. When we use simplicity and parsimony as the criteria for knowing, then we push for simpler and smaller explanations, and if we push for them, then we find them. The pursuit of simplicity and parsimony is not necessarily simpler or shorter. This is why scientists and philosophers have to toil hard to simplify and shorten things, so that other people can access it easily. This is why an academic holds an important role in society—he is contributing to the simplification and summarization of knowledge, which doesn't need to be done by everyone. Thus, long and complex answers are the norm—if they are at all true—and short and simple answers are generally false. But despite this general falsity of short and simple answers, we believe that answers must be short and simple. That belief—sometimes called Occam's Razor—drives us toward simpler and shorter answers before we find them. If we did not *a priori* believe in this idea, then we would never try for it, and because it is not itself easy and simple, therefore, we would never get it.

Using these simple and fewer ideas we must be able to construct a rational prediction and explanation, which means that there cannot be gaps in our thought process, and nothing can appear 'magically' and suddenly. Rationality is the capacity to *understand* the truth, which is different from *knowing* the truth. For example, we can teach someone a theory of nature, and they can memorize it, but they might not understand why this theory and not another theory. Unless they see that this explanation is not just consistent and complete, simple and parsimonious, necessary and sufficient, but also *intuitive*, they would not accept its truth. What is intuitive? Something becomes intuitive if it is the way we understand

and know ourselves. Intuition is a matter of familiarity, and we can know new things based on what we already know. If we don't know something already, we cannot classify, categorize, and organize the world even if we are given some new ideas. Therefore, intuitiveness is the existence of some *a priori* knowledge. What can exist *a priori*? Only that which is the most fundamental. What is most fundamental? It is the idea about the self. We don't know the self by looking into the world. At the least, we have an intuitive understanding of the distinction between a knower, a known, and knowing. We can intuitively understand that the knower must apply some conditions of knowing. And we can intuitively grasp the 12 conditions of knowing because we apply each of these conditions to knowing the self. Thus, these 12 conditions are intuitive—and we can call them 'rational'—because they are axiomatic.

If knowledge could not be operationalized, then every interpretation of data would be considered truth, because knowledge would simply be observation and interpretation, without the ability to make a difference to anyone's life. Indeed, knowing the truth and not knowing it would be identical for everyone, because knowledge would make no difference to anyone's life. We believe that knowing must make a difference to our lives, and we strive for that knowledge that makes a difference, and neglect everything else. To a long-winded philosophical discussion, the typical response is: So, what? Again, because we believe that knowledge must be operationalized, and then instrumentalized to make a difference in our life, therefore, we seek that thing that makes a difference and call that knowledge. Since that difference actually works, therefore, we now seek that truth which works, and which is also true in an ultimate sense. Hence, all religious philosophy must lead to a practice, and all practice is sustained by an underlying philosophy. In short, because we use our *a priori* assumptions about operational and instrumental truth, we find that truth, and we use it to design better operational and instrumental truths, which leads us to the logical conclusion that there must be some operational and instrumental truth that can solve all our problems. If our *a priori* belief did not exist, then we would not seek to test knowledge as a method of alleviating suffering, and without that attempt, religion would not exist as a method of practice that alleviates misery. Religious practice is thus the idea of pragmatism pushed to its limits.

Finally, we use the idea of originality and stability to create originality and stability. Our quest for originality is not simply to solve the practical day-to-day problems, but also because life must be thrilling and exciting, and it is indeed thrilling and exciting to discover new things. Most scientists, who have enough to solve their day-to-day problems, are still working hard only to find something exciting and thrilling that others have not found yet. But just as they would like to discover new things, they don't want them to be so disruptive as to take away the stability in their lives—i.e. make their lives more fearful, scary, or uncertain. Indeed, under the fear of losing their careers, most academics dare not say unpleasant or unpopular things, even though they may be much more exciting, because they seek stability too.

It is in the confluence of this paradoxical search for novelty without instability that most science is conducted: when the stability becomes too boring without the novelty, then novelty takes precedence, but when the novelty becomes too disruptive, then stability takes precedence. These are not considerations about nature; nothing tells us that nature is indeed hiding secrets from us. Rather, we believe that nature has secrets and the discovery of these secrets is the intellectual treasure hunt that we must embark upon. In this treasure hunt, we look for clues that might point us in the direction of the treasure. But we must go only so far in this hunt as our supplies would permit us. In short, we seek the excitement with stability, and then we find that nature gradually reveals its secrets to us, such that everything is not known at once because we are not prepared for the full truth—after all, it can disrupt everything that we currently believe in. Therefore, even if radical ideas are presented to us, we shy away from them to maintain stability.

This is then what I mean by *reflexivity*: we have ideas about knowledge, and we use them to define what we mean by knowledge. There is no reason for us to believe that nature is consistent or complete, simple or parsimonious, necessary or sufficient. There are no reasons to believe that by observation and reason we can know the true nature of reality. There is nothing telling us that knowledge can be operationalized to become the instrument of solving our day-to-day problems. And there is nothing telling us that nature is secretive, and sends us on a treasure hunt, to make our life thrilling, and yet, this thrilling life of discovery and novelty also creates stability. These are things that we believe in, and we use these beliefs to define what we mean by knowledge. If we take away these beliefs one by one, then we would also chip away at what we mean by knowledge, and if all the beliefs are gone, then there would be nothing called 'knowledge' to talk about.

If we don't agree upon one or some of these criteria, then different people would have different definitions of knowing. For example, some people would claim that we can have fragmented and incomplete theories, and we can still call them knowledge, because consistency and completeness are not criteria for knowing—this is not facetious; many people do claim that it is impossible to know everything consistently. Similarly, some people believe that experience and reason don't tell us anything about reality; that we must accept everything on faith, and even this faith should never be tested against evidence. The result is that there are many varieties of faiths that people believe in and nobody can claim their truth, except through coercion and violence. Likewise, some people would believe that whatever works pragmatically can be called truth, and we don't need ultimate theories of nature, just a loosely gathered assemblage of different tools that work for different tasks. In this way, there are many disagreements about the nature of knowledge today, and if we put them all together, then there would be nothing to know, and the thing we call knowledge just would not exist.

The argument that says that nature is not telling us what knowledge should be is correct. Yes, nature doesn't tell us. But *we* have these ideas innate in us. If we can apply these ideas simultaneously, then we can find what we call 'knowledge'. But if we give up these ideas then we would also be left with ignorance—the more we reject these ideas the greater is the ignorance. Upon this principle I can assert that knowledge cannot be thrust upon anyone. Truth will not force itself upon you. Rather, you have to seek the truth. And in this search, you are simply seeking *perfection* as defined by the above 12 criteria. The contention in Vedic philosophy is that if these principles of perfection are applied to knowledge, then the knowledge of God is obtained, because He is that thrilling, novel, exciting thing that is also stable; He is the consistent, complete, necessary and simple truth; He is beauty personified as the ability in everyone to understand Him easily (provided you accept that the truth is simple and parsimonious); His knowledge is pragmatically useful to solve all the problems of our life; and He can be known by direct observation as well as logical reasoning.

Thus, the 12 principles, perfection, and knowledge are synonymous, when they are attained. The same thing that is perfect, is also the ultimate truth, and the embodiment of the 12 principles that define perfection. That thing is sometimes called 'God', sometimes the 'Supreme Truth', sometimes the 'Absolute Truth' or 'Universal Truth'. Based on which of these 12 principles are given greater importance, there are innumerable other names by which the same thing can be called. The name only symbolizes what we mean by perfection, but if all these 12 qualities are present to a *sufficient* degree then that thing can be called 'God'. Sufficiency simply means that they are present completely in God, but *we* may not know them completely.

To the extent that we see these principles partially, we know God partially. When this partial knowing becomes completely devoid of one of the 12 qualities, then the material world is produced. This material world is now contrasted to knowledge—it is not knowledge but *ignorance*. That ignorance is not merely within us; the world is itself ignorance due to the absence of one of the 12 principles. However, due to consistency, we seek those things that are similarly ignorant as we are, and this is then the basis of modern science in which we are ready to discard everything except *consistency*.

Many not-so-thrilling theories, theories that have no practical benefit, empirically unconfirmable theories, theories that reject the reality of meaning, theories that are not necessary and sufficient, complicated and long descriptions, and finally incomplete models, are all considered 'knowledge' in modern time, but illogical is still not considered scientific. Those illogical fantasies are then suitable to be called literature, art, poetry, or religion.

In this way, out of the 12 conditions of knowledge, we only use one—*consistency*—dominantly. Practically all of modern academia is divided into compartments, which deal in separate areas, and because of that our knowledge is incomplete. People don't understand that laws of nature are symmetries, knowledge must be symmetric. That we must use the simplest and fewest number of ideas, and that simplicity is defined by that which can never be dispensed with. We don't see how knowledge must be necessary and sufficient in explaining all the world; a narrow explanation of a narrow phenomenon is also considered some 'knowledge'. Our rationality relies not on discovering the most intuitive ideas that we use to know ourselves; it rather relies on speculation by which enormous complexity is constructed. We postulate the reality of physical properties, which cannot be perceived, and we reject the reality of that which is intuitively accessible—i.e. the sensations and concepts. We do use pragmatism to create technology, but we don't apply it all the way—namely, that knowledge is that which solves the problems and doesn't create new problems. Indeed, we don't even believe that knowledge is only that which can solve *all* the problems. We don't think that knowledge is only that which will never change; we rather believe in competition by which one idea is thrown away in favor of another, and change is eulogized because it is thrilling. At the same time, our fears of instability prevent even thrilling new ideas and thrilling is confined to incremental changes to established ways of thinking, due to which our knowledge has become stagnant; it costs a lot to discover new things, and their value remains questionable; but we are unable to reject this expensive process.

Even consistency is adopted in a narrow sense, because we don't believe that we can obtain a consistent description of everything. Moreover, we don't consider inconsistency between various models a serious problem. This is because, under skepticism, we have learned to believe that we can never know the nature of truth, or even that this truth must be consistent. We are quite comfortable applying piecemeal models to separate problems, thus undermining even the most fundamental criterion for knowing.

If all these principles are undermined by our attitudes, we can say that we are not *seeking* knowledge. We are seeking ignorance, that may not be righteous, and that may not be good for everyone. As long as it works to get me what I want, it is proclaimed to be true, right, and good. The main casualty in this process is the idea of *perfection*. We have given up the idea that perfection is the goal of life; it has been replaced by survival. In this struggle for existence, enormous confusion is created in the minds of the people because they cannot decide what is true, right, and good. They jump from one thing to another, under the fear of their extinction. Science and philosophy have themselves become the channels not for creating perfection, but as tools in the hands of people to aid in their own survival. The philosopher and the scientist are so worried about their existence, that they do what suits them best, not what is truthful, righteous, and good.

Therefore, I will argue that we must rethink what we are doing. And that rethink requires us to go back to the meaning of truth and knowledge. If we can accept these 12 conditions of knowing, then all that we currently call knowledge would fall by the wayside, and at least we will have a strong criterion for defining something as knowledge. With that criterion we can judge the difference between knowing and ignorance. We will find that most of what we consider philosophy, science, etc. are ignorance. Practically all of literature, art, poetry, and most religions, will also become ignorance. If stringent criteria of knowledge are applied then we will see the nature of truth by the method of elimination—not this, not that. As we shed our ignorance about the nature of truth, we become better equipped to appreciate the nature of truth, because the false crutches of 'knowledge', upon which we currently lean, will cease to exist. When we are free of these distractions, which masquerade as knowledge, then we can try to seek the truth.

This search for the Absolute Truth is the search for God. His six qualities constitute the nature of knowing, which, as those qualities are transcendent, but because they can be applied to everything in this world, they are also immanent. The Absolute Truth is therefore one thing, and yet, it is present in everything. We can say that the Absolute Truth is *demonstrated* in everything, and yet those things cannot be *described* as the Absolute Truth. By virtue of this pervasiveness, the Absolute Truth is also demonstrated in us by the very nature of our consciousness, namely, that we accept as true only that which is consistent, complete, simple, parsimonious, necessary, sufficient, empirical, rational, operational, instrumental, novel, and stable. However, each of these proclivities are dominant at different times. When the other proclivities are completely neglected, a false idea about knowledge is produced, and under those false ideas, even if the other proclivities are seen, they are rejected, because we are ourselves not seeking them.

We don't find God because we are not seeking God. We are seeking something that is contrary to God, so, even though God is all-pervading, we cannot see His presence. The change doesn't lie in the world; it lies within us. We have to 'clean' the filters of our consciousness and stop filtering the pure nature of knowledge, and filter that which is impure. Philosophy and science can aid in this process, but how can they aid in the process unless we desire to attain the perfection of understanding ourselves?

Index

Printed in the USA
CPSIA information can be obtained
at www.ICGtesting.com
LVHW091646120224
771669LV00037B/684